Allergies
SOURCEBOOK

Fifth Edition

Health Reference Series

Fifth Edition

Allergies
SOURCEBOOK

Basic Consumer Health Information about the Immune System and Allergic Disorders, including Rhinitis (Hay Fever), Sinusitis, Conjunctivitis (Pink Eye), Asthma, Atopic Dermatitis, and Anaphylaxis, and Allergy Triggers Such as Pollen, Mold, Dust Mites, Animal Dander, Chemicals, Food Additives, Latex, and Vaccines

Along with Facts about Allergy Diagnosis and Treatment, Tips on Avoiding Triggers, and Preventing Symptoms, a Glossary of Related Terms, and Directories of Resources for Additional Help and Information

OMNIGRAPHICS

155 W. Congress, Suite 200 Detroit, MI 48226

MAY 2 6 2017

Bibliographic Note

Because this page cannot legibly accommodate all the copyright notices, the Bibliographic Note portion of the Preface constitutes an extension of the copyright notice.

* * *

Omnigraphics, Inc.

Editorial Services provided by Omnigraphics, Inc.,
a division of Relevant Information, Inc.

Keith Jones, *Managing Editor*

* * *

Copyright © 2016 Relevant Information, Inc.

ISBN 978-0-7808-1451-6
E-ISBN 978-0-7808-1452-3

Library of Congress Cataloging-in-Publication Data

Names: Omnigraphics, Inc.

Title: Allergies sourcebook : basic consumer health information about the immune system and allergic disorders, including rhinitis (hay fever), sinusitis, conjunctivitis, asthma, atopic dermatitis, and anaphylaxis, and allergy triggers such as pollen, mold, dust mites, animal dander, chemicals, foods and additives, and medications; along with facts about allergy diagnosis and treatment, tips on avoiding triggers and preventing symptoms, a glossary of related terms, and directories of resources for additional help / Keith Jones, managing editor.

Description: Fifth edition. | Detroit, MI Omnigraphics, Inc., [2016] | Includes bibliographical references and index.

Identifiers: LCCN 2015038048 | ISBN 9780780814516 (hardcover : alk. paper) | ISBN 9780780814523 (ebook)

Subjects: LCSH: Allergy--Popular works.

Classification: LCC RC584 .A3443 2016 | DDC 616.97--dc23

LC record available at http://lccn.loc.gov/2015038048

Table of Contents

Part III: Foods and Food Additives That Trigger Allergic Reactions

Part IV: Airborne, Chemical, and Other Environmental Allergy Triggers

Part V: Diagnosing and Treating Allergies

Part VII: Avoiding Allergy Triggers, Preventing Symptoms, and Getting Support

Part VIII: Additional Help and Information

Preface

About This Book

More than 50 million Americans suffer from allergies each year. Allergies are the sixth leading cause of chronic illness in the United States, and according to the National Institute of Allergy and Infectious Diseases (NIAID), about fifty percent of the Americans test positive for at least one of the most common allergens: ragweed, pollen, mold, animal dander, dust mite, cockroaches, milk, eggs, tree nuts, and peanuts. Symptoms associated with allergic reactions can range from mild annoyances to anaphylaxis, a life-threatening emergency. Combined, allergies cost the U.S. healthcare system more than $18 billion annually.

Despite their widespread occurrence, however, many people do not understand the basic biological processes involved in allergic reactions and the role the immune system plays in causing common symptoms. Furthermore, medical science has yet to identify the specific genetic and environmental interactions that lead to the development of allergies or to fully understand why the prevalence of allergic diseases is increasing.

Allergies Sourcebook, Fifth Edition provides updated information about the causes, triggers, treatments, and prevalence of common allergic disorders, including rhinitis, sinusitis, conjunctivitis, allergic asthma, dermatitis, eczema, hives, and anaphylaxis. It discusses the immune system and its role in the development of allergic disorders and describes such commonly encountered allergens as pollen, mold, dust mites, and animal dander. Facts about allergies to foods and food additives, insect stings, medications, and chemicals are also included, along with information about allergy diagnosis, treatments, coping strategies, and prevention efforts. The book concludes with a glossary of related terms and directories of resources, including one to help people with food allergies find allergen-free foods.

How to Use This Book

This book is divided into parts and chapters. Parts focus on broad areas of interest. Chapters are devoted to single topics within a part.

Part I: Introduction to Allergies and the Immune System discusses the components and function of the immune system and how allergic responses work. It further discusses the impact of allergies on children, and provides current information on trends in allergic conditions among children.

Part II: Types of Allergic Reactions identifies the signs and symptoms of common allergic reactions, including rhinitis (hay fever), sinusitis, conjunctivitis (eye allergies), asthma, atopic dermatitis (eczema), rashes, Urticaria (hives), life-threatening anaphylaxis, and some rare allergic disorders.

Part III: Foods and Food Additives That Trigger Allergic Reactions provides information about the most common food allergens, including milk, egg, fish, and shellfish, peanuts and tree nuts, wheat, and soy. Information about food additives and ingredients that trigger reactions, food intolerances, and tips on living with a food allergy are also included.

Part IV: Airborne, Chemical, and Other Environmental Allergy Triggers discusses symptoms of allergies to pollen and ragweed, mold, dust mites, cockroaches, animal dander, insect stings, medications, and latex. Air quality and the impact of climate change on allergies is also discussed. People whose allergies flare when exposed to tobacco smoke, environmental odors, or building materials will also find suggestions on coping at home and in the workplace.

Part V: Diagnosing and Treating Allergies identifies tests, therapies, and medications that alleviate allergy symptoms, including antihistamines, decongestants, nasal sprays, and allergy shots. This part also includes complementary health practices and safety concerns regarding their use in the treatment of allergies.

Part VI: Avoiding Allergy Triggers, Preventing Symptoms, and Getting Support provides information about reducing indoor allergy triggers and improving air quality. This part also offers strategies for preventing allergy symptoms during travel, exercise, and remaining free of symptoms at school. Readers will also find updated information on the role of the NIAID in global allergic and infectious diseases research.

Part VII: Additional Help and Information provides a glossary of important terms related to allergies and the immune system. A directory of organizations that provide health information about allergies and asthma is also included, along with a list of cookbooks and websites.

Bibliographic Note

This volume contains documents and excerpts from publications issued by the following U.S. government agencies: Agency for Healthcare Research and Quality (AHRQ); Agency for Toxic Substances and Disease Registry (ATSDR); Centers for Disease Control and Prevention (CDC); Eunice Kennedy Shriver National Institute of Child Health and Human Development (NICHD); Genetic and Rare Diseases Information Center (GARD); National Center for Complementary and Integrative Health (NCCIH); National Heart, Lung, and Blood Institute (NHLBI); National Institute for Occupational Safety and Health (NIOSH); National Institute of Allergy and Infectious Diseases (NIAID); National Institute of Arthritis and Musculoskeletal and Skin Diseases (NIAMS); National Institute of Environmental Health Sciences (NIEHS); National Institutes of Health (NIH); National Toxicology Program (NTP); Occupational Safety and Health Administration (OSHA); Office on Women's Health (OWH); U.S. Department of Agriculture (USDA); U.S. Environmental Protection Agency (EPA); U.S. Food and Drug Administration (FDA).

It may also contain original material produced by Omnigraphics, Inc. and reviewed by medical consultants.

About the Health Reference Series

The *Health Reference Series* is designed to provide basic medical information for patients, families, caregivers, and the general public. Each volume takes a particular topic and provides comprehensive coverage. This is especially important for people who may be dealing with a newly diagnosed disease or a chronic disorder in themselves or in a family member. People looking for preventive guidance, information about disease warning signs, medical statistics, and risk factors for health problems will also find answers to their questions in the *Health Reference Series*. The *Series*, however, is not intended to serve as a tool for diagnosing illness, in prescribing treatments, or as a substitute for the physician/patient relationship. All people concerned about medical symptoms or the possibility of disease are encouraged to seek professional care from an appropriate health care provider.

A Note about Spelling and Style

Health Reference Series editors use *Stedman's Medical Dictionary* as an authority for questions related to the spelling of medical terms and the *Chicago Manual of Style* for questions related to grammatical structures, punctuation, and other editorial concerns. Consistent adherence is not always possible, however, because the individual volumes within the *Series* include many documents from a wide variety of different producers, and the editor's primary goal is to present material from each source as accurately as is possible. This sometimes means that information in different chapters or sections may follow other guidelines and alternate spelling authorities.

Medical Review

Omnigraphics contracts with a team of qualified, senior medical professionals who serve as medical consultants for the *Health Reference Series*. As necessary, medical consultants review reprinted and originally written material for currency and accuracy. Citations including the phrase,

"Reviewed (month, year)" indicate material reviewed by this team. Medical consultation services are provided to the *Health Reference Series* editors by:

Dr. Senthil Selvan, MBBS, DCH, MD
Dr. K. Sivanandham, MBBS, DCH, MS (Research), PhD

Our Advisory Board

We would like to thank the following board members who provided initial guidance on the development of this Series:

- Dr. Lynda Baker, Associate Professor of Library and Information Science, Wayne State University, Detroit, MI

- Nancy Bulgarelli, William Beaumont Hospital Library, Royal Oak, MI

- Karen Imarisio, Bloomfield Township Public Library, Bloomfield Township, MI

- Karen Morgan, Mardigian Library, University of Michigan-Dearborn, Dearborn, MI

- Rosemary Orlando, St. Clair Shores Public Library, St. Clair Shores, MI

Health Reference Series *Update Policy*

The inaugural book in the *Health Reference Series* was the first edition of Cancer Sourcebook published in 1989. Since then, the Series has been enthusiastically received by librarians and in the medical community. In order to maintain the standard of providing high-quality health information for the layperson the editorial staff at Omnigraphics felt it was necessary to implement a policy of updating volumes when warranted.

Medical researchers have been making tremendous strides, and it is the purpose of the *Health Reference Series* to stay current with the most recent advances. Each decision to update a volume is made on an individual basis. Some of the considerations include how much new information is available and the feedback we receive from people who use the books. If there is a topic you would like to see added to the update list, or an area of medical concern you feel has not been adequately addressed, please write to:

Managing Editor
Health Reference Series
Omnigraphics, Inc.
155 W. Congress, Suite 200
Detroit, MI 48226

Part One

Introduction to Allergies and the Immune System

Chapter 1

Understanding the Immune System

Overview of the Immune System

Function

The overall function of the immune system is to prevent or limit infection. An example of this principle is found in immune-compromised people, including those with genetic immune disorders, immune-debilitating infections like HIV, and even pregnant women, who are susceptible to a range of microbes that typically do not cause infection in healthy individuals.

The immune system can distinguish between normal, healthy cells and unhealthy cells by recognizing a variety of "danger" cues called danger-associated molecular patterns (DAMPs). Cells may be unhealthy because of infection or because of cellular damage caused by non-infectious agents like sunburn or cancer. Infectious microbes

This chapter includes excerpts from "Overview of the Immune System," National Institute of Allergy and Infectious Diseases (NIAID), December 30, 2013; text from "Cold, Flu, or Allergy?" National Institutes of Health (NIH), October 2015; text from "Features of an Immune Response," National Institute of Allergy and Infectious Diseases (NIAID), January 16, 2014; text from "Immune Tolerance," National Institute of Allergy and Infectious Diseases (NIAID), January 17, 2014; and text from "Disorders of the Immune System," National Institute of Allergy and Infectious Diseases (NIAID), January 17, 2014.

such as viruses and bacteria release another set of signals recognized by the immune system called pathogen-associated molecular patterns (PAMPs).

When the immune system first recognizes these signals, it responds to address the problem. If an immune response cannot be activated when there is sufficient need, problems arise, like infection. On the other hand, when an immune response is activated without a real threat or is not turned off once the danger passes, different problems arise, such as allergic reactions and autoimmune disease.

The immune system is complex and pervasive. There are numerous cell types that either circulate throughout the body or reside in a particular tissue. Each cell type plays a unique role, with different ways of recognizing problems, communicating with other cells, and performing their functions. By understanding all the details behind this network, researchers may optimize immune responses to confront specific issues, ranging from infections to cancer.

Location

All immune cells come from precursors in the bone marrow and develop into mature cells through a series of changes that can occur in different parts of the body.

Skin: The skin is usually the first line of defense against microbes. Skin cells produce and secrete important antimicrobial proteins, and immune cells can be found in specific layers of skin.

Bone marrow: The bone marrow contains stems cells that can develop into a variety of cell types. The common myeloid progenitor stem cell in the bone marrow is the precursor to innate immune cells—neutrophils, eosinophils, basophils, mast cells, monocytes, dendritic cells, and macrophages—that are important first-line responders to infection.

The common lymphoid progenitor stem cell leads to adaptive immune cells—B cells and T cells—that are responsible for mounting responses to specific microbes based on previous encounters (immunological memory). Natural killer (NK) cells also are derived from the common lymphoid progenitor and share features of both innate and adaptive immune cells, as they provide immediate defenses like innate cells but also may be retained as memory cells like adaptive cells. B, T, and NK cells also are called lymphocytes.

Bloodstream: Immune cells constantly circulate throughout the bloodstream, patrolling for problems. When blood tests are used to monitor white blood cells, another term for immune cells, a snapshot of the immune system is taken. If a cell type is either scarce or over-abundant in the bloodstream, this may reflect a problem.

Thymus: T cells mature in the thymus, a small organ located in the upper chest.

Lymphatic system: The lymphatic system is a network of vessels and tissues composed of lymph, an extracellular fluid, and lymphoid organs, such as lymph nodes. The lymphatic system is a conduit for travel and communication between tissues and the bloodstream. Immune cells are carried through the lymphatic system and converge in lymph nodes, which are found throughout the body.

Lymph nodes are a communication hub where immune cells sample information brought in from the body. For instance, if adaptive immune cells in the lymph node recognize pieces of a microbe brought in from a distant area, they will activate, replicate, and leave the lymph node to circulate and address the pathogen. Thus, doctors may check patients for swollen lymph nodes, which may indicate an active immune response.

Spleen: The spleen is an organ located behind the stomach. While it is not directly connected to the lymphatic system, it is important for processing information from the bloodstream. Immune cells are enriched in specific areas of the spleen, and upon recognizing blood-borne pathogens, they will activate and respond accordingly.

Mucosal tissue: Mucosal surfaces are prime entry points for pathogens, and specialized immune hubs are strategically located in mucosal tissues like the respiratory tract and gut. For instance, Peyer's patches are important areas in the small intestine where immune cells can access samples from the gastrointestinal tract.

Cold, Flu, or Allergy?

Know the Difference for Best Treatment

You're feeling pretty lousy. You've got sniffles, sneezing, and a sore throat. Is it a cold, flu, or allergies? It can be hard to tell them apart because they share so many symptoms. But understanding the differences will help you choose the best treatment.

"If you know what you have, you won't take medications that you don't need, that aren't effective, or that might even make your symptoms worse," says an expert on infectious diseases that affect breathing.

Cold, flu, and allergy all affect your respiratory system, which can make it hard to breathe. Each condition has key symptoms that set them apart.

Colds and flu are caused by different viruses. As a rule of thumb, the symptoms associated with the flu are more severe. Both illnesses can lead to a runny, stuffy nose; congestion; cough; and sore throat. But the flu can also cause high fever that lasts for 3–4 days, along with a headache, fatigue, and general aches and pain. These symptoms are less common when you have a cold.

Allergies are a little different, because they are not caused by a virus. Instead, it's your body's immune system reacting to a trigger, or allergen, which is something you're allergic to. If you have allergies and breathe in things like pollen or animal dander, the immune cells in your nose and airways may overreact to these harmless substances. Your delicate respiratory tissues may then swell, and your nose may become stuffed up or runny.

Allergies can also cause itchy, watery eyes, which you don't normally have with a cold or flu.

Allergy symptoms usually last as long as you're exposed to the allergen, which may be about 6 weeks during pollen seasons in the spring, summer, or fall. Colds and flu rarely last beyond 2 weeks.

Most people with a cold or flu recover on their own without medical care. But check with a health care provider if symptoms last beyond 10 days or if symptoms aren't relieved by over-the-counter medicines.

To treat colds or flu, get plenty of rest and drink lots of fluids. If you have the flu, pain relievers such as aspirin, acetaminophen, or ibuprofen can reduce fever or aches. Allergies can be treated with antihistamines or decongestants.

Be careful to avoid "drug overlap" when taking medicines that list two or more active ingredients on the label. For example, if you take 2 different drugs that contain acetaminophen—one for a stuffy nose and the other for headache—you may be getting too much acetaminophen.

Read medicine labels carefully—the warnings, side effects, dosages. If you have questions, talk to your doctor or pharmacist, especially if you have children who are sick. You don't want to overmedicate, and you don't want to risk taking a medication that may interact with another.

Table 1.1. Cold, Flu, or Allergy? Tips and Treatments

Symptoms	Cold	Flu	Airborne Allergy
Fever	Rare	Usual, high (100–102 °F), sometimes higher, especially in young children); lasts 3–4 days	Never
Headache	Uncommon	Common	Uncommon
General Aches, Pains	Slight	Usual; often severe	Never
Fatigue, Weakness	Sometimes	Usual, can last up to 3 weeks	Sometimes
Extreme Exhaustion	Never	Usual, at the beginning of the illness	Never
Stuffy, Runny Nose	Common	Sometimes	Common
Sneezing	Usual	Sometimes	Usual
Sore Throat	Common	Sometimes	Sometimes
Cough	Common	Common, can become severe	Sometimes
Chest Discomfort	Mild to moderate	Common	Rare, except for those with allergic asthma
Treatment	Get plenty of rest. Stay hydrated. (Drink plenty of fluids.) Decongestants. Aspirin (ages 18 and up), acetaminophen, or ibuprofen for aches and pains	Get plenty of rest. Stay hydrated. Aspirin (ages 18 and up), acetaminophen, or ibuprofen for aches, pains, and fever Antiviral medicines (see your doctor)	Avoid allergens (things that you're allergic to) Antihistamines Nasal steroids Decongestants
Prevention	Wash your hands often. Avoid close contact with anyone who has a cold.	Get the flu vaccine each year. Wash your hands often. Avoid close contact with anyone who has the flu.	Avoid allergens, such as pollen, house dust mites, mold, animal dander, cockroaches.
Complications	Sinus infection middle ear infection, asthma	Bronchitis, pneumonia; can be life-threatening	Sinus infection, middle ear infection, asthma

Features of an Immune Response

An immune response is generally divided into innate and adaptive immunity. Innate immunity occurs immediately, when circulating innate cells recognize a problem. Adaptive immunity occurs later, as it relies on the coordination and expansion of specific adaptive immune cells. Immune memory follows the adaptive response, when mature adaptive cells, highly specific to the original pathogen, are retained for later use.

Innate Immunity

Innate immune cells express genetically encoded receptors, called Toll-like receptors (TLRs), which recognize general danger- or pathogen-associated patterns. Collectively, these receptors can broadly recognize viruses, bacteria, fungi, and even non-infectious problems. However, they cannot distinguish between specific strains of bacteria or viruses.

There are numerous types of innate immune cells with specialized functions. They include neutrophils, eosinophils, basophils, mast cells, monocytes, dendritic cells, and macrophages. Their main feature is the ability to respond quickly and broadly when a problem arises, typically leading to inflammation. Innate immune cells also are important for activating adaptive immunity. Innate cells are critical for host defense, and disorders in innate cell function may cause chronic susceptibility to infection.

Adaptive Immunity

Adaptive immune cells are more specialized, with each adaptive B or T cell bearing unique receptors, B-cell receptors (BCRs) and T-cell receptors (TCRs), that recognize specific signals rather than general patterns. Each receptor recognizes an antigen, which is simply any molecule that may bind to a BCR or TCR. Antigens are derived from a variety of sources including pathogens, host cells, and allergens. Antigens are typically processed by innate immune cells and presented to adaptive cells in the lymph nodes.

The genes for BCRs and TCRs are randomly rearranged at specific cell maturation stages, resulting in unique receptors that may potentially recognize anything. Random generation of receptors allows the immune system to respond to new or unforeseen problems. This concept is especially important because environments may frequently change, for instance when seasons change or a person relocates, and pathogens are constantly evolving to survive. Because BCRs and TCRs are so specific, adaptive cells may only recognize one strain of a particular pathogen, unlike innate cells, which recognize broad classes of pathogens. In fact, a group of adaptive cells that recognize the same strain will likely recognize different areas of that pathogen.

If a B or T cell has a receptor that recognizes an antigen from a pathogen and also receives cues from innate cells that something is wrong, the B or T cell will activate, divide, and disperse to address the problem. B cells make antibodies, which neutralize pathogens, rendering them harmless. T cells carry out multiple functions, including killing infected cells and activating or recruiting other immune cells. The adaptive response has a system of checks and balances to prevent unnecessary activation that could cause damage to the host. If a B or T cell is autoreactive, meaning its receptor recognizes antigens from the body's own cells, the cell will be deleted. Also, if a B or T cell does not receive signals from innate cells, it will not be optimally activated.

Immune memory is a feature of the adaptive immune response. After B or T cells are activated, they expand rapidly. As the problem resolves, cells stop dividing and are retained in the body as memory cells. The next time this same pathogen enters the body, a memory cell is already poised to react and can clear away the pathogen before it establishes itself.

Vaccination

Vaccination, or immunization, is a way to train your immune system against a specific pathogen. Vaccination achieves immune memory without an actual infection, so the body is prepared when the virus or bacterium enters. Saving time is important to prevent a pathogen from establishing itself and infecting more cells in the body.

An effective vaccine will optimally activate both the innate and adaptive response. An immunogen is used to activate the adaptive immune response so that specific memory cells are generated. Because BCRs and TCRs are unique, some memory cells are simply better at eliminating the pathogen. The goal of vaccine design is to select immunogens that will generate the most effective and efficient memory response against a particular pathogen. Adjuvants, which are important for activating innate immunity, can be added to vaccines to optimize the immune response. Innate immunity recognizes broad patterns, and without innate responses, adaptive immunity cannot be optimally achieved.

Immune Tolerance

Tolerance is the prevention of an immune response against a particular antigen. For instance, the immune system is generally tolerant of self-antigens, so it does not usually attack the body's own cells, tissues, and organs. However, when tolerance is lost, disorders like autoimmune disease or food allergy may occur. Tolerance is maintained in a number of ways:

- When adaptive immune cells mature, there are several checkpoints in place to eliminate autoreactive cells. If a B cell produces antibodies that strongly recognize host cells, or if a T cell strongly recognizes self-antigen, they are deleted.

- Nevertheless, there are autoreactive immune cells present in healthy individuals. Autoreactive immune cells are kept in a non-reactive, or anergic, state. Even though they recognize the body's own cells, they do not have the ability to react and cannot cause host damage.

- Regulatory immune cells circulate throughout the body to maintain tolerance. Besides limiting autoreactive cells, regulatory cells are important for turning an immune response off after the problem is resolved. They can act as drains, depleting areas of essential nutrients that surrounding immune cells need for activation or survival.

- Some locations in the body are called immunologically privileged sites. These areas, like the eye and brain, do not typically elicit strong immune responses. Part of this is because of physical barriers, like the blood-brain barrier, that limit the degree to which immune cells may enter. These areas also may express higher levels of suppressive cytokines to prevent a robust immune response.

Fetomaternal tolerance is the prevention of a maternal immune response against a developing fetus. Major histocompatibility complex (MHC) proteins help the immune system distinguish between host and foreign cells. MHC also is called human leukocyte antigen (HLA). By expressing paternal MHC or HLA proteins and paternal antigens, a fetus can potentially trigger the mother's immune system. However, there are several barriers that may prevent this from occurring: The placenta reduces the exposure of the fetus to maternal immune cells, the proteins expressed on the outer layer of the placenta may limit immune recognition, and regulatory cells and suppressive signals may play a role.

Transplantation of a donor tissue or organ requires appropriate MHC or HLA matching to limit the risk of rejection. Because MHC or HLA matching is rarely complete, transplant recipients must continuously take immunosuppressive drugs, which can cause complications like higher susceptibility to infection and some cancers. Researchers are developing more targeted ways to induce tolerance to transplanted tissues and organs while leaving protective immune responses intact.

Disorders of the Immune System

Complications arise when the immune system does not function properly. Some issues are less pervasive, such as pollen allergy, while others are extensive, such as genetic disorders that wipe out the presence or function of an entire set of immune cells.

Immune Deficiencies

Immune deficiencies may be temporary or permanent. Temporary immune deficiency can be caused by a variety of sources that weaken the immune system. Common infections, including influenza and mononucleosis, can suppress the immune system.

When immune cells are the target of infection, severe immune suppression can occur. For example, HIV specifically infects T cells, and their elimination allows for secondary infections by other pathogens. Patients receiving chemotherapy, bone marrow transplants, or immunosuppressive drugs experience weakened immune systems until immune cell levels are restored. Pregnancy also suppresses the maternal immune system, increasing susceptibility to infections by common microbes.

Primary immune deficiency diseases (PIDDs) are inherited genetic disorders and tend to cause chronic susceptibility to infection. There are over 150 PIDDs, and almost all are considered rare (affecting fewer than 200,000 people in the United States). They may result from altered immune signaling molecules or the complete absence of mature immune cells. For instance, X-linked severe combined immunodeficiency (SCID) is caused by a mutation in a signaling receptor gene, rendering immune cells insensitive to multiple cytokines. Without the growth and activation signals delivered by cytokines, immune cell subsets, particularly T and natural killer cells, fail to develop normally.

Allergy

Allergies are a form of hypersensitivity reaction, typically in response to harmless environmental allergens like pollen or food. Hypersensitivity reactions are divided into four classes. Class I, II, and III are caused by antibodies, IgE or IgG, which are produced by B cells in response to an allergen. Overproduction of these antibodies activates immune cells like basophils and mast cells, which respond by releasing inflammatory chemicals like histamine. Class IV reactions are caused by T cells, which may either directly cause damage themselves or activate macrophages and eosinophils that damage host cells.

Autoimmune Diseases

Autoimmune diseases occur when self-tolerance is broken. Self-tolerance breaks when adaptive immune cells that recognize host cells persist unchecked. B cells may produce antibodies targeting host cells, and active T cells may recognize self-antigen. This amplifies when they recruit and activate other immune cells.

Autoimmunity is either organ-specific or systemic, meaning it affects the whole body. For instance, type I diabetes is organ-specific and caused by immune cells erroneously recognizing insulin-producing pancreatic β cells as foreign. However, systemic lupus erythematosus, commonly called lupus, can result from antibodies that recognize antigens expressed by nearly all healthy cells. Autoimmune diseases have a strong genetic component, and with advances in gene sequencing tools, researchers have a better understanding of what may contribute to specific diseases.

Sepsis

Sepsis may refer to an infection of the bloodstream, or it can refer to a systemic inflammatory state caused by the uncontrolled, broad release of cytokines that quickly activate immune cells throughout the body. Sepsis is an extremely serious condition and is typically triggered by an infection. However, the damage itself is caused by cytokines (the adverse response is sometimes referred to as a "cytokine storm"). The systemic release of cytokines may lead to loss of blood pressure, resulting in septic shock and possible multi-organ failure.

Cancer

Some forms of cancer are directly caused by the uncontrolled growth of immune cells. Leukemia is cancer caused by white blood cells, which is another term for immune cells. Lymphoma is cancer caused by lymphocytes, which is another term for adaptive B or T cells. Myeloma is cancer caused by plasma cells, which are mature B cells. Unrestricted growth of any of these cell types causes cancer.

In addition, an emerging concept is that cancer progression may partially result from the ability of cancer cells to avoid immune detection. The immune system is capable of removing infectious pathogens and dangerous host cells like tumors. Cancer researchers are studying how the tumor microenvironment may allow cancer cells to evade immune cells. Immune evasion may result from the abundance of suppressive, regulatory immune cells, excessive inhibitory cytokines, and other features that are not well understood.

Chapter 2

How Does an Allergic Response Work

In allergy-prone people, initial encounters with an allergy-triggering substance, or allergen, prompt changes in the immune system that eventually may lead to allergy symptoms. This stage is called sensitization. When an allergy-prone person inhales pollen, for example, immune cells in the lining of the nose or lungs engulf the pollen allergen and process it into small fragments. These cells, called antigen-presenting cells (APCs), display the allergen fragments on their surfaces.

When white blood cells called type 2 T helper (Th2) cells come into contact with the allergen fragments on APCs, they become activated. The Th2 cells then interact with immune cells known as B cells and release chemical signals that help the B cells develop into antibody-producing plasma cells. These plasma cells make large amounts of a type of antibody called immunoglobulin E (IgE). Each IgE molecule is specific to a particular allergen. IgE produced after exposure to grass pollen, for example, is specific for grass and will not cause a reaction to ragweed pollen. IgE binds to the surface of specialized cells called

Text in this chapter is excerpted from "Allergic Diseases," National Institute of Allergy and Infectious Diseases (NIAID), April 21, 2015; and text from "Asthma: The Hygiene Hypothesis," U.S. Food and Drug Administration (FDA), January 1, 2015.

mast cells that reside in the tissues, particularly in the skin and at mucous membranes.

When a person who has made IgE to an allergen is exposed to the same allergen again, the allergen interacts with IgE on the surface of mast cells. The binding of allergen to IgE triggers these cells to release histamine, leukotrienes, and other chemicals, leading to allergy symptoms. For example, histamine acts on nerves, which can cause sneezing, an itchy feeling, and a runny nose. Leukotrienes contribute to the widening of blood vessels, which can result in swelling inside the nose, causing a stuffy nose. In people with asthma, if mast cells in the airways are triggered by allergens, leukotrienes can make the muscles surrounding the airways contract, narrowing the airways and causing an asthma attack. Drugs known as antihistamines or leukotriene receptor antagonists block the action of histamine and leukotrienes and can provide relief from allergy symptoms.

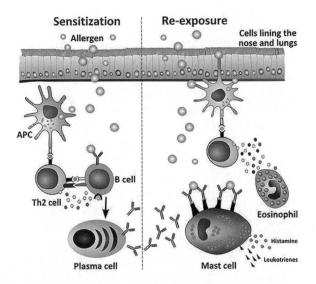

Figure 2.1. *Sensitization and Re-exposure*

During sensitization, an antigen-presenting cell (APC) picks up the allergen and presents part of it to a Th2 cell, which helps a B cell become a plasma cell. Plasma cells produce allergen-specific antibodies called IgE, which binds to mast cells. When allergen returns, mast cells release histamine and other chemicals. In addition, Th2 cells release many different chemicals that attract inflammatory cells such as eosinophils. This results in allergy symptoms such as sneezing, mucus production, swelling, itching, runny nose, coughing, and wheezing.

Re-exposure to an allergen also causes mast cells and Th2 cells to release chemical messengers that attract and activate other inflammatory cells, such as eosinophils and basophils, which release more chemicals and cause allergy symptoms to worsen and last longer. Nasal steroids are anti-inflammatory medications that help decrease the inflammatory cell responses to an allergen.

What do clean houses have in common with childhood infections?

One of the many explanations for asthma being the most common chronic disease in the developed world is the "hygiene hypothesis." This hypothesis suggests that the critical post-natal period of immune response is derailed by the extremely clean household environments often found in the developed world. In other words, the young child's environment can be "too clean" to pose an effective challenge to a maturing immune system.

According to the "hygiene hypothesis," the problem with extremely clean environments is that they fail to provide the necessary exposure to germs required to "educate" the immune system so it can learn to launch its defense responses to infectious organisms. Instead, its defense responses end up being so inadequate that they actually contribute to the development of asthma.

Scientists based this hypothesis in part on the observation that, before birth, the fetal immune system's "default setting" is suppressed to prevent it from rejecting maternal tissue. Such a low default setting is necessary before birth—when the mother is providing the fetus with her own antibodies. But in the period immediately after birth the child's own immune system must take over and learn how to fend for itself.

The "hygiene hypothesis" is supported by epidemiologic studies demonstrating that allergic diseases and asthma are more likely to occur when the incidence and levels of endotoxin (bacterial lipopolysaccharide, or LPS) in the home are low. LPS is a bacterial molecule that stimulates and educates the immune system by triggering signals through a molecular "switch" called TLR4, which is found on certain immune system cells.

Science behind the hygiene hypothesis

The Inflammatory Mechanisms Section of the Laboratory of Immunobiochemistry is working to better understand the hygiene hypothesis, by looking at the relationship between respiratory viruses and allergic diseases and asthma, and by studying the respiratory syncytial virus (RSV) in particular.

What does RSV have to do with the hygiene hypothesis?

- RSV is often the first viral pathogen encountered by infants.

- RSV pneumonia puts infants at higher risk for developing childhood asthma. (Although children may outgrow this type of asthma, it can account for clinic visits and missed school days.)

- RSV carries a molecule on its surface called the F protein, which flips the same immune system "switch" (TLR4) as do bacterial endotoxins.

It may seem obvious that, since both the RSV F protein and LPS signal through the same TLR4 "switch," they both would educate the infant's immune system in the same beneficial way. But that may not be the case.

The large population of bacteria that normally lives inside humans educates the growing immune system to respond using the TLR4 switch. When this education is lacking or weak, the response to RSV by some critical cells in the immune system's defense against infections—called "T-cells"—might inadvertently trigger asthma instead of protecting the infant and clearing the infection.

In order to determine RSV's role in triggering asthma, the laboratory studied how RSV blocks T-cell proliferation.

Studying the effect of RSV on T-cells in the laboratory, however, has been very difficult. That's because when RSV is put into the same culture as T-cells, it blocks them from multiplying as they would naturally do when they are stimulated. To get past this problem, most researchers kill RSV with ultraviolet light before adding the virus to T-cell cultures. However we did not have the option of killing the RSV because that would have prevented us from determining the virus's role in triggering asthma.

The first major discovery at the laboratory was that, RSV causes the release from certain immune system cells of signaling molecules called Type I and Type III interferons that can suppress T-cell proliferation.

Conclusion

The hygiene hypothesis suggests that a newborn baby's immune system must be educated so it will function properly during infancy and the rest of life. One of the key elements of this education is a switch on T cells called TLR4. The bacterial protein LPS normally plays a key role by flipping that switch into the "on" position.

Prior research suggested that since RSV flips the TLR4 switch, RSV should "educate" the child's immune system to defend against infections just like LPS does.

But it turns out that RSV does not flip the TLR switch in the same way as LPS. This difference in switching on TLR, combined with other characteristics of RSV, can prevent proper education of the immune system.

One difference in the way that RSV flips the TLR4 switch may be through the release of interferons, which suppresses the proliferation of T-cells. We still do not know whether these interferons are part of the reason the immune system is not properly educated or simply an indicator of the problem. Therefore, we plan to continue our studies about how RSV can contribute to the development of asthma according to the hygiene hypothesis.

Chapter 3

Allergen Immunotherapy

Most people manage their allergies by avoiding allergy-triggering substances (allergens) and taking medications to provide temporary relief from symptoms. For some types of allergies, allergen immunotherapy is an additional and often useful approach that involves introducing increasing amounts of allergens to the immune system. Immunotherapy is a long-term treatment that may help prevent or reduce the severity of allergic reactions and can change the course of allergic disease by modifying the body's immune response to allergens. Immunotherapy can be used to treat environmental allergies and is particularly effective at reducing the risk of severe allergic reactions to stings from some insects, such as bees and yellow jackets. Improvements in allergy symptoms may last for several years after stopping immunotherapy. Scientists are attempting to use immunotherapy to prevent and treat food allergy. However, the balance between the benefits and risks of immunotherapy for food allergy has not yet been well-studied, and it currently is not recommended except as an experimental approach.

National Institute of Allergy and Infectious Diseases (NIAID) research efforts on allergen immunotherapy focus on the prevention and treatment of asthma, allergic rhinitis (hay fever), and food allergy.

This chapter includes excerpts from "Allergen Immunotherapy," National Institute of Allergy and Infectious Diseases (NIAID), April 22, 2015; text from "Immunotherapy for Environmental Allergies," National Institute of Allergy and Infectious Diseases (NIAID), May 12, 2015; and text from "Immunotherapy for Food Allergy," National Institute of Allergy and Infectious Diseases (NIAID), May 12, 2015.

NIAID-supported research aims to increase the effectiveness and safety of immunotherapy, reduce the duration of treatment, advance the development of safe and effective immunotherapy for food allergy, and improve understanding of how immunotherapy helps reduce allergic symptoms in these diseases.

Types of Allergen Immunotherapies

1. Immunotherapy for environmental allergies
2. Immunotherapy for food allergies

Immunotherapy for Environmental Allergies

Allergic rhinitis, commonly known as hay fever, occurs when the immune system overreacts to airborne allergens, such as those from pollens, animal dander, dust mites, cockroaches, and molds. These environmental allergies can cause symptoms such as sneezing, a runny and stuffy nose, and itchy or watery eyes. Reactions to allergens often also play an important role in asthma. Surveys performed at clinical practices suggest that many patients do not get complete relief from medications and may be candidates for immunotherapy.

Allergy shots, or subcutaneous immunotherapy, have been used for more than 100 years and can provide long-lasting symptom relief. In 2014, the Food and Drug Administration approved three types of under-the-tongue tablets for allergies to grass and ragweed. The treatments, called sublingual immunotherapy, offer a potential alternative to allergy shots for people with these allergies.

Subcutaneous Immunotherapy

Subcutaneous immunotherapy (SCIT) involves a series of shots containing small amounts of allergen into the fat under the skin.

SCIT includes two phases: a buildup phase and a maintenance phase. During the buildup phase, doctors administer injections containing gradually increasing amounts of allergen once or twice per week. This phase generally lasts from three to six months, depending on how often the shots are given and the body's response. The aim is to reach a target dose that has been shown to be effective. Once the target dose is reached, the maintenance phase begins. Shots are given less frequently during the maintenance phase, typically every two to four weeks. Some people begin experiencing a decrease in symptoms during the buildup phase, but others may not notice an improvement until the maintenance phase.

Maintenance therapy generally lasts three to five years. The decision about how long to continue SCIT is based on how well it is working and how well a person tolerates the shots. For example, if after one year of maintenance therapy there is no evidence of improvement, it is hard to justify continuing immunotherapy for another two to four years. On the other hand, if a person is entirely symptom-free, he or she may choose to stop after three years rather than complete five years of treatment. Many people continue to experience benefits for several years after the shots are stopped, and the theoretical potential of "curing" allergy makes the concept of immunotherapy very attractive.

Side-effects from SCIT are usually minor and may include swelling or redness at the injection site. However, there is a small risk of serious allergic reactions such as anaphylaxis. Because most severe reactions occur shortly after injection, it is recommended that patients remain under medical supervision for at least half an hour after receiving a shot. Patients whose asthma is not under control are recommended to postpone their shot until their asthma is stable.

An estimated 5 percent of people with environmental allergies receive SCIT for allergic rhinitis and asthma, and less than 20 percent of people who begin SCIT finish the entire treatment course. The time and cost commitments that SCIT requires likely discourage some people from starting or completing treatment. Development of new forms of immunotherapy that require shorter treatment duration may result in more patients being interested in receiving allergen immunotherapy.

NIAID funds research to investigate several approaches to improve the effectiveness and safety of SCIT and decrease the duration of treatment. Scientists are exploring the use of modified allergens that may elicit the same or better effects with fewer shots, while decreasing the risk of side effects. Scientists also are developing treatment approaches that combine SCIT with other medications. For example, researchers from the NIAID-sponsored Immune Tolerance Network are testing a combination of SCIT and an investigational allergy drug as a potential treatment for cat allergy.

Sublingual Immunotherapy

People taking sublingual immunotherapy (SLIT) place a tablet containing allergen under the tongue. SLIT tablets are taken daily and kept under the tongue for one to two minutes, then swallowed. The allergen doses used in SLIT typically are higher than those used in SCIT. For example, a daily SLIT dose for grass pollen is roughly equivalent to a monthly SCIT dose.

SLIT has been widely used in Europe for several years and is available in the United States for treatment of grass and ragweed allergies.

Studies show that there are fewer allergic reactions to SLIT compared to SCIT. After the first SLIT dose is given at the doctor's office, patients can take subsequent doses at home. However, even though therapy is taken at home, many people do not complete the recommended three years of treatment.

Side effects of SLIT are usually minor and may include itching of the mouth, lips, or throat. Severe allergic reactions (anaphylaxis) are extremely rare, and this represents a clear advantage over allergy shots. Nevertheless, because treatment takes place at home, doctors may prescribe an epinephrine autoinjector (EpiPen) to people receiving SLIT for use in the event of a severe allergic reaction.

The NIAID-funded Immune Tolerance Network is conducting a side-by-side evaluation of SLIT or SCIT for grass allergy. This will help determine whether there are any differences in the effectiveness of these two types of immunotherapy.

How Does Immunotherapy Work?

Scientists have developed a general understanding of how SCIT and SLIT may work to prevent and treat allergies, although many of the details of this process have yet to be unraveled.

An allergic response begins when an allergen is taken up by cells known as antigen-presenting cells (APCs). The APCs break down the allergen and display fragments of it on their surfaces, alerting other cells to become active and starting a chain of events that leads to allergy symptoms. The amount of allergen given in an allergy shot or as an under-the-tongue tablet is much larger than the amount that would be encountered during a natural exposure. This difference in quantity may be responsible for the change in the kind of immune response that is started by the APCs. Instead of activating type 2 T helper (Th2) cells, which play a key role in promoting an allergic response, APCs activate specialized immune cells called regulatory T cells (Tregs). Tregs begin to release a variety of chemical messengers that lead to the suppression, change in function, or elimination of the Th2 cells. Tregs can also influence B cells, the cells that develop into antibody-producing plasma cells. As a result, plasma cells produce less IgE, the main type of antibody involved in allergic reactions and also may make more of other types of allergen-specific antibodies known as "blocking" antibodies. Blocking antibodies recognize and bind to the allergen, preventing it from binding to IgE and triggering an allergic reaction.

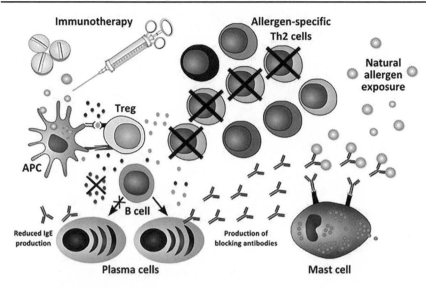

Figure 3.1. *Immunotherapy*

Allergen introduced to the body by allergy shots or under-the-tongue tablets is processed by antigen-presenting cells (APCs), which activate regulatory cells (Tregs). Signals sent by the APCs and Tregs lead to changes in production of chemical messengers, increasing those that are anti-allergic and decreasing those that are pro-allergic. In addition, allergy-promoting type 2 T helper (Th2) cells that specifically recognize the allergen are suppressed or deleted. However, other Th2 cells that do not contribute to the allergic response are not affected. Tregs can also influence B cells, which develop into antibody-producing plasma cells. Plasma cells are driven to produce less IgE and more blocking antibodies. Blocking antibodies bind to allergen and do not allow it to reach the mast cells and start an allergic reaction.

Immunotherapy for Food Allergy

Current strategies to manage food allergy involve avoiding foods that may cause an allergic reaction and treating severe reactions as they arise. However, avoiding food allergens can be difficult because they are often "hidden" in unexpected foods. For example, the coating of a fruit-flavored jelly bean may contain peanut allergen. Therefore, scientists are working to develop immunotherapy approaches to prevent and treat food allergy. These experimental therapies include oral immunotherapy, therapy with baked milk or egg, sublingual (under-the-tongue) immunotherapy, and epicutaneous (skin patch) immunotherapy. Initial attempts to use allergy shots, or subcutaneous immunotherapy, to treat food allergy have been stopped because too many people experienced severe allergic reactions after receiving the injections.

All forms of immunotherapy for food allergy are experimental, and although some trained clinicians offer them, these therapies are not approved by the U.S. Food and Drug Administration (FDA). People should not try immunotherapy on their own because of the risk of severe reactions. The therapy should be administered only under the guidance of trained clinicians.

Oral Immunotherapy

Oral immunotherapy (OIT) currently is being tested in several NIAID-funded and other clinical trials. It involves eating small but gradually increasing doses of the food that causes the allergy every day, usually in the form of a powder mixed with a harmless food.

The most common side effects associated with OIT are mouth itching and swelling and stomach aches. However, severe allergic reactions requiring treatment with epinephrine, an emergency rescue medication that is given by injection, have occurred in some cases. Some people who have participated in OIT studies discontinued OIT due to side effects. The gastrointestinal side effects of OIT sometimes can be severe and may be due to the development of a condition called eosinophilic esophagitis, which often is associated with food allergy.

OIT has shown some benefits in small clinical trials for treatment of milk, egg, and peanut allergies. However, there are still many issues that need to be addressed, including the safety of the treatment, the number of people who will benefit, the duration of improvement, and the effectiveness of OIT for a wider variety of foods.

NIAID supports research to evaluate the role of OIT in treating and managing food allergy. A study from the NIAID-funded Consortium of Food Allergy Research suggested that egg OIT can benefit children with egg allergy. Most of the study participants could be safely exposed to egg while on egg OIT, and some were able to safely eat egg after stopping OIT for four to six weeks.

NIAID also is funding peanut OIT trials in older children and adults, as well as another trial to evaluate OIT for multiple food allergies at the same time.

Baked Milk and Egg Therapy

Consumption of baked milk and egg is a potential alternative to OIT for treatment of milk and egg allergies. Temperature-associated changes in certain milk and egg proteins may render baked versions of these foods less allergenic. However, the same does not hold true for all allergy-triggering foods. Roasting peanuts, for example, can make them more likely to cause allergic reactions.

Studies have suggested that some children who are allergic to uncooked egg and milk can tolerate small amounts of these foods in fully cooked products such as muffins. An NIAID-funded study found that more than half of baked-milk-tolerant children who followed specific instructions to include baked milk products into their diets eventually were able to tolerate foods containing uncooked milk. The results also suggested that children who ate baked milk outgrew their milk allergies more quickly than children who did not eat baked milk. However, many children treated with baked products may never be able to eat unheated milk without allergic reactions. More studies need to be done to determine whether the baked food approach benefits some people with food allergy.

Sublingual Immunotherapy

Sublingual immunotherapy (SLIT) involves holding drops containing food allergen extract under the tongue, then swallowing or spitting them out. Currently, very little information is available regarding food allergen SLIT. More work is needed to determine the potential role of this therapy in treating food allergy, including appropriate dosing and length of treatment, before SLIT can be considered a safe or effective option.

Epicutaneous Immunotherapy

In epicutaneous immunotherapy (EPIT), another experimental form of immunotherapy, allergen is delivered to the skin surface by a patch. The NIAID-funded Consortium of Food Allergy Research currently is conducting a clinical trial evaluating EPIT for the treatment of peanut allergy in children and young adults.

Prevention of Food Allergy

For many years, parents of children at high risk of developing food allergies were advised to wait to put common food allergens into their children's diet. For example, it was recommended that eggs be avoided until 2 years of age and peanuts until 3 years. However, food allergy continued to become more common, suggesting that delayed introduction was not helping, and in 2008, this practice was no longer recommended by the American Academy of Pediatrics. In fact, by 2008, there was some evidence to suggest that early introduction might decrease the likelihood of developing food allergy.

In February 2015, scientists reported results from the Learning Early About Peanut Allergy (LEAP) study, a large clinical trial conducted by the NIAID-funded Immune Tolerance Network. The goal of this trial was to determine whether early exposure to peanut-containing foods can prevent the development of peanut allergy. The study enrolled 640 children under a year of age thought to be at high risk of peanut allergy because they had severe eczema, an allergy to egg, or both. These children were divided into a group that avoided peanuts until they were 5 years old and a group that immediately started eating peanut-containing foods at least three times per week. When the children reached 5 years of age, the rate of peanut allergy was 80 percent lower in the group that had eaten peanut products compared to the group that had avoided them. These results suggest that the early introduction of peanut into the diet may prevent the development of peanut allergy. Medical experts currently are discussing how the LEAP findings will change recommendations about introducing peanuts into the diet of infants and young children.

Chapter 4

Allergies in Children

Chapter Contents

Section 4.1

Allergy Relief for Your Child

Text in this section is excerpted from "Allergy Relief for Your Child,"
U.S. Food and Drug Administration (FDA), August 30, 2015.

How Allergies Affect Your Child

Children are magnets for colds. But when the "cold" won't go away
for weeks, the culprit may be allergies.

Long-lasting sneezing, with a stuffy or runny nose, may signal the
presence of allergic rhinitis—the collection of symptoms that affect the
nose when you have an allergic reaction to something you breathe in
and that lands on the lining inside the nose.

Allergies may be seasonal or they can strike year-round (perennial).
In most parts of the United States, plant pollens are often the cause
of seasonal allergic rhinitis—more commonly called hay fever. Indoor
substances, such as mold, dust mites, and animal dander, may cause
the perennial kind.

Up to 40 percent of children suffer from allergic rhinitis, according
to the National Institute of Allergy and Infectious Diseases (NIAID).
And children are more likely to develop allergies if one or both parents
have allergies.

The Food and Drug Administration (FDA) regulates both over-the-
counter (OTC) and prescription medicines that offer allergy relief as
well as allergen extracts used to diagnose and treat allergies.

Immune System Reaction

An allergy is a reaction of the immune system to a specific substance, or allergen. The immune system responds to the invading
allergen by releasing histamine and other chemicals that typically
trigger symptoms in the nose, lungs, throat, sinuses, ears, eyes, skin,
or stomach lining, according to the American Academy of Allergy,
Asthma and Immunology.

In some children, allergies can also trigger symptoms of asthma—a
disease that causes wheezing or difficulty breathing.

If a child has allergies and asthma, "not controlling the allergies can make asthma worse," says Anthony Durmowicz, M.D., a pediatric pulmonary doctor in FDA's Division of Pulmonary, Allergy, and Rheumatology Products.

Avoiding the Culprit

If your child has seasonal allergies, you may want to pay attention to pollen counts and try to keep your child inside when the levels are high.

- In the late summer and early fall, during ragweed pollen season, pollen levels are highest in the morning.

- In the spring and summer, during the grass pollen season, pollen levels are highest in the evening.

- Some molds, another allergy trigger, may also be seasonal. For example, leaf mold is more common in the fall.

- Sunny, windy days can be especially troublesome for pollen allergy sufferers.

It may also help to keep windows closed in your house and car and run the air conditioner when pollen counts are high.

Allergy Medicines

For most children, symptoms may be controlled by avoiding the allergen, if known, and using OTC medicines. However, if a child's symptoms are persistent and not relieved by OTC medicines, it is wise to see a health care professional to assess your child's symptoms and see if other treatments, including prescription medicines, may be appropriate. Five types of drugs are generally available to help bring your child relief.

While some allergy medicines are approved for use in children as young as six months, always read the label to make sure the product is appropriate for your child's age. Just because a product's box says that it is intended for children does not mean it is intended for children of all ages.

Children are more sensitive than adults to many drugs. For example, some antihistamines can have adverse effects at lower doses on young patients, causing excitability or excessive drowsiness.

More Child-Friendly Medicines

Recent pediatric legislation, including a combination of incentives and requirements for drug companies, has significantly increased research and development of drugs for children and has led to more products with new pediatric information in their labeling. Since 1997, a combination of legislative activities has helped generate studies in children for 400 products.

Many of the older drugs were only tested in adults, but the FDA now has more information available for the newer allergy medications. With the passing of this legislation, there should be more confidence in pediatric dosing and safety with the newer drugs.

The legislation also requires drugs for children to be in a child-friendly formulation. So if the drug was initially developed as a capsule, it has to also be made in a form that a child can take, such as a liquid with cherry flavoring, rapidly dissolving tablets, or strips for placing under the tongue.

Allergy Shots

Children who don't respond to either OTC or prescription medications, or who suffer from frequent complications of allergic rhinitis, may be candidates for allergen immunotherapy—commonly known as allergy shots. According to NIAID, about 80 percent of people with allergic rhinitis will see their symptoms and need for medicine drop significantly within a year of starting allergy shots.

After allergy testing, typically by skin testing to detect what allergens your child may react to, a health care professional injects the child with "extracts"—small amounts of the allergens that trigger a reaction. The doses are gradually increased so that the body builds up immunity to these allergens.

Allergen extracts are manufactured from natural substances, such as pollens, insect venoms, animal hair, and foods. More than 1,200 extracts are licensed by FDA.

Some doctors are buying extracts licensed for injection and instructing the parents to administer the extracts using a dropper under the child's tongue, says Jay E. Slater, M.D., director of FDA's Division of Bacterial, Parasitic and Allergenic Products. "While FDA considers this the practice of medicine (and the agency does not regulate the practice of medicine), parents and patients should be aware that there are no allergenic extracts currently licensed by FDA for oral use."

"Allergy shots are never appropriate for food allergies," adds Slater, who is also a pediatrician and allergist. But it's common to use extracts to test for food allergies so the child can avoid those foods.

Transformation in Treatment

"In the last 20 years, there has been a remarkable transformation in allergy treatments," says Slater. "Kids used to be miserable for months out of the year, and drugs made them incredibly sleepy. But today's products are outstanding in terms of safety and efficacy."

Forgoing treatment can make for an irritable, sleepless, and unhappy child, adds Slater, recalling a mother saying, after her child's successful treatment, "I didn't realize I had a nice kid!"

Table 4.1. FDA-Approved Drug Options for Treatment of Allergic Rhinitis (Hay Fever) in Children

Drug Type	How Used	Some Examples of Over-the-Counter (OTC) or Prescription (Rx) Drugs (many are available in generic form)	Common Side Effects
Nasal corticosteroids	Usually sprayed in nose once a day	Rx: Nasonex (mometasone furoate) Flonase (fluticasone propionate)	Stinging in nose
Oral and topical antihistamines	Orally (pills, liquid, or strip placed under the tongue), nasally (spray or drops), or eye drops	Oral OTC: Benadryl (diphenhydramine) Chlor-Trimeton (chlorpheniramine) Allegra (fexofenadine) Claritin (loratadine) Zyrtec (cetirizine) Oral Rx: Clarinex (desloratadine) Nasal Rx: Astelin (azelastine) Non-sedating	Some antihistamines may cause drowsiness Some nasal sprays may cause a bitter taste in mouth, headache, and stinging in nose

Table 4.1. Continued

Drug Type	How Used	Some Examples of Over-the-Counter (OTC) or Prescription (Rx) Drugs (many are available in generic form)	Common Side Effects
Decongestants	Orally and nasally (some-times taken with antihistamines, which used alone do not treat nasal congestion)	Oral Sudafed (pseudoephedrine*), Sudafed PE (phenylephrine)Oral Rx: Allegra D, which has both an antihistamine (fexofenadine) and decongestant (pseudoephedrine*) Nasal OTC: Neo-Synephrine (phenylephrine) Afrin (oxymetazoline) Drugs that contain pseudoephedrine are non-prescription but are kept behind the pharmacy counter because of their illegal use to make methamphetamine. You'll need to ask your pharmacist and show identification to buy these drugs.	Using nose sprays or drops more than a few days may cause "rebound" effect, in which nasal congestion gets worse
Non-steroidal nasal sprays	Nasally used 3–4 times a day	OTC: NasalCrom (cromolyn sodium) Rx: Atrovent (ipratropium bromide)	Stinging in nose or sneezing; can help prevent symptoms of allergic rhinitis if used before symptoms start
Leukotriene receptor antagonist	Orally once a day (comes in granules to mix with food, and chewable tablets)	Rx: Singulair (montelukast sodium)	Headache, ear infection, sore throat, upper respiratory infection

Section 4.2

Trends in Allergic Conditions among Children in the United States

Text in this section is excerpted from "NCHS Data Brief," Centers for Disease Control and Prevention (CDC), May 2, 2013.

Key findings

Data from the National Health Interview Survey

- The prevalence of food and skin allergies increased in children under age 18 years.

- The prevalence of skin allergies decreased with age. In contrast, the prevalence of respiratory allergies increased with age.

- Hispanic children had a lower prevalence of food allergy, skin allergy, and respiratory allergy compared with children of other race or ethnicities. Non-Hispanic black children were more likely to have skin allergies and less likely to have respiratory allergies compared with non-Hispanic white children.

- Food and respiratory allergy prevalence increased with income level. Children with family income equal to or greater than 200% of the poverty level had the highest prevalence rates.

Allergic conditions are among the most common medical conditions affecting children in the United States. An allergic condition is a hypersensitivity disorder in which the immune system reacts to substances in the environment that are normally considered harmless. Food or digestive allergies, skin allergies (such as eczema), and respiratory allergies (such as hay fever) are the most common allergies among children. Allergies can affect a child's physical and emotional health and can interfere with daily activities, such as sleep, play, and attending school. A severe allergic reaction with rapid onset, anaphylaxis, can be life threatening. Foods represent the most common cause of anaphylaxis among children and adolescents. Early detection and appropriate interventions can help to decrease the negative impact of allergies on quality of life. This report presents recent trends in the prevalence of allergies and differences by selected sociodemographic characteristics for children under age 18 years.

The prevalence of food and skin allergies increased in children aged 0–17 years from 1997–2011.

Among children aged 0–17 years, the prevalence of food allergies increased from 3.4% in 1997–1999 to 5.1% in 2009–2011. The prevalence of skin allergies increased from 7.4% in 1997–1999 to 12.5% in 2009–2011. There was no significant trend in respiratory allergies from 1997–1999 to 2009–2011, yet respiratory allergy remained the most common type of allergy among children throughout this period (17.0% in 2009–2011). Skin allergy prevalence was also higher than food allergy prevalence for each period. (Figure 4.1).

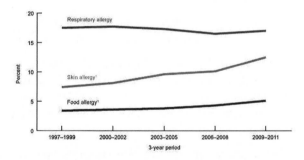

Figure 4.1. *Percentage of children aged 0–17 years with a reported allergic condition in the past 12 months: United States, 1997–2011*

1. Significant increasing linear trend for food and skin allergy.
SOURCE: CDC/NCHS, Health Data Interactive, National Health Interview Survey.

Younger children were more likely to have skin allergies, while older children were more likely to have respiratory allergies.

Food allergy prevalence was similar among all age groups. Skin allergy prevalence decreased with the increase of age (14.2% among 0–4 years, 13.1% among 5–9 years, and 10.9% among 10–17 years); while respiratory allergy prevalence increased with the increase of age (10.8% among 0–4 years, 17.4% among 5–9 years, and 20.8% among 10–17 years). (Figure 4.2).

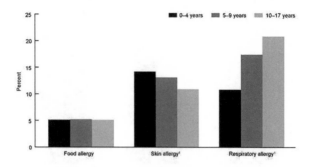

Figure 4.2. *Percentage of children aged 0–17 years with a reported allergic condition in the past 12 months, by age group: United States, average annual 2009–2011*

1. Significant trend by age group.
SOURCE: CDC/NCHS, Health Data Interactive, National Health Interview Survey.

Hispanic children had lower rates of all three types of allergies compared with children of other race or ethnicities. Non-Hispanic black children were more likely to have skin allergies and less likely to have respiratory allergies compared with non-Hispanic white children.

Hispanic children had a lower prevalence of food allergy (3.6%), skin allergy (10.1%), and respiratory allergy (13.0%) compared with non-Hispanic white and non-Hispanic black children. Non-Hispanic black children had a higher percentage of reported skin allergy (17.4%) compared with non-Hispanic white children (12.0%) and a lower percentage of respiratory allergy (15.6%) compared with non-Hispanic white children (19.1%).

The prevalence of food and respiratory allergy, but not skin allergy, increased with higher income levels.

The prevalence of both food allergy and respiratory allergy increased with the increase of income level. Among children with family income less than 100% of the poverty level, 4.4% had a food allergy and 14.9% had a respiratory allergy. Food allergy prevalence among children with family income between 100% and 200% of the poverty level was 5.0%, and respiratory allergy prevalence was 15.8%. Among children with family income above 200% of the poverty level, food allergy prevalence was 5.4%, and respiratory allergy prevalence was 18.3%. There was no significant difference in the prevalence of skin allergy by poverty status.

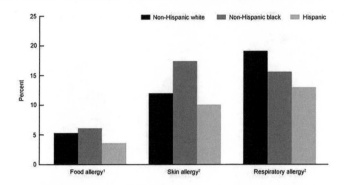

Figure 4.3. *Percentage of children aged 0–17 years with a reported allergic condition in the past 12 months, by race and ethnicity: United States, average annual 2009–2011.*

1. Hispanic significantly different than all other race groups.
2. The differences between all race groups are statistically significant.
SOURCE: CDC/NCHS, Health Data Interactive, National Health Interview Survey.

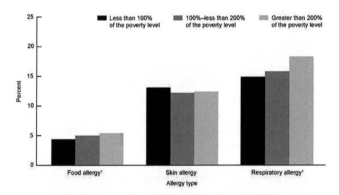

Figure 4.4. *The prevalence of both food allergy and respiratory allergy increased with the increase of income level. Among children with family income less than 100% of the poverty level, 4.4% had a food allergy and 14.9% had a respiratory allergy. Food allergy prevalence among children with family income between 100% and 200% of the poverty level was 5.0%, and respiratory allergy prevalence was 15.8%. Among children with family income above 200% of the poverty level, food allergy prevalence was 5.4%, and respiratory allergy prevalence was 18.3%. There was no significant difference in the prevalence of skin allergy by poverty status.*

1. Significant trend by poverty status.
SOURCE: CDC/NCHS, Health Data Interactive, National Health Interview Survey.

Summary

Among children under age 18 years in the United States, the prevalence of food and skin allergies increased from 1997–1999 to 2009–2011. The prevalence of respiratory allergy, which is the most prevalent type of allergy among children, did not change during this period. There was no significant difference in food allergy prevalence between age groups. However, skin allergy decreased with the increase of age, and respiratory allergy increased with the increase of age. The prevalence of allergies varies by race and ethnicity, with Hispanic children having the lowest prevalence of food, skin, and respiratory allergies compared with non-Hispanic white and non-Hispanic black children. Non-Hispanic black children were more likely to have skin allergies and less likely to have respiratory allergies compared with non-Hispanic white children. The prevalence of allergies differed by poverty status. Food allergy and respiratory allergy increased with the increase of income level, but there was no difference in the prevalence of skin allergy by poverty status.

Part Two

Types of Allergic Reactions

Chapter 5

Overview of Allergic Diseases and Types

Allergic Diseases

Asthma and allergic diseases, such as allergic rhinitis (hay fever), food allergy, and atopic dermatitis (eczema), are common for all age groups in the United States. For example, asthma affects more than 17 million adults and more than 7 million children. Hay fever, respiratory allergies, and other allergies affect approximately 10 percent of children under 18 years old. In addition, food allergy affects an estimated 5 percent of children under 5 years old and 4 percent of children ages 5 to 17 years old and adults.

Types of Allergic Diseases

Anaphylaxis

Anaphylaxis is a serious, potentially life-threatening allergic reaction. It involves many of the body's organs and can begin very rapidly.

This chapter includes excerpts from "Allergic Diseases," National Institute of Allergy and Infectious Diseases (NIAID), October 27, 2015; and text from "Types of Allergic Diseases," National Institute of Allergy and Infectious Diseases (NIAID), May 29, 2015.

Asthma

Asthma is a chronic disease that inflames and narrows the airways of the lungs, causing wheezing, breathlessness, chest tightness, and coughing. In people with allergic asthma, asthma symptoms can be triggered by exposure to an allergy-triggering substance, or allergen.

Atopic Dermatitis (Eczema)

Atopic dermatitis, also known as eczema, is a non-contagious inflammatory skin condition characterized by dry, itchy skin that can weep clear fluid when scratched.

Environmental Allergies

Environmental allergies occur when the body's immune system reacts abnormally to a harmless substance such as pollen or animal dander. This can trigger allergic reactions in the nose (allergic rhinitis, or hay fever) and in the lung (asthma).

Food Allergy

Food allergy occurs when the immune system responds to a harmless food as if it were a threat. In the United States, the most common foods that trigger allergic reactions are milk, eggs, peanuts, tree nuts, soy, wheat, fish, and shellfish.

Chapter 6

Allergic Rhinitis (Hay Fever)

Pollen Allergy

Pollen is one of the most common triggers of seasonal allergies. Many people know pollen allergy as "hay fever," but health experts usually refer to it as "seasonal allergic rhinitis." Pollen allergy affects approximately 7 percent of adults and 9 percent of children in the United States.

An allergic reaction is a specific response of the body's immune system to a normally harmless substance called an allergen. People who have allergies often are sensitive to more than one allergen. In addition to pollen, other airborne allergens that can cause allergic reactions include materials from house dust mites, animal dander, and cockroaches.

Pollen Overview

Each spring, summer, and fall, plants release tiny pollen grains to fertilize other plants of the same species. Most of the pollens that cause allergic reactions come from trees, weeds, and grasses. These plants make small, light, and dry pollen grains that are carried by the wind. Among North American plants, grasses are the most common cause of allergy. Ragweed is a main culprit among the weeds, but other major sources of weed pollen include sagebrush, pigweed, lamb's quarters,

Text in this chapter is excerpted from "Pollen Allergy," National Institute of Allergy and Infectious Diseases (NIAID), July 2015.

and tumbleweed. Certain species of trees, including birch, cedar, and oak, also produce highly allergenic pollen. Plants that are pollinated with the help of insects, such as roses and ornamental flowering trees like cherry and pear trees, usually do not cause allergic rhinitis.

People with pollen allergy only have symptoms for the period or season when the pollen grains to which they are allergic are in the air. For example, in most parts of the United States, grass pollen is present during the spring.

What Is a Pollen Count?

A pollen count, which is often reported by local weather broadcasts or allergy websites, is a measure of how much pollen is in the air. Pollen counts tend to be highest early in the morning on warm, dry, breezy days and lowest during chilly, wet periods. Although pollen counts reflect the last 24 hours, they are useful as a general guide for when it may be wise to stay indoors with windows closed to avoid contact with a certain pollen.

Symptoms

Pollen allergy can cause symptoms such as a runny nose and watery eyes. Reactions to allergens often also play an important role in asthma. Common symptoms of allergic rhinitis and asthma include the following:

- Runny nose and mucus production
- Swelling around the eyes
- Sneezing
- Coughing
- Itchy nose, eyes, ears, and mouth
- Wheezing
- Stuffy nose
- Chest tightness
- Red and watery eyes
- Shortness of breath

However, not all of these seasonal symptoms are due to pollen. Rhinovirus, the cause of the common cold, also can cause runny noses in the fall and spring. It is not always easy to figure out whether an allergy or a common cold is the cause of these symptoms, although some clues can help distinguish between the two. For example, a fever suggests a cold rather than an allergy, and symptoms lasting more than 2 weeks suggest allergies rather than a cold.

Diagnosis

Skin Tests

A skin prick test can detect if a person is sensitive to a specific allergen. Being "sensitive" means that the immune system produces a type of antibody called immunoglobulin E (IgE) that recognizes that allergen. IgE attaches to specialized cells called mast cells. This happens throughout the body, including the skin.

During a skin prick test, a health care provider uses a piece of plastic to prick the skin on a person's arm or back and places a tiny amount of allergen extract just below the skin's surface. In sensitive people, the allergen binds to IgE on mast cells in the skin and causes them to release histamine and other chemicals that produce itching, redness, and minor swelling.

A positive skin prick test to a particular pollen allergen does not necessarily indicate that a person has allergic rhinitis caused by that allergen. Therefore, health care providers must compare the skin test results with the time and place of a person's symptoms to see if they match.

Blood Tests

Instead of performing a skin test, doctors may take a blood sample to measure levels of allergen-specific IgE antibodies. Most people who are sensitive to a particular allergen will have IgE antibodies detectable by both skin and blood tests. As with skin testing, a positive blood test to an allergen does not necessarily mean that a person's symptoms are caused by that allergen.

One reason why a positive skin or blood test does not always indicate that a person's symptoms are caused by a particular allergen is that allergens include many different components, some of which are more likely to cause symptoms than others. For example, birch tree pollen contains proteins, sugars, and fats. IgE antibodies to birch pollen proteins are likely to cause allergic reactions, but IgE antibodies to the sugars in birch pollen, although common, are less likely to cause allergic reactions.

Medications

Certain over-the-counter and prescription medications may help reduce the severity of pollen allergy symptoms.

Antihistamines

Antihistamines, which are taken by mouth or as a nasal spray, can relieve sneezing and itching in the nose and eyes. They also reduce runny nose and, to a lesser extent, nasal stuffiness. Some older antihistamines can cause side effects such as drowsiness and loss of alertness and coordination. Effective, newer antihistamines cause fewer or no side effects.

Nasal Corticosteroids

Nasal corticosteroid sprays are anti-inflammatory medicines that help block allergic reactions. They are widely considered to be the most effective medication type for allergic rhinitis and can reduce all symptoms, including nasal congestion. Unlike corticosteroids taken by mouth or as an injection, nasal corticosteroids have few side effects. Combining a nasal antihistamine with a nasal corticosteroid appears to be more effective than using either of the sprays alone. However, it is not clear if taking an oral antihistamine with a nasal corticosteroid is helpful.

Decongestants

Oral and nasal decongestants help shrink the lining of the nasal passages, relieving nasal stuffiness. Decongestant nose drops and sprays are intended for short-term use. When used for more than a few days, these medicines may lead to even more congestion and swelling inside the nose. Doctors may recommend using decongestants along with an antihistamine because antihistamines do not have a strong decongestant effect.

Leukotriene Receptor Antagonists

Leukotriene receptor antagonists, such as the prescription drug montelukast, block the action of important chemical messengers other than histamine that are involved in allergic reactions.

Cromolyn Sodium

Cromolyn sodium is a nasal spray that blocks the release of chemicals that cause allergy symptoms, including histamine and leukotrienes. The drug causes few side effects but must be taken four times a day.

Allergen Immunotherapy

Many people with pollen allergy do not get complete relief from medications and may be candidates for immunotherapy. Immunotherapy is a long-term treatment that can help prevent or reduce the severity of allergic reactions and change the course of allergic disease by modifying the body's immune response to allergens.

Allergy Shots (Subcutaneous Immunotherapy)

Allergy shots, also known as subcutaneous immunotherapy (SCIT), have been used for more than 100 years and can provide long-lasting symptom relief. SCIT involves a series of shots containing small amounts of allergen into the fat under the skin.

SCIT includes two phases: a buildup phase and a maintenance phase. During the buildup phase, doctors administer injections containing gradually increasing amounts of allergen once or twice per week. This phase generally lasts from 3 to 6 months, depending on how often the shots are given and the body's response. The aim is to reach a target dose that has been shown to be effective. Once the target dose is reached, the maintenance phase begins. Shots are given less frequently during the maintenance phase, typically every 2 to 4 weeks. Some people begin experiencing a decrease in symptoms during the buildup phase, but others may not notice an improvement until the maintenance phase. Maintenance therapy generally lasts 3 to 5 years. The decision about how long to continue SCIT is based on how well it is working and how well a person tolerates the shots. Many people continue to experience benefits for several years after the shots are stopped.

Side effects from SCIT are usually minor and may include swelling or redness at the injection site. However, there is a small risk of serious allergic reactions such as anaphylaxis, a potentially life-threatening reaction that can develop very rapidly. Because most severe reactions occur shortly after injection, it is recommended that patients remain under medical supervision for at least 30 minutes after receiving a shot.

Sublingual Immunotherapy

In 2014, the U.S. Food and Drug Administration (FDA) approved three types of under-the-tongue tablets to treat allergies to grass and ragweed. The treatments, called sublingual immunotherapy (SLIT), offer people with these allergies a potential alternative to allergy shots. People taking SLIT place a tablet containing allergen under the tongue for 1 to 2 minutes and then swallow it. SLIT tablets are taken daily before and during grass or ragweed season.

Studies show that there are fewer allergic reactions to SLIT compared with SCIT. After the first SLIT dose is given at the doctor's office, patients can take subsequent doses at home. Side effects of SLIT are usually minor and may include itching of the mouth, lips, or throat. Although severe allergic reactions to SLIT are extremely rare, because SLIT treatment takes place at home, doctors usually prescribe an epinephrine auto-injector (EpiPen) for use in the event of a serious reaction.

Chapter 7

Sinusitis

Chapter Contents

Section 7.1

Sinusitis: An Overview

Text in this section is excerpted from "Sinusitis," National Institute
of Allergy and Infectious Diseases (NIAID), June 2015.

Sinusitis

Sinusitis is an inflammation of the membranes lining the paranasal
sinuses—small air-filled spaces located within the skull or bones of
the head surrounding the nose. Sinusitis can be caused by an infection
or other health problem. Symptoms include facial pain and nasal discharge, or "runny nose." Nearly 30 million adults in the United States
are diagnosed with sinusitis each year, according to the Centers for
Disease Control and Prevention.

The paranasal sinuses comprise four pairs of air-filled spaces:

1. Frontal sinuses—over the eyes in the brow area

2. Ethmoid sinuses—just behind the bridge of the nose, between
   the eyes

3. Maxillary sinuses—inside each cheekbone

4. Sphenoid sinuses—behind the ethmoids in the upper region of
   the nose and behind the eyes

There are two basic types of sinusitis:

1. Acute, which lasts up to 4 weeks

2. Chronic, which lasts more than 12 weeks and can continue for
   months or years

What Are the Symptoms of Sinusitis?

Most people with sinusitis have facial pain or tenderness in several places, and their symptoms usually do not clearly indicate which
sinuses are inflamed. The pain of a sinus attack arises because trapped
air and mucus put pressure on the membranes of the sinuses and the
bony wall behind them. Also, when a swollen membrane at the opening

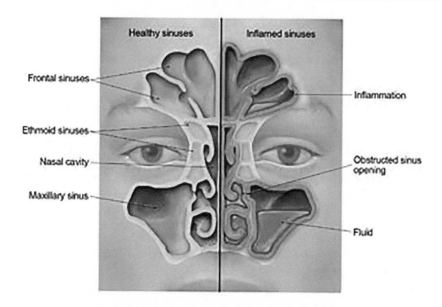

Figure 7.1. *Sinusitis*

Source: Centers for Disease Control and Prevention

of a paranasal sinus prevents air from entering into the sinuses, it can create a vacuum that causes pain.

People with sinusitis also have thick nasal secretions that can be white, yellowish, greenish, or bloodtinged. Sometimes these secretions drain in the back of the throat and are difficult to clear. This is referred to as "post-nasal drip" or "post-nasal drainage." Chronic post-nasal discharge may indicate sinusitis, even in people who do not have facial pain.

However, facial pain without either nasal or post-nasal drainage is rarely caused by inflammation of the sinuses. People who experience facial pain but no nasal discharge often are diagnosed with a pain disorder—such as migraines, cluster headaches, or tension-type headaches—rather than sinusitis.

Less common symptoms of acute or chronic sinusitis include the following:

• Tiredness

• Decreased sense of smell

• Cough that may be worse at night

- Sore throat

- Bad breath

- Fever

On very rare occasions, acute sinusitis can result in brain infection and other serious complications.

What Causes Sinusitis?

Colds, bacterial infections, allergies, asthma, and other health conditions can cause sinusitis.

Acute Sinusitis

Acute sinusitis usually is caused by a viral or bacterial infection. The common cold, which is caused by a virus, may lead to swelling of the sinuses, trapping air and mucus behind the narrowed sinus openings. Both the nasal and the sinus symptoms usually go away within 2 weeks. Sometimes, viral infections are followed by bacterial infections. Many cases of acute sinusitis are caused by bacteria that frequently colonize the nose and throat, such as *Streptococcus pneumoniae*, *Haemophilus influenzae*, and *Moraxella catarrhalis*. These bacteria typically do not cause problems in healthy people, but in some cases they begin to multiply in the sinuses, causing acute sinusitis. NIAID supports studies to better understand the factors that put people at risk for bacterial sinusitis.

People who have allergies or other chronic nasal problems are prone to episodes of acute sinusitis. In general, people who have reduced immune function, such as those with HIV infection, are more likely to have sinusitis. Sinusitis also is common in people who have abnormal mucus secretion or mucus movement, such as people with cystic fibrosis, an inherited disease in which thick and sticky mucus clogs the lungs.

Chronic Sinusitis (Rhinosinusitis)

In chronic sinusitis, also known as chronic rhinosinusitis, the membranes of both the paranasal sinuses and the nose thicken because they are constantly inflamed. This condition can occur with or without nasal polyps, grape-like growths on the mucous membranes that protrude into the sinuses or nasal passages. The causes of chronic rhinosinusitis are largely unknown. NIAID supports basic research to help explain why people develop this chronic inflammation.

People with asthma and allergies, recurrent acute sinusitis, and other health conditions are at higher risk of developing chronic rhinosinusitis. In fact, some evidence suggests that chronic rhinosinusitis and asthma may be the same disease occurring in the upper and lower parts of the respiratory system, respectively. NIAID supports research to understand the causes of chronic airway inflammation in asthma and its link to chronic rhinosinusitis. For example, NIAID-supported researchers are investigating and developing improved treatments for aspirin-exacerbated respiratory disease (AERD). People with AERD have asthma and chronic rhinosinusitis with nasal polyps, and they experience potentially severe respiratory reactions to aspirin and other nonsteroidal anti-inflammatory drugs. NIAID-supported scientists also are examining whether viral infections cause worsening of chronic rhinosinusitis and identifying differences in genes and proteins in people with chronic rhinosinusitis and those whose sinuses are healthy.

How Is Sinusitis Diagnosed?

Often, healthcare providers can diagnose acute sinusitis by reviewing a person's symptoms and examining the nose and face. Doctors may perform a procedure called rhinoscopy, in which they use a thin, flexible tube-like instrument to examine the inside of the nose.

If symptoms do not clearly indicate sinusitis or if they persist for a long time and do not get better with treatment, the doctor may order a computerized tomography (CT) scan—a form of X-ray that shows some soft tissue and other structures that cannot be seen in conventional X-rays—to confirm the diagnosis of sinusitis and to evaluate how severe it is.

Laboratory tests that a healthcare professional may use to check for possible causes of chronic rhinosinusitis include the following:

- Allergy testing

- Blood tests to rule out conditions that are associated with sinusitis, such as an immune deficiency disorder

- A sweat test or a blood test to rule out cystic fibrosis

- Tests on the material inside the sinuses to detect a bacterial or fungal infection

- An aspirin challenge to test for AERD. In an aspirin challenge, a person takes small but gradually increasing doses of aspirin under the careful supervision of a healthcare professional

How Is Sinusitis Treated?

Acute Sinusitis

Medications can help ease the symptoms of acute sinusitis. Health-care providers may recommend pain relievers or decongestants—medicines that shrink the swollen membranes in the nose and make it easier to breathe. Decongestant nose drops and sprays should be used for only a few days, as longer term use can lead to even more congestion and swelling of the nasal passages. A doctor may prescribe antibiotics if the sinusitis is caused by a bacterial infection.

Chronic Rhinosinusitis

Chronic rhinosinusitis can be difficult to treat. Medicines may offer some symptom relief. Surgery can be helpful if medication fails.

Medicine

Nasal steroid sprays are helpful for many people, but most do not get full relief of symptoms with these medicines. Saline (salt water) washes or nasal sprays can be helpful because they remove thick secretions and allow the sinuses to drain. Doctors may prescribe oral steroids, such as prednisone, for severe chronic rhinosinusitis. However, oral steroids are powerful medicines that can cause side effects such as weight gain and high blood pressure if used over the long term. Oral steroids typically are prescribed when other medicines have failed. Desensitization to aspirin may be helpful for patients with AERD. During desensitization, which is performed under close medical supervision, a person is given gradually increasing doses of aspirin over time to induce tolerance to the drug.

Surgery

When medicine fails, surgery may be the only alternative for treating chronic rhinosinusitis. The goal of surgery is to improve sinus drainage and reduce blockage of the nasal passages. Sinus surgery usually is performed to:

- Enlarge the natural openings of the sinuses

- Remove nasal polyps

- Correct significant structural problems inside the nose and the sinuses if they contribute to sinus obstruction

Although most people have fewer symptoms and a better quality of life after surgery, problems can reoccur, sometimes even after a short period of time.

In children, problems can sometimes be eliminated by removing the adenoids. These gland-like tissues, located high in the throat behind and above the roof of the mouth, can obstruct the nasal passages.

Can Sinusitis Be Prevented?

There is little information about the prevention of acute or chronic sinusitis, but the following measures may help:

- Avoid exposure to irritants such as cigarette and cigar smoke or strong chemicals.

- To avoid infections, wash hands frequently during common cold season and try to avoid touching your face.

- If you have allergies, avoid exposure to allergy-inducing substances, or consider asking your healthcare provider for an allergy evaluation or a referral to an allergy specialist.

Section 7.2

Nasal Polyps

"Nasal Polyps," © 2016 Omnigraphics, Inc.
Reviewed November 2015.

What Is a Nasal Polyp?

Nasal polyps are small, polypoidal, noncancerous growths that can occur anywhere in the mucous membranes lining the nose or the paranasal sinuses. They may occur singly or in clusters, and they usually form where the sinuses open into the nasal cavity. While small polyps may not cause problems as they are freely movable, larger ones can block the sinuses or the nasal airway.

Nasal polyps can develop at any age, but they are most common in adults over age 40. Men are more prone to this disease, while it is uncommon in children under ten years. When young children are diagnosed with nasal polyps, in fact, doctors should conduct further tests to rule out cystic fibrosis, a genetic disorder characterized by a buildup of mucus in the lungs. Nasal polyps occur in nearly two-thirds of cystic fibrosis patients.

Causes

It is not entirely clear why some people develop nasal polyps and others do not. Although there is no definite cause of nasal polyposis, some factors may contribute to an increased risk of developing nasal polyps. One of the most common triggers is nasal congestion arising from chronic inflammation of the sinuses,which may be caused by allergies or recurring sinus infections. A certain degree of genetic predisposition has been observed in patients with nasal polyps, and it may explain why the mucosa in some people reacts differently to inflammation. Polyps are also commonly seen in patients with late onset of asthma and aspirinsensitivity, allergic rhinitis, and sinusitis.

Types of Nasal Polyps

Nasal polyps can be classified as a) Antrochoanal and b) Ethmoidal. Antrochoanal nasal polyp is single, unilateral, and originates from maxillary sinus; it is mostly found in children. Ethmoidal polyps are bilateral and usually found in adults.

Symptoms and Diagnosis

Polyposis may be asymptomatic in some people, particularly if the polyps are small. Larger polyps are usually associated with catarrh (excessive secretion of mucus), breathing difficulties, inflammation of the paranasal cavities, and loss of smell and taste. Other symptoms of nasal polyps may include postnasal drip (drainage of mucous down the back of the throat) and a dull, achy feeling in the face because of fluid buildup.

Diagnosis of nasal polyps is generally made using a procedure called nasal endoscopy. Although a routine examination with a rhinoscope (a lighted device fitted with a lens that can be inserted into the nose) can find polyps located in the nasal cavity, an endoscope (a long, flexible tool fitted with a miniature camera on its end) is required to find polyps that are deep-seated in the sinuses. The doctor may also request a Computerized Tomography (CT) scan to diagnose polyps and additional tests such as biopsy to rule out nasal and sinus cancer, and non-malignant conditions such as nasal papilloma.

Treatment Options

Although various forms of medicine can alleviate symptoms associated with nasal polyps, they may provide only temporary relief. The first line of treatment is usually nasal drops or sprays containing steroids. Steroid treatment is often beneficial if the polyps are small, and the patient is likely to experience marked improvement in breathing as the polyps shrink and free up the airways. Tapered oral steroid medications can prevent sinus inflammation associated with allergies and effectively reduce the size of inflammatory polyps, but these drugs are used sparingly because they may increase the risk of such health concerns as diabetes, high blood pressure, and osteoporosis. Steroids, both topical and oral, are also frequently used after surgery to prevent the recurrence of polyps.

Doctors may also prescribe antibiotics to treat chronic sinusitis that may be associated with nasal polyps.

Endoscopic nasal surgery is the most commonly used treatment option for polyposis when the polyps are too large to respond to corticosteroids. This minimally invasive surgical procedure, known as a polypectomy, is performed with a nasal endoscope and can be done on an outpatient basis. The procedure, which is done in approximately 45 minutes to an hour, is carried out under general anaesthesia using a suction device or a microdebrider (a minuscule, motorized shaver) to remove the polyps. If there is no bleeding, the patient is discharged after a few hours of observation. Antibiotics are usually prescribed to prevent infection at the site of surgery.

Although surgery can provide symptomatic relief for a few years, the nasal polyps grow back in at least 15 percent of patients. In such cases, postoperative use of steroidal sprays and saline washes is usually prescribed to extend the period before the polyps recur.

References:

1. Case-Lo, Christine. "Nasal Polyps." Healthline, October 5, 2015.

2. "Nasal Polyps—Treatment." NHS Choices, February 12, 2015.

Chapter 8

Conjunctivitis (Pink Eye)

Pink Eye: Usually Mild and Easy to Treat

Pink eye, also known as conjunctivitis, is one of the most common and treatable eye conditions in children and adults. It is an inflammation of the conjunctiva, the thin, clear tissue that lines the inside of the eyelid and the white part of the eyeball. This inflammation makes blood vessels more visible and gives the eye a pink or reddish color.

What Causes Pink Eye?

There are four main causes of pink eye:

1. Viruses

2. Bacteria

3. Allergens (like animal dander or dust mites)

4. Irritants (like smog or swimming pool chlorine) that infect or irritate the eye and eyelid lining

It can be difficult to determine the exact cause of pink eye because some signs and symptoms may be the same no matter the cause.

This chapter includes excerpts from "Pink Eye: Usually Mild and Easy to Treat," Centers for Disease Control and Prevention (CDC), May 5, 2015; and text from "Conjunctivitis (Pink Eye)," Centers for Disease Control and Prevention (CDC), January 9, 2014.

What Are the Symptoms of Pink Eye?

The symptoms of pink eye may vary depending on the cause but usually include:

- Redness or swelling of the white of the eye or inside the eyelids
- Increased amount of tears
- White, yellow or green eye discharge
- Itchy, irritated, and/or burning eyes
- Increased sensitivity to light
- Gritty feeling in the eye
- Crusting of the eyelids or lashes

When to See a Healthcare Provider?

Most cases of pink eye are mild and get better on their own, even without treatment. However, there are times when it is important to see a healthcare provider for specific treatment and/or close follow-up. You should see a healthcare provider if you have pink eye along with any of the following:

- Moderate to severe pain in your eye(s)
- Sensitivity to light or blurred vision
- Intense redness in the eye(s)
- A weakened immune system, for example from HIV or cancer treatment
- Symptoms that get worse or don't improve, including bacterial pink eye that does not improve after 24 hours of antibiotic use
- Pre-existing eye conditions that may put you at risk for complications or severe infection

How Do I Stop Pink Eye from Spreading?

Pink eye caused by a virus or bacteria is very contagious and spreads easily and quickly from person to person. Pink eye that is caused by allergens or irritants is not contagious, but it is possible to develop a secondary infection caused by a virus or bacteria that is contagious. You can reduce the risk of getting or spreading pink eye by following some simple self-care steps:

- Wash your hands.

- Avoid touching or rubbing your eyes.

- Avoid sharing eye and face makeup, makeup brushes, contact lenses and containers, and eyeglasses.

Pink Eye in Newborns

A newborn baby who has symptoms of pink eye should see a healthcare provider. Pink eye in newborns can be caused by an infection, irritation, or a blocked tear duct.

Neonatal pink eye caused by sexually transmitted infections, like gonorrhea or chlamydia, can be very serious. If you are pregnant and think you may have a sexually transmitted infection, visit your healthcare provider for testing and treatment. If you don't know whether you have a sexually transmitted infection but have recently given birth and your newborn shows signs of pink eye, visit your child's healthcare provider right away.

Most hospitals are required by state law to put drops or ointment in a newborn's eyes to prevent pink eye.

Treatment

The treatment for conjunctivitis depends on the cause. It is not always necessary to see a healthcare provider for conjunctivitis. But, as noted below, there are times when it is important to seek medical care.

Allergic Conjunctivitis

Conjunctivitis caused by an allergy usually improves when the allergen (such as pollen or animal dander) is removed. Allergy medications and certain eye drops (topical antihistamine and vasoconstrictors), including some prescription eye drops, can also provide relief from allergic conjunctivitis. For conjunctivitis caused by contact lenses, an eye doctor may recommend removing lenses and keeping them out for a period of time. In some cases, a combination of drugs may be needed to improve symptoms. Your doctor can help if you have conjunctivitis caused by an allergy.

When to Seek Medical Care

A healthcare provider should be seen if:

- Conjunctivitis is accompanied by moderate to severe pain in the eye(s).

- Conjunctivitis is accompanied by vision problems, such as sensitivity to light or blurred vision, that does not improve when any discharge that is present is wiped from the eye(s).

- Conjunctivitis is accompanied by intense redness in the eye(s).

- Conjunctivitis symptoms become worse or persist when a patient is suspected of having a severe form of viral conjunctivitis—for example, a type caused by herpes simplex virus or varicella-zoster virus (the cause of chickenpox and shingles).

- Conjunctivitis occurs in a patient who is immunocompromised (has a weakened immune system) from HIV infection, cancer treatment, or other medical conditions or treatments.

- Bacterial conjunctivitis is being treated with antibiotics and does not begin to improve after 24 hours of treatment.

Chapter 9

Allergic Asthma

Chapter Contents

Section 9.1

Understanding Asthma

Text in this section is excerpted from "Asthma," National Heart,
Lung, and Blood Institute (NHLBI), August 4, 2014.

What Is Asthma?

Asthma is a chronic (long-term) lung disease that inflames and
narrows the airways. Asthma causes recurring periods of wheezing
(a whistling sound when you breathe), chest tightness, shortness of
breath, and coughing. The coughing often occurs at night or early in
the morning.

Asthma affects people of all ages, but it most often starts during
childhood. In the United States, more than 25 million people are known
to have asthma. About 7 million of these people are children.

Overview

To understand asthma, it helps to know how the airways work. The
airways are tubes that carry air into and out of your lungs. People who
have asthma have inflamed airways. The inflammation makes the
airways swollen and very sensitive. The airways tend to react strongly
to certain inhaled substances.

When the airways react, the muscles around them tighten. This
narrows the airways, causing less air to flow into the lungs. The swelling also can worsen, making the airways even narrower. Cells in the
airways might make more mucus than usual. Mucus is a sticky, thick
liquid that can further narrow the airways.

This chain reaction can result in asthma symptoms. Symptoms can
happen each time the airways are inflamed.

Sometimes asthma symptoms are mild and go away on their own
or after minimal treatment with asthma medicine. Other times, symptoms continue to get worse.

When symptoms get more intense and/or more symptoms occur,
you're having an asthma attack. Asthma attacks also are called fla-
reups or exacerbations.

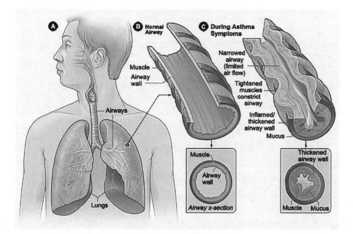

Figure 9.1. *Asthma – Figure A shows the location of the lungs and airways in the body. Figure B shows a cross-section of a normal airway. Figure C shows a cross-section of an airway during asthma symptoms.*

Treating symptoms when you first notice them is important. This will help prevent the symptoms from worsening and causing a severe asthma attack. Severe asthma attacks may require emergency care, and they can be fatal.

Outlook

Asthma has no cure. Even when you feel fine, you still have the disease and it can flare up at any time.

However, with today's knowledge and treatments, most people who have asthma are able to manage the disease. They have few, if any, symptoms. They can live normal, active lives and sleep through the night without interruption from asthma.If you have asthma, you can take an active role in managing the disease. For successful, thorough, and ongoing treatment, build strong partnerships with your doctor and other health care providers.

What Causes Asthma?

The exact cause of asthma isn't known. Researchers think some genetic and environmental factors interact to cause asthma, most often early in life. These factors include:

- An inherited tendency to develop allergies, called atopy

- Parents who have asthma

- Certain respiratory infections during childhood

- Contact with some airborne allergens or exposure to some viral infections in infancy or in early childhood when the immune system is developing

If asthma or atopy runs in your family, exposure to irritants (for example, tobacco smoke) may make your airways more reactive to substances in the air.

Some factors may be more likely to cause asthma in some people than in others. Researchers continue to explore what causes asthma.

Asthma and The "Hygiene Hypothesis"

One theory researchers have for what causes asthma is the "hygiene hypothesis." They believe that our Western lifestyle— with its emphasis on hygiene and sanitation—has resulted in changes in our living conditions and an overall decline in infections in early childhood.

Many young children no longer have the same types of environmental exposures and infections as children did in the past. This affects the way that young children's immune systems develop during very early childhood, and it may increase their risk for atopy and asthma. This is especially true for children who have close family members with one or both of these conditions.

Who Is at Risk for Asthma?

Asthma affects people of all ages, but it most often starts during childhood. In the United States, more than 22 million people are known to have asthma. Nearly 6 million of these people are children.

Young children who often wheeze and have respiratory infections— as well as certain other risk factors—are at highest risk of developing asthma that continues beyond 6 years of age. The other risk factors include having allergies, eczema (an allergic skin condition), or parents who have asthma.

Among children, more boys have asthma than girls. But among adults, more women have the disease than men. It's not clear whether or how sex and sex hormones play a role in causing asthma.

Most, but not all, people who have asthma have allergies.

Some people develop asthma because of contact with certain chemical irritants or industrial dusts in the workplace. This type of asthma is called occupational asthma.

What Are the Signs and Symptoms of Asthma?

Common signs and symptoms of asthma include:

- Coughing. Coughing from asthma often is worse at night or early in the morning, making it hard to sleep.

- Wheezing. Wheezing is a whistling or squeaky sound that occurs when you breathe.

- Chest tightness. This may feel like something is squeezing or sitting on your chest.

- Shortness of breath. Some people who have asthma say they can't catch their breath or they feel out of breath. You may feel like you can't get air out of your lungs.

Not all people who have asthma have these symptoms. Likewise, having these symptoms doesn't always mean that you have asthma. The best way to diagnose asthma for certain is to use a lung function test, a medical history (including type and frequency of symptoms), and a physical exam.

The types of asthma symptoms you have, how often they occur, and how severe they are may vary over time. Sometimes your symptoms may just annoy you. Other times, they may be troublesome enough to limit your daily routine.

Severe symptoms can be fatal. It's important to treat symptoms when you first notice them so they don't become severe.

With proper treatment, most people who have asthma can expect to have few, if any, symptoms either during the day or at night.

What Causes Asthma Symptoms to Occur?

Many things can trigger or worsen asthma symptoms. Your doctor will help you find out which things (sometimes called triggers) may cause your asthma to flare up if you come in contact with them. Triggers may include:

- Allergens from dust, animal fur, cockroaches, mold, and pollens from trees, grasses, and flowers

- Irritants such as cigarette smoke, air pollution, chemicals or dust in the workplace, compounds in home decor products, and sprays (such as hairspray)

- Medicines such as aspirin or other nonsteroidal anti-inflammatory drugs and nonselective beta-blockers

- Sulfites in foods and drinks

- Viral upper respiratory infections, such as colds

- Physical activity, including exercise

Other health conditions can make asthma harder to manage. Examples of these conditions include a runny nose, sinus infections, reflux disease, psychological stress, and sleep apnea. These conditions need treatment as part of an overall asthma care plan.

Asthma is different for each person. Some of the triggers listed above may not affect you. Other triggers that do affect you may not be on the list. Talk with your doctor about the things that seem to make your asthma worse.

How Is Asthma Diagnosed?

Your primary care doctor will diagnose asthma based on your medical and family histories, a physical exam, and test results

Your doctor also will figure out the severity of your asthma—that is, whether it's intermittent, mild, moderate, or severe. The level of severity will determine what treatment you'll start on.

You may need to see an asthma specialist if:

- You need special tests to help diagnose asthma

- You've had a life-threatening asthma attack

- You need more than one kind of medicine or higher doses of medicine to control your asthma, or if you have overall problems getting your asthma well controlled

- You're thinking about getting allergy treatments

Medical and Family Histories

Your doctor may ask about your family history of asthma and allergies. He or she also may ask whether you have asthma symptoms and when and how often they occur.

Let your doctor know whether your symptoms seem to happen only during certain times of the year or in certain places, or if they get worse at night.

Your doctor also may want to know what factors seem to trigger your symptoms or worsen them.

Your doctor may ask you about related health conditions that can interfere with asthma management. These conditions include a runny nose, sinus infections, reflux disease, psychological stress, and sleep apnea.

Physical Exam

Your doctor will listen to your breathing and look for signs of asthma or allergies. These signs include wheezing, a runny nose or swollen nasal passages, and allergic skin conditions (such as eczema).

Keep in mind that you can still have asthma even if you don't have these signs on the day that your doctor examines you.

Diagnostic Tests

Lung Function Test

Your doctor will use a test called spirometry to check how your lungs are working. This test measures how much air you can breathe in and out. It also measures how fast you can blow air out.

Your doctor also may give you medicine and then test you again to see whether the results have improved.

If the starting results are lower than normal and improve with the medicine, and if your medical history shows a pattern of asthma symptoms, your diagnosis will likely be asthma.

Other Tests

Your doctor may recommend other tests if he or she needs more information to make a diagnosis. Other tests may include:

- Allergy testing to find out which allergens affect you, if any.

- A test to measure how sensitive your airways are. This is called a bronchoprovocation test. Using spirometry, this test repeatedly measures your lung function during physical activity or after you receive increasing doses of cold air or a special chemical to breathe in.

- A test to show whether you have another condition with the same symptoms as asthma, such as reflux disease, vocal cord dysfunction, or sleep apnea.

- A chest X-ray or an EKG (electrocardiogram). These tests will help find out whether a foreign object or other disease may be causing your symptoms.

Diagnosing Asthma in Young Children

Most children who have asthma develop their first symptoms before 5 years of age. However, asthma in young children (aged 0 to 5 years) can be hard to diagnose.

Sometimes it's hard to tell whether a child has asthma or another childhood condition. This is because the symptoms of asthma also occur with other conditions.

Also, many young children who wheeze when they get colds or respiratory infections don't go on to have asthma after they're 6 years old.

A child may wheeze because he or she has small airways that become even narrower during colds or respiratory infections. The airways grow as the child grows older, so wheezing no longer occurs when the child gets colds.

A young child who has frequent wheezing with colds or respiratory infections is more likely to have asthma if:

- One or both parents have asthma

- The child has signs of allergies, including the allergic skin condition eczema

- The child has allergic reactions to pollens or other airborne allergens

- The child wheezes even when he or she doesn't have a cold or other infection

The most certain way to diagnose asthma is with a lung function test, a medical history, and a physical exam. However, it's hard to do lung function tests in children younger than 5 years. Thus, doctors must rely on children's medical histories, signs and symptoms, and physical exams to make a diagnosis.

Doctors also may use a 4–6 week trial of asthma medicines to see how well a child responds.

How Can Asthma Be Prevented?

You can't prevent asthma. However, you can take steps to control the disease and prevent its symptoms. For example:

- Learn about your asthma and ways to control it.

- Follow your written asthma action plan.

- Use medicines as your doctor prescribes.

- Identify and try to avoid things that make your asthma worse (asthma triggers). However, one trigger you should not avoid is physical activity. Physical activity is an important part of a healthy lifestyle. Talk with your doctor about medicines that can help you stay active.

- Keep track of your asthma symptoms and level of control.

- Get regular checkups for your asthma.

Living with Asthma

If you have asthma, you'll need long-term care. Successful asthma treatment requires that you take an active role in your care and follow your asthma action plan.

Learn How to Manage Your Asthma

Partner with your doctor to develop an asthma action plan. This plan will help you know when and how to take your medicines. The plan also will help you identify your asthma triggers and manage your disease if asthma symptoms worsen.

Children aged 10 or older—and younger children who can handle it—should be involved in creating and following their asthma action plans.

Most people who have asthma can successfully manage their symptoms by following their asthma action plans and having regular checkups. However, knowing when to seek emergency medical care is important.

Learn how to use your medicines correctly. If you take inhaled medicines, you should practice using your inhaler at your doctor's office. If you take long-term control medicines, take them daily as your doctor prescribes.

Record your asthma symptoms as a way to track how well your asthma is controlled. Also, your doctor may advise you to use a peak flow meter to measure and record how well your lungs are working.

Your doctor may ask you to keep records of your symptoms or peak flow results daily for a couple of weeks before an office visit. You'll bring these records with you to the visit.

These steps will help you keep track of how well you're controlling your asthma over time. This will help you spot problems early and prevent or relieve asthma attacks. Recording your symptoms and peak flow results to share with your doctor also will help him or her decide whether to adjust your treatment.

Ongoing Care

Have regular asthma checkups with your doctor so he or she can assess your level of asthma control and adjust your treatment as needed. Remember, the main goal of asthma treatment is to achieve the best control of your asthma using the least amount of medicine. This may require frequent adjustments to your treatments.

If you find it hard to follow your asthma action plan or the plan isn't working well, let your health care team know right away. They will work with you to adjust your plan to better suit your needs.

Get treatment for any other conditions that can interfere with your asthma management.

Watch for Signs That Your Asthma Is Getting Worse

Your asthma might be getting worse if:

- Your symptoms start to occur more often, are more severe, or bother you at night and cause you to lose sleep.

- You're limiting your normal activities and missing school or work because of your asthma.

- Your peak flow number is low compared to your personal best or varies a lot from day to day.

- Your asthma medicines don't seem to work well anymore.

- You have to use your quick-relief inhaler more often. If you're using quick-relief medicine more than 2 days a week, your asthma isn't well controlled.

- You have to go to the emergency room or doctor because of an asthma attack.

If you have any of these signs, see your doctor. He or she might need to change your medicines or take other steps to control your asthma.

Partner with your health care team and take an active role in your care. This can help you better control your asthma so it doesn't interfere with your activities and disrupt your life.

Section 9.2

Asthma and Its Environmental Triggers

Text in this section is excerpted from "Asthma Triggers:
Gain Control," U.S. Environmental Protection Agency (EPA),
October 26, 2015.

Americans spend up to 90 percent of their time indoors. Indoor allergens and irritants play a significant role in triggering asthma attacks. Triggers are things that can cause asthma symptoms, an episode or attack or make asthma worse. If you have asthma, you may react to just one trigger or you may find that several things act as triggers. Be sure to work with a doctor to identify triggers and develop a treatment plan that includes ways to reduce exposures to your asthma triggers.

About Secondhand Smoke and Asthma

Secondhand smoke is the smoke from a cigarette, cigar or pipe, and the smoke exhaled by a smoker. Secondhand smoke contains more than 4,000 substances, including several compounds that cause cancer.

Secondhand smoke can trigger asthma episodes and increase the severity of attacks. Secondhand smoke is also a risk factor for new cases of asthma in preschool-aged children. Children's developing bodies make them more susceptible to the effects of secondhand smoke and, due to their small size, they breathe more rapidly than adults, thereby taking in more secondhand smoke. Children receiving high doses of secondhand smoke, such as those with smoking parents, run the greatest relative risk of experiencing damaging health effects.

Actions You Can Take

- Don't let anyone smoke near your child.

- If you smoke—until you can quit, don't smoke in your home or car.

About Dust Mites and Asthma

Dust mites are tiny bugs that are too small to see. Every home has dust mites. They feed on human skin flakes and are found in mattresses, pillows, carpets, upholstered furniture, bedcovers, clothes, stuffed toys and fabric and fabric-covered items.

Body parts and droppings from dust mites can trigger asthma in individuals with allergies to dust mites. Exposure to dust mites can cause asthma in children who have not previously exhibited asthma symptoms.

Actions You Can Take

- Common house dust may also contain asthma triggers. These simple steps can help:

- Wash bedding in hot water once a week. Dry completely.

- Use dust proof covers on pillows and mattresses.

- Vacuum carpets and furniture every week.

- Choose stuffed toys that you can wash. Wash stuffed toys in hot water. Dry completely before your child plays with the toy.

- Dust often with a damp cloth.

- Use a vacuum with a High efficiency Particulate air (HEPA) filter on carpet and fabric-covered furniture to reduce dust build-up. People with asthma or allergies should leave the area being vacuumed.

About Molds and Asthma

Molds create tiny spores to reproduce, just as plants produce seeds. Mold spores float through the indoor and outdoor air continually. When mold spores land on damp places indoors, they may begin growing. Molds are microscopic fungi that live on plant and animal matter. Molds can be found almost anywhere when moisture is present.

For people sensitive to molds, inhaling mold spores can trigger an asthma attack.

Actions You Can Take

- If mold is a problem in your home, you need to clean up the mold and eliminate sources of moisture.

- If you see mold on hard surfaces, clean it up with soap and water. Let the area dry completely.

- Use exhaust fans or open a window in the bathroom and kitchen when showering, cooking or washing dishes.

- Fix water leaks as soon as possible to keep mold from growing.

- Dry damp or wet things completely within one to two days to keep mold from growing.

- Maintain low indoor humidity, ideally between 30-50% relative humidity. Humidity levels can be measured by hygrometers, which are available at local hardware stores.

About Cockroaches, Other Pests, and Asthma

Droppings or body parts of cockroaches and other pests can trigger asthma. Certain proteins are found in cockroach feces and saliva and can cause allergic reactions or trigger asthma symptoms in some individuals.

Cockroaches are commonly found in crowded cities and the southern regions of the United States. Cockroach allergens likely play a significant role in asthma in many urban areas.

Actions You Can Take

- Insecticides and pesticides are not only toxic to pests—they can harm people too. Try to use pest management methods that pose less of a risk. Keep counters, sinks, tables, and floors clean and free of clutter.

- Clean dishes, crumbs and spills right away.

- Store food in airtight containers.

- Seal cracks or openings around or inside cabinets.

About Pets and Asthma

Proteins in your pet's skin flakes, urine, feces, saliva, and hair can trigger asthma. Dogs, cats, rodents (including hamsters and guinea pigs), and other warm-blooded mammals can trigger asthma in individuals with an allergy to animal dander.

The most effective method to control animal allergens in the home is to not allow animals in the home. If you remove an animal from the home, it is important to thoroughly clean the floors, walls, carpets and upholstered furniture.

Some individuals may find isolation measures to be sufficiently effective. Isolation measures that have been suggested include keeping pets out of the sleeping areas, keeping pets away from upholstered furniture, carpets and stuffed toys, keeping the pet outdoors as much as possible and isolating sensitive individuals from the pet as much as possible.

Actions You Can Take

- Find another home for your cat or dog.

- Keep pets outside if possible.

- If you have to have a pet inside, keep it out of the bedroom of the person with asthma.

- Keep pets off of your furniture.

- Vacuum carpets and furniture when the person with asthma is not around.

About Nitrogen Dioxide NO_2 and Asthma

Nitrogen dioxide (NO_2) is an odorless gas that can irritate your eyes, nose and throat and cause shortness of breath. NO_2 can come from appliances inside your home that burn fuels such as gas, kerosene and wood. NO_2 forms quickly from emissions from cars, trucks and buses, power plants and off-road equipment. Smoke from your stove or fireplace can trigger asthma.

In people with asthma, exposure to low levels of NO_2 may cause increased bronchial reactivity and make young children more susceptible to respiratory infections. Long-term exposure to high levels of NO_2 can lead to chronic bronchitis. Studies show a connection between breathing elevated short-term NO_2 concentrations, and increased visits to emergency departments and hospital admissions for respiratory issues, especially asthma.

Actions You Can Take

If possible, use fuel-burning appliances that are vented to the outside. Always follow the manufacturer's instructions on how to use these appliances.

- Gas cooking stoves: If you have an exhaust fan in the kitchen, use it when you cook. Never use the stove to keep you warm or heat your house.

- Unvented kerosene or gas space heaters: Use the proper fuel and keep the heater adjusted the right way. Open a window slightly or use an exhaust fan when you are using the heater.

About Outdoor Air Pollution and Asthma

Outdoor air pollution is caused by small particles and ground level ozone that comes from car exhaust, smoke, road dust, and factory emissions. Outdoor air quality is also affected by pollen from plants, crops and weeds. Particle pollution can be high any time of year and are higher near busy roads and where people burn wood.

When inhaled, outdoor pollutants and pollen can aggravate the lungs, and can lead to:

- Chest pain
- Coughing
- Digestive problems
- Dizziness
- Fever
- Lethargy
- Sneezing
- Shortness of breath
- Throat irritation
- Watery eyes

Outdoor air pollution and pollen may also worsen chronic respiratory diseases, such as asthma.

Actions You Can Take

- Monitor the Air Quality Index on your local weather report.

- Know when and where air pollution may be bad.

- Regular exercise is healthy. Check your local air quality to know when to play and when to take it a little easier.

- Schedule outdoor activities at times when the air quality is better. In the summer, this may be in the morning.

- Stay inside with the windows closed on high pollen days and when pollutants are high.
- Use your air conditioner to help filter the air coming into the home. Central air systems are the best.
- Remove indoor plants if they irritate or produce symptoms for you or your family.
- Pay attention to asthma warning signs. If you start to see signs, limit outdoor activity. Be sure to talk about this with your child's doctor.

About Chemical Irritants and Asthma

Chemical irritants are found in some products in your house and may trigger asthma. Your asthma or your child's asthma may be worse around products such as cleaners, paints, adhesives, pesticides, cosmetics or air fresheners. Chemical irritants are also present in schools and can be found in commonly used cleaning supplies and educational kits.

Chemical irritants may exacerbate asthma. At sufficient concentrations in the air, many products can trigger a reaction.

Actions You Can Take

If you find that your asthma or your child's asthma gets worse when you use a certain product, consider trying different products. If you must use a product, then you should:

- Make sure your child is not around.
- Open windows or doors, or use an exhaust fan.
- Always follow the instructions on the product label.

About Wood Smoke and Asthma

Smoke from wood-burning stoves and fireplaces contain a mixture of harmful gases and small particles. Breathing these small particles can cause asthma attacks and severe bronchitis, aggravate heart and lung disease and may increase the likelihood of respiratory illnesses. If you're using a wood stove or fireplace and smell smoke in your home, it probably isn't working as it should.

Actions You Can Take

- To help reduce smoke, make sure to burn dry wood that has been split, stacked, covered, and stored for at least 6 months.

- Have your stove and chimney inspected every year by a certified professional to make sure there are no gaps, cracks, unwanted drafts or to remove dangerous creosote build-up.

- If possible, replace your old wood stove with a new, cleaner heating appliance. Newer wood stoves are at least 50% more efficient and pollute 70% less than older models.

- This can help make your home healthier and safer and help cut fuel costs.

Section 9.3

Occupational Asthma

Text in this section is excerpted from "Do You Have Work-Related Asthma? A Guide for You and Your Doctor," Occupational Safety and Health Administration (OSHA), March 2014.

Occupational Asthma due to Allergen Exposure at Work

Do you have any of these symptoms: cough, wheezing, difficulty breathing, shortness of breath, or chest tightness? If the answer is yes, you may have work-related asthma.

What Is Work-Related Asthma?

Work-related asthma is a lung disease caused or made worse by exposures to substances in the workplace. Common exposures include chemicals, dust, mold, animals, and plants. Exposure can occur from both inhalation (breathing) and skin contact. Asthma symptoms may start at work or within several hours after leaving work and may occur with no clear pattern. People who never had asthma can develop asthma due to workplace exposures. People who have had asthma for years may find that their condition worsens due to workplace exposures. Both of these situations are considered work-related asthma.

A group of chemicals called isocyanates are one of the most common chemical causes of work-related asthma. Occupational Safety and Health Administration (OSHA) is working to reduce exposures to isocyanates and has identified their use in numerous workplaces. See table below for common products (both at home and work) and common jobs where exposure to isocyanates may occur.

Why You Should Care about Work-Related Asthma

Work-related asthma may result in long-term lung damage, loss of work days, disability, or even death. The good news is that early diagnosis and treatment of work-related asthma can lead to a better health outcome.

What to Do If You Think You Have Work-Related Asthma

If you think that you may have work-related asthma, see your doctor as soon as possible.

Work-Related Asthma Quick Facts

- Work-related asthma can develop over ANY period of time (days to years).

- Work-related asthma may occur with changes in work exposures, jobs, or processes.

- It is possible to develop work-related asthma even if your workplace has protective equipment, such as exhaust ventilation or respirators.

- Work-related asthma can continue to cause symptoms even when the exposure stops.

Table 9.1. Products and Jobs Where Exposure to Isocyanates may Occur

Common Products*	Common Jobs and Job Processes*	
Polyurethane foam	Car manufacture and repair	Foundry work (casting)
Paints, lacquers, ink, varnishes, sealants, finishes	Building construction (plaster, insulation)	Textile, rubber and plastic manufacturing
Insulation materials	Foam blowing and cutting	Printing
Polyurethane rubber	Painting	Furniture manufacturing
Glues and adhesives	Truck bed liner application	Electric cable insulation

Many more jobs and products may also cause work-related asthma.

- Before working with isocyanates or any other asthma-causing substances, ask your employer for training, as required under OSHA's Hazard Communication standard.

Helpful Resources for Workers

- If you have a workplace health and safety question contact the Occupational Safety and Health Administration (OSHA) at 1-800-321-OSHA (6742) or go to OSHA's Workers web page at www.osha.gov/workers.html.

- Additional information on worker protection from isocyanates can be found on OSHA's Isocyanates Safety and Health Topics page: www.osha.gov/SLTC/isocyanates.

Section 9.4

Aspergillosis: People with Asthma at Highest Risk

Text in this section is excerpted from "Fungal Diseases," Centers for Disease Control and Prevention (CDC), September 8, 2014.

What Is Aspergillosis?

Aspergillosis is a disease caused by *Aspergillus*, a common mold (a type of fungus) that lives indoors and outdoors. Most people breathe in *Aspergillus* spores every day without getting sick. However, people with weakened immune systems or lung diseases are at a higher risk of developing health problems due to *Aspergillus*. There are different types of aspergillosis. Some types are mild, but some of them are very serious.

Types of Aspergillosis

- **Allergic bronchopulmonary aspergillosis (ABPA):** *Aspergillus* causes inflammation in the lungs and allergy symptoms such as coughing and wheezing, but doesn't cause an infection.

- **Allergic Aspergillus sinusitis:** *Aspergillus* causes inflammation in the sinuses and symptoms of a sinus infection (drainage, stuffiness, headache) but doesn't cause an infection.

- **Aspergilloma:** also called a "fungus ball." As the name suggests, it is a ball of *Aspergillus* that grows in the lungs or sinuses, but usually does not spread to other parts of the body.

- **Chronic pulmonary aspergillosis:** a long-term (3 months or more) condition in which *Aspergillus* can cause cavities in the lungs. One or more fungal balls (aspergillomas) may also be present in the lungs.

- **Invasive aspergillosis:** a serious infection that usually affects people who have weakened immune systems, such as people who have had an organ transplant or a stem cell transplant. Invasive aspergillosis most commonly affects the lungs, but it can also spread to other parts of the body.

- **Cutaneous (skin) aspergillosis:** *Aspergillus* enters the body through a break in the skin (for example, after surgery or a burn wound) and causes infection, usually in people who have weakened immune systems. Cutaneous aspergillosis can also occur if invasive aspergillosis spreads to the skin from somewhere else in the body, such as the lungs.

Symptoms of Aspergillosis

The different types of aspergillosis can cause different symptoms. The symptoms of **allergic bronchopulmonary aspergillosis (ABPA)** are similar to asthma symptoms, including:

- Wheezing

- Shortness of breath

- Cough

- Fever (in rare cases)

Symptoms of **allergic Aspergillus** sinusitis include:

- Stuffiness

- Runny nose

- Headache

- Reduced ability to smell

Symptoms of an **aspergilloma** ("fungus ball") include:

- Cough
- Coughing up blood
- Shortness of breath

Symptoms of **chronic pulmonary aspergillosis** include:

- Weight loss
- Cough
- Coughing up blood
- Fatigue
- Shortness of breath

Invasive aspergillosis usually occurs in people who are already sick from other medical conditions, so it can be difficult to know which symptoms are related to an *Aspergillus* infection. However, the symptoms of invasive aspergillosis in the lungs include:

- Fever
- Chest pain
- Cough
- Coughing up blood
- Shortness of breath
- Other symptoms can develop if the infection spreads from the lungs to other parts of the body.

Contact your healthcare provider if you have symptoms that you think are related to any form of aspergillosis.

People at Risk and Prevention

Who Gets Aspergillosis?

The different types of aspergillosis affect different groups of people.

- Allergic bronchopulmonary aspergillosis (ABPA) most often occurs in people who have cystic fibrosis or asthma.
- Aspergillomas usually affect people who have other lung diseases like tuberculosis.

- Chronic pulmonary aspergillosis typically occurs in people who have other lung diseases, including tuberculosis, chronic obstructive pulmonary disease (COPD), or sarcoidosis.

- Invasive aspergillosis affects people who have weakened immune systems, such as people who have had a stem cell transplant or organ transplant, are getting chemotherapy for cancer, or are taking high doses of corticosteroids.

How Does Someone Get Aspergillosis?

People can get aspergillosis by breathing in microscopic *Aspergillus* spores from the environment. Most people breathe in *Aspergillus* spores every day without getting sick. However, people with weakened immune systems or lung diseases are at a higher risk of developing health problems due to *Aspergillus*.

Is Aspergillosis Contagious?

No. Aspergillosis can't spread between people or between people and animals from the lungs.

How Can I Prevent Aspergillosis?

- It's difficult to avoid breathing in *Aspergillus* spores because the fungus is common in the environment. For people who have weakened immune systems, there may be some ways to lower the chances of developing a severe *Aspergillus* infection.

- Protect yourself from the environment. It's important to note that although these actions are recommended, they haven't been proven to prevent aspergillosis.

  - Try to avoid areas with a lot of dust like construction or excavation sites. If you can't avoid these areas, wear an N95 respirator (a type of face mask) while you're there.

  - Avoid activities that involve close contact to soil or dust, such as yard work or gardening. If this isn't possible,

- Wear shoes, long pants, and a long-sleeved shirt when doing outdoor activities such as gardening, yard work, or visiting wooded areas.

- Wear gloves when handling materials such as soil, moss, or manure.

- To reduce the chances of developing a skin infection, clean skin injuries well with soap and water, especially if they have been exposed to soil or dust.

- Antifungal medication. If you are at high risk for developing invasive aspergillosis (for example, if you've had an organ transplant or a stem cell transplant), your healthcare provider may prescribe medication to prevent aspergillosis. Scientists are still learning about which transplant patients are at highest risk and how to best prevent fungal infections.

- Testing for early infection. Some high-risk patients may benefit from blood tests to detect invasive aspergillosis. Talk to your doctor to determine if this type of test is right for you.

Sources of Aspergillosis

Aspergillus lives in the environment

Aspergillus, the mold (a type of fungus) that causes aspergillosis, is very common both indoors and outdoors, so most people breathe in fungal spores every day. It's probably impossible to completely avoid breathing in some *Aspergillus* spores. For people with healthy immune systems, breathing in *Aspergillus* isn't harmful. However, for people who have weakened immune systems, breathing in *Aspergillus* spores can cause an infection in the lungs or sinuses which can spread to other parts of the body.

I'm worried that the mold in my home is Aspergillus. Should someone test the mold to find out what it is?

No. Generally, it's not necessary to identify the species of mold growing in a home, and CDC doesn't recommend routine sampling for molds.

Types of Aspergillus

There are approximately 180 species of *Aspergillus,* but fewer than 40 of them are known to cause infections in humans. *Aspergillus fumigatus* is the most common cause of human *Aspergillus* infections. Other common species include A. *flavus,* A. *terreus,* and A. *niger.*

Diagnosis and Testing for Aspergillosis

Healthcare providers consider your medical history, risk factors, symptoms, physical examinations, and lab tests when diagnosing aspergillosis. You may need imaging tests such as a chest X-ray or a CT scan of your lungs or other parts of your body depending on the location of the suspected infection. If your healthcare provider suspects that you have an *Aspergillus* infection in your lungs, he or she might collect a sample of fluid from your respiratory system to send to a laboratory. Healthcare providers may also perform a tissue biopsy, in which a small sample of affected tissue is analyzed in a laboratory for evidence of *Aspergillus* under a microscope or in a fungal culture. A blood test can help diagnose invasive aspergillosis early in people who have severely weakened immune systems.

Treatment for Aspergillosis

Allergic Forms of Aspergillosis

For allergic forms of aspergillosis such as allergic bronchopulmonary aspergillosis (ABPA) or allergic *Aspergillus* sinusitis, the recommended treatment is itraconazole, a prescription antifungal medication. Corticosteroids may also be helpful.

Invasive Aspergillosis

Invasive aspergillosis needs to be treated with prescription antifungal medication, usually voriconazole. There are other medications that can be used to treat invasive aspergillosis in patients who can't take voriconazole or whose infections don't get better after taking voriconazole. These include itraconazole, lipid amphotericin formulations, caspofungin, micafungin, and posaconazole. Whenever possible, immunosuppressive medications should be discontinued or decreased. People who have severe cases of aspergillosis may need surgery.

Chapter 10

Atopic Dermatitis (Eczema)

Chapter Contents

Section 10.1

Atopic Dermatitis (Eczema): Overview

Text in this section is excerpted from "Eczema," National Institute of
Allergy and Infectious Diseases (NIAID), August 28, 2015.

What Is Atopic Dermatitis?

Atopic dermatitis (AD), also known as eczema, is a non-contagious
inflammatory skin condition that affects an estimated 30 percent of
the U.S. population, mostly children and adolescents. It is a chronic
disease characterized by dry, itchy skin that can weep clear fluid when
scratched. People with eczema also may be particularly susceptible to
bacterial, viral, and fungal skin infections.

Researchers estimate that 65 percent of people with atopic dermatitis develop symptoms during the first year of life, sometimes as early
as age 2 to 6 months, and 85 percent develop symptoms before the age
of 5. Many people outgrow the disease by early adulthood.

Causes

A combination of genetic and environmental factors appears to be
involved in the development of eczema. The condition often is associated with other allergic diseases such as asthma, hay fever, and food
allergy. Children whose parents have asthma and allergies are more
likely to develop atopic dermatitis than children of parents without
allergic diseases. Approximately 30 percent of children with atopic
dermatitis have food allergies, and many develop asthma or respiratory allergies. People who live in cities or drier climates also appear
more likely to develop the disease.

The condition tends to worsen when a person is exposed to certain
triggers, such as

- Pollen, mold, dust mites, animals, and certain foods (for allergic
  individuals)

- Cold and dry air

- Colds or the flu

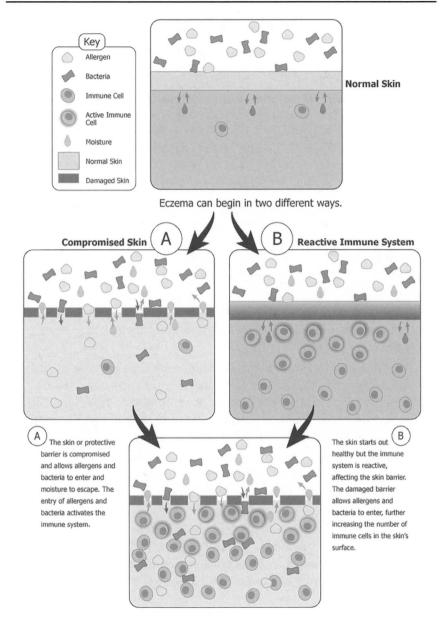

Figure 10.1. *Two Possible Causes of Eczema*

- Skin contact with irritating chemicals

- Skin contact with rough materials such as wool

- Emotional factors such as stress

- Fragrances or dyes added to skin lotions or soaps.

Taking too many baths or showers and not moisturizing the skin properly afterward may also make eczema worse.

Symptoms

Atopic dermatitis is characterized by red and itchy dry skin. Itching may start before the rash appears and sometimes can be intense. Persistent scratching of itchy skin can lead to redness, swelling, cracking, weeping of clear fluid, crusting, and scaling.

Both the type of rash and where the rash appears depend on a person's age.

- Infants as young as 6 to 12 weeks develop a scaly rash on their face and chin. As they begin to crawl and move about, other exposed areas may be affected.

- In childhood, the rash begins with bumps that become hard and scaly when scratched. It occurs behind the knees; inside the elbows; on the wrists, ankles, and hands; on the sides of the neck; and around the mouth. Constant licking of the lips can cause small, painful cracks in the skin.

- In some children, the disease goes into remission for a long time, only to come back at the onset of puberty when hormones, stress, and the use of irritating skin care products or cosmetics may cause the disease to flare.

- Some people develop atopic dermatitis for the first time as adults. The rash is more commonly seen on the insides of the knees and elbows, as well as on the neck, hands, and feet. The symptoms can be localized or widespread throughout the body.

During a severe flare-up, rashes may occur anywhere on the body.

Diagnosis

If your doctor suspects that you have atopic dermatitis, he or she may:

- Perform a physical exam and specifically inspect the appearance of the skin

- Take a personal and family history

- Perform a skin biopsy (the removal of a small piece of skin for examination) to confirm the diagnosis or to rule out other causes of dry, itchy skin

- Perform allergy skin testing, which may be helpful for individuals with hard-to-treat atopic dermatitis or who have symptoms of other allergic diseases

Treatment

Skin Care at Home

You and your doctor should discuss the best treatment plan and medications for your atopic dermatitis. But taking care of your skin at home may reduce the need for prescription medications. Some recommendations include:

- Avoid scratching the rash or skin.

- Relieve the itch by using a moisturizer or topical steroids. Take antihistamines to reduce severe itching.

- Keep your fingernails cut short. Consider light gloves if night-time scratching is a problem.

- Lubricate or moisturize the skin two to three times a day using ointments such as petroleum jelly. Moisturizers should be free of alcohol, scents, dyes, fragrances, and other skin-irritating chemicals. A humidifier in the home also can help.

- Avoid anything that worsens symptoms, including

  - Irritants such as wool and lanolin (an oily substance derived from sheep wool used in some moisturizers and cosmetics)

  - Strong soaps or detergents

  - Sudden changes in body temperature and stress, which may cause sweating

- When washing or bathing

  - Keep water contact as brief as possible and use gentle body washes and cleansers instead of regular soaps. Lukewarm baths are better than long, hot baths.

- Do not scrub or dry the skin too hard or for too long.

- After bathing, apply lubricating ointments to damp skin. This will help trap moisture in the skin.

Wet Wrap Therapy

Researchers at NIAID and other institutions are studying an innovative treatment for severe eczema called wet wrap therapy. It includes three lukewarm baths a day, each followed by an application of topical medicines and moisturizer that is sealed in by a wrap of wet gauze.

People with severe eczema have come to the National Institutes of Health Clinical Center in Bethesda, Maryland, for research evaluation. Treatment may include wet wrap therapy to bring the condition under control. Patients and their caregivers also receive training on home-based skin care to properly manage flare-ups once they leave the hospital.

Medications

A variety of medications are used to treat atopic dermatitis.

Corticosteroid creams and ointments have been used for many years to treat atopic dermatitis and other autoimmune diseases affecting the skin.

When topical corticosteroids are not effective, the doctor may prescribe a systemic corticosteroid, which is taken by mouth or injected instead of being applied directly to the skin. Typically, these medications are used only in resistant cases and only given for short periods of time.

Antibiotics to treat skin infections may necessary. If viral or fungal infections are present, the doctor may also prescribe specific medications to treat those infections.

Certain antihistamines that cause drowsiness can reduce nighttime scratching and allow more restful sleep when taken at bedtime. This effect can be particularly helpful for patients whose nighttime scratching makes the disease worse.

Topical calcineurin inhibitors decrease inflammation in the skin and help prevent flares.

Barrier repair moisturizers reduce water loss and work to rebuild the skin.

Phototherapy

Use of ultraviolet A or B light waves, alone or combined, can be an effective treatment for mild to moderate dermatitis. If the doctor thinks that phototherapy may be useful to treat the symptoms of atopic dermatitis, he or she will use the minimum exposure necessary and monitor the skin carefully.

Treating Atopic Dermatitis in Infants and Children

- Give lukewarm baths.
- Apply lubricant immediately following the bath.
- Keep child's fingernails filed short.
- Select soft cotton fabrics when choosing clothing.
- Consider using sedating antihistamines to promote sleep and reduce scratching at night.
- Keep the child cool; avoid situations where overheating occurs.
- Learn to recognize skin infections and seek treatment promptly.
- Attempt to distract the child with activities to keep him or her from scratching.
- Identify and remove irritants and allergens.

Protection from allergen exposure

The doctor may suggest reducing exposure to a suspected allergen. For example, the presence of the house dust mite can be limited by encasing mattresses and pillows in special dust-proof covers, frequently washing bedding in hot water, and removing carpeting. However, there is no way to completely rid the environment of airborne allergens.

Changing the diet may not always relieve symptoms of atopic dermatitis. A change may be helpful, however, when the medical history, laboratory studies, and specific symptoms strongly suggest a food allergy. It is up to the patient and his or her family and physician to decide whether the dietary restrictions are appropriate. Unless properly monitored by a physician or dietitian, diets with many restrictions can contribute to serious nutritional problems, especially in children.

Complications

The skin of people with atopic dermatitis lacks infection-fighting proteins, making them susceptible to skin infections caused by bacteria and viruses. Fungal infections also are common in people with atopic dermatitis.

Bacterial Infections

A major health risk associated with atopic dermatitis is skin colonization or infection by bacteria such as *Staphylococcus aureus*. Sixty to 90 percent of people with atopic dermatitis are likely to have staph bacteria on their skin. Many eventually develop infection, which worsens the atopic dermatitis.

Viral Infections

People with atopic dermatitis are highly vulnerable to certain viral infections of the skin. For example, if infected with herpes simplex virus, they can develop a severe skin condition called atopic dermatitis with eczema herpeticum.

Those with atopic dermatitis should not receive the currently licensed smallpox vaccine, even if their disease is in remission, because they are at risk of developing a severe infection called eczema vaccinatum. This infection is caused when the live vaccinia virus in the smallpox vaccine reproduces and spreads throughout the body. Furthermore, those in close contact with people who have atopic dermatitis or a history of the disease should not receive the smallpox vaccine because of the risk of transmitting the live vaccine virus to the person with atopic dermatitis.

Section 10.2

Factors That Make Atopic Dermatitis Worse

Text in this section is excerpted from "Atopic Dermatitis," National Institute of Arthritis and Musculoskeletal and Skin Diseases (NIAMS), May 2013.

Many factors or conditions can make symptoms of atopic dermatitis worse, further triggering the already overactive immune system, aggravating the itch-scratch cycle, and increasing damage to the skin. These factors can be broken down into two main categories: irritants and allergens. Emotional factors and some infections and illnesses can also influence atopic dermatitis.

Irritants are substances that directly affect the skin and, when present in high enough concentrations with long enough contact, cause the skin to become red and itchy or to burn. Frequent wetting and drying of the skin may affect the skin barrier function. Also, wool or synthetic fibers and rough or poorly fitting clothing can rub the skin, trigger inflammation, and cause the itch-scratch cycle to begin. Soaps and detergents may have a drying effect and worsen itching, and some perfumes and cosmetics may irritate the skin. Exposure to certain substances, such as solvents, dust, or sand, may also make the condition worse. Cigarette smoke may irritate the eyelids.

Allergens are substances from foods, plants, animals, or the air that inflame the skin because the immune system overreacts to the substance. Inflammation occurs even when the person is exposed to small amounts of the substance for a limited time. Although it is known that allergens in the air, such as dust mites, pollens, molds, and dander from animal hair or skin, may worsen the symptoms of atopic dermatitis in some people, scientists aren't certain whether inhaling these allergens or their actual penetration of the skin causes the problems.

When people with atopic dermatitis come into contact with an irritant or allergen they are sensitive to, inflammation producing cells become active. These cells release chemicals that cause itching and redness. As the person responds by scratching and rubbing the skin, further damage occurs.

Common Irritants

- Wool or synthetic fibers
- Soaps and detergents
- Some perfumes and cosmetics
- Substances such as chlorine, mineral oil, or solvents
- Dust or sand
- Cigarette smoke

Children with atopic disease tend to have a higher prevalence of food allergy than those in the general population. An allergic reaction to food can cause skin inflammation (generally an itchy red rash), gastrointestinal (GI) symptoms (abdominal pain, vomiting, diarrhea), and/or upper respiratory tract symptoms (congestion, sneezing, and wheezing). The most common allergenic (allergy-causing) foods are eggs, milk, peanuts, wheat, soy, tree nuts, shellfish, and fish.

In addition to irritants and allergens, emotional factors, skin infections, and temperature and climate play a role in atopic dermatitis. Although the disease itself is not caused by emotional factors, it can be made worse by stress, anger, and frustration. Interpersonal problems or major life changes, such as divorce, job changes, or the death of a loved one, can also make the disease worse.

Bathing without proper moisturizing afterward is a common factor that triggers a flare of atopic dermatitis. The low humidity of winter or the dry year-round climate of some geographic areas can make the disease worse, as can overheated indoor areas and long or hot baths and showers. Alternately sweating and chilling can trigger a flare in some people. Bacterial infections can also trigger or increase the severity of atopic dermatitis. If a patient experiences a sudden flare of illness, the doctor may check for infection.

Section 10.3

Atopic Dermatitis and Quality of Life

Text in this section is excerpted from "Atopic Dermatitis," National Institute of Arthritis and Musculoskeletal and Skin Diseases (NIAMS), May 2013.

Although the symptoms of atopic dermatitis can be difficult and uncomfortable, the disease can be successfully managed. People with atopic dermatitis can lead healthy, productive lives. The keys to quality of life lie in being well-informed; being aware of symptoms and their possible cause; and developing a partnership involving the patient or caregiving family member, medical doctor, and other health professionals.

When a child has atopic dermatitis, the entire family may be affected. It is helpful if families have additional support to help them cope with the stress and frustration associated with the disease.

A child may be fussy and difficult and unable to keep from scratching and rubbing the skin. Distracting the child and providing activities that keep the hands busy are helpful but require much effort on the part of the parents or caregivers. Another issue families face is the social and emotional stress associated with changes in appearance caused by atopic dermatitis. The child may face difficulty in school or with social relationships and may need additional support and encouragement from family members.

Adults with atopic dermatitis can enhance their quality of life by caring regularly for their skin and being mindful of the effects of the disease and how to treat them. Adults should develop a skin care regimen as part of their daily routine, which can be adapted as circumstances and skin conditions change. Stress management and relaxation techniques may help decrease the likelihood of flares. Developing a network of support that includes family, friends, health professionals, and support groups or organizations can be beneficial. Chronic anxiety and depression may be relieved by psychological therapy.

Recognizing the situations when scratching is most likely to occur may also help. For example, many patients find that they scratch more when they are idle, and they do better when engaged in activities that keep the hands occupied. Counseling also may be helpful to identify or change career goals if a job involves contact with irritants or involves frequent hand washing, such as work in a kitchen or auto machine shop.

Tips for Working with Your Doctor

- Provide complete, accurate medical information.
- Make a list of your questions and concerns in advance.
- Be honest and share your point of view with the doctor.
- Ask for clarification or further explanation if you need it.
- Talk to other members of the health care team, such as nurses, therapists, or pharmacists.
- Don't hesitate to discuss sensitive subjects with your doctor.
- Discuss changes to medical treatment or medications with your doctor.

Chapter 11

Allergic Contact Dermatitis

Chapter Contents

Section 11.1

Contact Dermatitis: An Overview

Text in this section is excerpted from "Skin Exposures & Effects,"
Centers for Disease Control and Prevention (CDC), July 2, 2013.

Contact dermatitis, also called eczema, is defined as an inflammation of the skin resulting from exposure to a hazardous agent. It is the most common form of reported OSD, and represents an overwhelming burden for workers in developed nations. Epidemiological data indicate that contact dermatitis constitutes approximately 90-95% of all cases of OSD in the United States. Common symptoms of dermatitis include:

- Itching

- Pain

- Redness

- Swelling

- The formation of small blisters or wheals (itchy, red circles with a white centre) on the skin

- Dry, flaking, scaly skin that may develop cracks

Occupational contact dermatitis is frequently divided into two categories:

- **Irritant contact dermatitis (ICD)** is a non-immunologic reaction that manifests as an inflammation of the skin caused by direct damage to the skin following exposure to a hazardous agent. The reaction is typically localized to the site of contact. Available data indicates that ICD represents approximately 80% of all cases of occupational contact dermatitis.

  ICD may be caused by phototoxic responses (e.g., tar), acute exposures to highly irritating substances (e.g., acids, bases, oxiding/reducing agents), or chronic cumulative exposures to mild irritants (e.g., water, detergents, weak cleaning agents).

- **Allergic contact dermatitis (ACD)** is an inflammation of the skin caused by an immunologic reaction triggered by dermal contact to a skin allergen. For ACD to occur, a worker must be first sensitized to the allergen. Subsequent exposures of the skin to the allergenic agent may elicit an immunologic reaction resulting in inflammation of the skin. The reaction is not confined to the site of contact and may result in systemic responses.

ACD may be caused by industrial compounds (i.e., metals, epoxy and acrylic resins, rubber additives, chemical intermediates), agrochemicals (i.e., pesticides and fertilizers), and commercial chemicals.

Because the symptoms and presentation of ICD and ACD are so similar, it is extremely difficult to distinguish between the two forms of contact dermatitis without clinical testing (e.g., patch testing). The severity of contact dermatitis is highly variable and depends on many factors including:

- Characteristics of the hazardous agent (irritant and/or allergen)

- Concentration of the hazardous agent (irritant and/or allergen)

- Duration and frequency of exposure to the hazardous agent (irritant and/or allergen)

- Environmental factors (e.g., temperature, humidity)

- Condition of the skin (e.g., healthy vs. damaged skin, dry vs. wet)

Section 11.2

Outsmarting Poison Ivy and Other Poisonous Plants

Text in this section is excerpted from "Outsmarting Poison Ivy and Other Poisonous Plants," U.S. Food and Drug Administration (FDA), August 28, 2015.

First comes the itching, then a red rash, and then blisters. These symptoms of poison ivy, poison oak, and poison sumac can start from a few hours to several days after exposure to the plant oil found in the sap of these poisonous plants.

Recognizing Poison Ivy, Poison Oak, and Poison Sumac

- **Poison Ivy:** Found throughout the United States except Alaska, Hawaii, and parts of the West Coast. Can grow as a vine or small shrub trailing along the ground or climbing on low plants, trees and poles. Each leaf has three glossy leaflets, with smooth or toothed edges. Leaves are reddish in spring, green in summer, and yellow, orange, or red in fall. May have greenish-white flowers and whitish-yellow berries.

- **Poison Oak:** Grows as a low shrub in the eastern and southern United States, and in tall clumps or long vines on the Pacific Coast. Fuzzy green leaves in clusters of three are lobed or deeply toothed with rounded tips. May have yellow-white berries.

- **Poison Sumac:** Grows as a tall shrub or small tree in bogs or swamps in Northeast, Midwest, and parts of the Southeast. Each leaf has clusters of seven to 13 smooth-edged leaflets. Leaves are orange in spring, green in summer, and yellow, orange, or red in fall. May have yellow-greenish flowers and and whitish green fruits hang in loose clusters.

Not Contagious

Poison ivy and other poison plant rashes can't be spread from person to person. But it is possible to pick up the rash from plant oil that may have stuck to clothing, pets, garden tools, and other items that have come in contact with these plants. The plant oil lingers (sometimes for years) on virtually any surface until it's washed off with water or rubbing alcohol.

The rash will only occur where the plant oil has touched the skin, so a person with poison ivy can't spread it on the body by scratching. It may seem like the rash is spreading if it appears over time instead of all at once. But this is either because the plant oil is absorbed at different rates on different parts of the body or because of repeated exposure to contaminated objects or plant oil trapped under the fingernails. Even if blisters break, the fluid in the blisters is not plant oil and cannot further spread the rash.

Tips for Prevention

- Learn what poison ivy, oak, and sumac plants look like so you can avoid them.

- Wash your garden tools and gloves regularly. If you think you may be working around poison ivy, wear long sleeves, long pants tucked into boots, and impermeable gloves.

- Wash your pet if it may have brushed up against poison ivy, oak, or sumac. Use pet shampoo and water while wearing rubber gloves, such as dishwashing gloves. Most pets are not sensitive to poison ivy, but the oil can stick to their fur and cause a reaction in someone who pets them.

- Wash your skin in soap and cool water as soon as possible if you come in contact with a poisonous plant. The sooner you cleanse the skin, the greater the chance that you can remove the plant oil or help prevent further spread.

- Use the topical product "Ivy Block" if you know you will come into contact with the poisonous plants. This FDA-approved product is available over the counter (OTC).

Tips for Treatment

Don't scratch the blisters. Bacteria from under your fingernails can get into the blisters and cause an infection. The rash, blisters, and itch normally disappear in several weeks without any treatment. But you can relieve the itch by:

- using wet compresses or soaking in cool water

- applying OTC topical corticosteroid preparations or taking prescription oral corticosteroids

- applying topical OTC skin protectants, such as zinc acetate, zinc carbonate, zinc oxide, and calamine dry the oozing and weeping of poison ivy, poison oak, and poison sumac. Protectants such as baking soda or colloidal oatmeal relieve minor irritation and itching. Aluminum acetate is an astringent that relieves rash.

When to See a Doctor

- If you have a temperature over 100 °F

- If there is pus, soft yellow scabs, or tenderness on the rash

- If the itching gets worse or keeps you awake at night

- If the rash spreads to your eyes, mouth, genital area, or covers more than one-fourth of your skin area

- If the rash is not improving within a few weeks

Section 11.3

Why Should We Care about Contact Dermatitis?

Text in this section is excerpted from "3Rs Topics," National Toxicology Program (NTP), September 2014.

If you've ever had a case of poison ivy, you know how unpleasant it is. It produces red, itching, weeping and blistered skin. The effects can last for weeks and it can have a major effect on your daily life.

Poison ivy is an example of allergic contact dermatitis (ACD). To get the rash, you have to be *allergic* to poison ivy, and your bare skin must come in *contact* with the plant or its sap. The resulting rash is the *dermatitis* of ACD.

Sensitizers can cause allergic reactions

An allergy is an immune reaction to a foreign substance. Such a foreign substance is called an allergen or, in the case of ACD, a sensitizer. Except for their allergenic properties, sensitizers are generally (though not always) relatively harmless substances. Why sensitizers result in ACD in some people but not others is not fully understood— we do know that allergies can be hereditary, so sensitivity may be part of your genetic makeup.

The first time you encounter a sensitizer, you might become sensitized. You'll have no visible symptoms, but the sensitizer triggers a complex physiological reaction. This will cause your cells to produce substances that damage your body the next time you are exposed to the sensitizer. The outward symptom of that damage is the ACD rash.

ACD is a common occupational illness

Allergic Contact Dermatitis is often considered an occupational illness because it can develop in a variety of workplace settings. Workers in professions as diverse as farming, construction, food handling, or hairdressing may be at risk. Even office workers might be exposed to sensitizers such as rubber, nickel, or glue.

According to the U.S. Bureau of Labor Statistics, occupational skin diseases, including contact dermatitis, account for 15% to 20% of occupational diseases and are the second most common type of occupational illness. ACD is estimated to constitute about 20% to 25% of all contact dermatitis cases. A severe rash can result in lost workdays, and if the sensitizer is not removed from the home or workplace, the rash can reoccur. Sometimes, a worker is forced to leave the job to avoid exposures. The estimated total annual cost of occupational skin diseases (including lost workdays and loss of productivity) may reach $1 billion annually.

ACD diagnosis and treatment

ACD is difficult to diagnose unless you can establish a direct connection between the sensitizer and the rash. You may be uncertain what you were exposed to or where the exposure occurred. In severe cases of ACD, the rash can persist for years, even if the patient avoids additional exposure to the sensitizer, and have a significant impact on the patient's quality of life.

Your dermatologist can diagnose whether you have ACD with a patch test. This test involves placing small amounts of sensitizers (covered with patches) on your skin. The patches are left on for about 48 hours, long enough for an allergic reaction to occur. Then the skin beneath the patches is examined for signs of dermatitis. A positive reaction means that you have been sensitized to the applied substance or a closely related one.

Once the sensitizer has been identified, you can inspect your home and workplace for its presence and take steps to avoid exposure. Occasionally, all that is required is personal protective equipment such as gloves, long sleeves, or a mask, but sometimes you will need to completely avoid the environment where the exposure occurs. Allergy shots may provide a cure, but they are not always effective.

Testing and labeling can help prevent exposure to sensitizers

The best way to avoid developing ACD is to avoid becoming sensitized. This is easier said than done, however. Thousands of potential sensitizers are introduced into the environment every year. U.S. regulatory agencies require chemical and product testing to determine their potential to cause ACD. Substances identified as sensitizers must be labelled with a description of their potential hazard and the precautions necessary to minimize exposure. Proper labelling reduces the risk for inadvertent exposure.

Traditionally, substances were tested in guinea pigs to predict if they had the potential to be human sensitizers. Animals were exposed to the substance twice, several weeks apart, and observed after the second exposure to see if ACD developed. More recently, the mouse local lymph node assay has become the test of choice for determining the ACD hazard potential for most substances. Compared to the guinea pig tests, it requires fewer animals, takes less time to perform, and eliminates animal pain and distress.

Alternative tests have been developed that don't use live animals at all. For these, sensitizing potential is assessed by:

- measuring specific responses in cells grown in culture
- measuring the reactivity of a chemical in a test tube, or
- examining and comparing chemical structures using computer models.

While it is not yet possible to eliminate all animal testing for ACD, scientists are working to develop an integrated testing strategy that may replace animal testing in the future.

Sensitizers are everywhere

Among the top 10 identified sensitizers are nickel, the topical antibiotics neomycin and bacitracin, formaldehyde, and the chemicals Balsam of Peru and Quaterinium-15. Nickel is everywhere; it is found in coins and costume jewelry and has a myriad of other uses. Neomycin and bacitracin are common constituents of the nonprescription antibiotic ointments used to treat minor skin infections and abrasions. Formaldehyde is familiar to anyone who dissected a frog in high school as the strong-smelling preservative that made your eyes water; it's used in home construction materials, personal care products, clothing, and furniture. Balsam of Peru is an ingredient in many fragrances and processed foods. Quaternium-15 is a preservative used in many cosmetics.

It is important to remember that exposure to a sensitizer does not mean that you will automatically develop ACD. Some people are not allergic to even very strong sensitizers like poison ivy. However, if you experience a recurring skin rash, especially on your hands or face, you may wish to visit your dermatologist to determine if ACD is the problem.

Chapter 12

Other Allergic Skin Reactions

Chapter Contents

Section 12.1

Urticaria (Hives)

"Urticaria (Hives)," © 2016 Omnigraphics, Inc.
Reviewed November 2015.

What Is Urticaria

Urticaria, commonly known as hives, is a condition in which itchy, swollen red wheals or welts of different sizes appear on the skin. Although there are many possible causes of hives, they most commonly result from an allergic reaction to food or drugs. Hives can last from several minutes to several hours, or in some cases several weeks. They can be itchy, painful, and sometimes cause a burning sensation. Hives may form in one small area on the surface of the skin, or on a larger area of the body. They affect one out of every five people at some point in life.

There are two distinct types of urticaria, acute and chronic. Acute urticaria typically lasts for less than six weeks. The rashes appear suddenly and disappear within a short period of time. Chronic hives, on the other hand, last for more than six weeks and sometimes for months. Although the condition is not dangerous, it can cause considerable discomfort. Angioedema is another form of hives in which the swelling occurs beneath the surface of the skin, often around the eyes and lips.

Hives are generally not life threatening and do not have long-term health effects. However, when breathing difficulties, dizziness, and swelling of the throat or tongue occur along with an eruption of hives on the skin, it could signal anaphylaxis—a severe, life-threatening allergic reaction—and emergency medical care must be sought.

Causes and Treatment

Hives usually occur as a symptom of allergic reactions, when the body's immune system releases histamines and other chemicals into the bloodstream. Hives may be triggered by contact with a variety of common allergens, including foods, drugs, latex, pollen, insect bites, or dust mites. Urticaria may also occur as a result of bacterial and viral infections; immunizations; disease conditions such as vasculitis and lupus; adverse reactions to blood transfusions; or skin contact with plants such as poison ivy. In some cases, hives may also be caused by external triggers such as exercise, emotional stress, heat and cold, and sun exposure.

While the cause of hives may be obvious in people with known allergies, other people may need to undergo medical testing by specialists to identify the cause. In some people with chronic hives, the underlying cause may be difficult to find. It may be helpful to keep a diary of symptoms, noting the conditions under which they occur and improve. This information can help people identify and avoid any factors that can trigger the condition.

As the first course of treatment for hives, a healthcare provider will usually prescribe antihistamine medication to negate the effects of histamines released into the bloodstream. Corticosteroids may be prescribed if the symptoms are severe. If the patient experiences hives as part of a severe allergic reaction and has symptoms of anaphylaxis, they will require an immediate shot of epinephrine. Anti-itch medications or salves may also be prescribed to provide relief from itching. Applying wet compresses or taking a cool bath with baking soda or oatmeal sprinkled in the water can also help relieve symptoms of hives.

References:

1. Cole, Gary W. "Hives (Urticaria and Angiodema)." MedicineNet, n.d.

2. "Hives (Urticaria)." American College of Allergy, Asthma, and Immunology, 2014.

3. U.S. National Library of Medicine. "Hives." Medline Plus, September 8, 2014.

Section 12.2

Cold Urticaria – A Rare Disorder

Text in this section is excerpted from "Cold Urticaria," Genetic and
Rare Diseases Information Center (GARD), September 15, 2015.

Overview

Cold urticaria is a condition that affects the skin. Signs and symptoms generally include reddish, itchy welts (hives) and/or swelling when skin is exposed to the cold (i.e., cold weather or swimming in cold water). This rash is usually apparent within 2–5 minutes after exposure and can last for 1–2 hours. The exact cause of cold urticaria is poorly understood in most cases. Rarely, it may be associated with an underlying blood condition or infectious disease. Treatment generally consists of patient education, avoiding exposures that may trigger a reaction, and/or medications.

Symptoms

What are the signs and symptoms of cold urticaria?

The signs and symptoms of cold urticaria and the severity of the condition vary. Affected people generally develop reddish, itchy welts (hives) and/or swelling when skin is exposed to the cold (i.e. cold weather or swimming in cold water). This rash is usually apparent within 2–5 minutes after exposure and lasts for 1–2 hours. Other signs and symptoms may include:

- Headache
- Anxiety
- Tiredness
- Fainting
- Heart palpitations

- Wheezing

- Joint pain

- Low blood pressure

In very severe cases, exposure to cold could lead to loss of consciousness, shock or even death.

Cause

What causes cold urticaria?

In most cases of cold urticaria, the underlying cause is poorly understood. Although the symptoms are triggered by exposure of the skin to the cold (most often when the temperature is lower than 39 degrees Fahrenheit), it is unclear why this exposure leads to such a significant reaction.

Rarely, cold urticaria is associated with blood conditions or infectious disease such as cryoglobulinemia, chronic lymphocytic leukaemia, lymphosarcoma, chicken pox, viral hepatitis, and mononucleosis.

Inheritance

Is cold urticaria inherited?

Cold urticaria is not thought to be inherited. Most cases occur sporadically in people with no family history of the condition.

Tests and Diagnosis

How is cold urticaria diagnosed?

A diagnosis of cold urticaria is typically suspected based on the presence of characteristic signs and symptoms. Additional testing can then be ordered to confirm the diagnosis and determine if there are other associated conditions. This generally involves a cold simulation test in which a cold object (such as an ice cube) is applied against the skin of the forearm for 1–5 minutes. In people affected by cold urticaria, a distinct red and swollen rash will generally develop within minutes of exposure. A complete blood count and/or metabolic tests may also be performed to determine associated diseases.

Treatment

How might cold urticaria be treated?

The treatment of cold urticaria generally consists of patient education, avoiding scenarios that may trigger a reaction (i.e. cold temperatures, cold water), and/or medications. Prophylactic treatment with high-dose antihistimines may be recommended when exposure to cold is expected and can not be avoided. Additionally, affected people are often told to carry an epinephrine autoinjector due to the increased risk of anaphylaxis.

Several other therapies have reportedly been used to treat cold urticaria with varying degrees of success. These include:

- Leukotriene antagonists
- Ciclosporin
- Systemic corticosteroids
- Dapsone
- Oral antibiotics
- Synthetic hormones
- Danazol

Prognosis

What is the long-term outlook for people with cold urticaria?

The long-term outlook (prognosis) for people with cold urticaria varies. In approximately 50% of cases, the condition either completely resolves or drastically improves within five to six years. However, some people have the disorder for many years or even lifelong.

Living With

Medical Resources

- Many individuals want to know about healthcare professionals or researchers who have knowledge of their conditions. When a condition is rare, it can be difficult to find someone who has seen many cases. Although there is no list of experts in rare diseases, GARD's How to Find a Disease Specialist (www.rarediseases. info.nih.gov/gard/pages/25/how-to-find-a-disease-specialist) fact sheet provides several ways to identify healthcare professionals who have experience with a particular condition.

Parent and Caregiver Resources

- The Parent Technical Assistance Center Network (www.parent-centerhub.org/find-your-center) provides a list of the Parent Training and Information Centers in each state. These centers are funded by the United States Department of Education to provide early intervention and special education information and training to parents of children with disabilities from birth to age 26.

Section 12.3

Allergic Reaction Caused by Mast Cells

Text in this section is excerpted from "Mastocytosis," National Institute of Allergy and Infectious Diseases (NIAID), October 28, 2013

Mastocytosis

Mastocytosis is a disorder that can occur in both children and adults. It is caused by the presence of too many mast cells in your body.

You can find mast cells in skin, lymph nodes, internal organs (such as the liver and spleen) and the linings of the lung, stomach, and intestine. Mast cells play an important role in helping your immune system defend these tissues from disease. Mast cells attract other key players of the immune defense system to areas of your body where they are needed by releasing chemical "alarms" such as histamine and cytokines.

Mast cells seem to have other roles as well. Found to gather around wounds, they may play a part in wound healing. For example, the typical itching you feel around a healing scab may be caused by histamine released by mast cells. Researchers also think mast cells may have a role in the growth of blood vessels. No one with too few or no mast cells has ever been found. This fact indicates to some scientists that having too few mast cells may be incompatible with life.

The presence of too many mast cells, or mastocytosis, can occur in two forms—cutaneous and systemic. The most common cutaneous (skin) form is also called urticaria pigmentosa, which occurs when mast cells infiltrate the skin. Systemic mastocytosis is caused by mast cells accumulating in the tissues and can affect organs such as the liver, spleen, bone marrow, and small intestine.

Researchers first described urticaria pigmentosa in 1869. Systemic mastocytosis was first reported in the scientific literature in 1949. The true number of cases of either type of mastocytosis remains unknown, but mastocytosis generally is considered to be an "orphan disease." (Orphan diseases affect about 200,000 or fewer people in the United States.)

Symptoms

Chemicals released by mast cells cause changes in your body's functioning that lead to typical allergic responses such as flushing, itching, abdominal cramping, and even shock. When too many mast cells are in your body, the additional chemicals can cause

- Muscle and bone pain

- Abdominal discomfort

- Nausea and vomiting

- Ulcers

- Diarrhea

- Itching

It can also cause episodes of hypotension (very low blood pressure and faintness) or anaphylaxis (shock).

Diagnosis

Your healthcare provider can diagnose cutaneous mastocytosis by the appearance of your skin and confirm it by finding an abnormally high number of mast cells on a skin biopsy. Your provider can diagnose systemic mastocytosis by finding an increased number of abnormal mast cells during an examination of your bone marrow.

Other tests that are important in evaluating a suspected case of mastocytosis include

- Measurement of a protein (tryptase) from mast cells in your blood

- A search for specific genetic mutations that health experts associate with this disease

Treatment

Healthcare providers use several medicines to treat mastocytosis symptoms, including antihistamines (to prevent the effect of mast cell histamine—a chemical) and anticholinergics (to relieve intestinal cramping). A number of medicines treat specific symptoms of mastocytosis.

- Antihistamines frequently treat itching and other skin complaints.

- Certain antihistamines work specifically against ulcers; proton pump inhibitors also relieve ulcer-like symptoms.

- Epinephrine treats symptom flares which occur with shock, referred to as "anaphylaxis."

- Two types of antihistamines treat severe flushing and low blood pressure before symptoms appear.

- Steroids treat malabsorption, or impaired ability to take in nutrients.

- Cromolyn sodium may help reduce cramping in the abdomen.

In cases in which mastocytosis is malignant, cancerous, or associated with a blood disorder, steroids and/or chemotherapy may be necessary.

Research

NIAID scientists have studied and treated patients with mastocytosis for more than three decades at the National Institutes of Health (NIH) Clinical Center.

Some of the most important research advances for this rare disorder include

- Improved diagnosis of mast cell disease

- Identification of growth factors responsible for increased mast cell production

- Improved treatment

For example, researchers have developed drugs that help block the division of mast cells and the action of chemicals released from mast cells.

Scientists also are focusing on identifying gene mutations associated with the disease. Several such mutations have been identified at NIH in a cell receptor for a mast cell growth factor and in key molecules within mast cells that control cell activation. Understanding such mutations helps researchers understand the causes of mastocytosis, improve diagnosis, and develop better treatment.

Chapter 13

Anaphylaxis: Life-Threatening Allergies

Chapter Contents

Section 13.1

Signs of Anaphylaxis

Text in this section is excerpted from "Anaphylaxis," National
Institute of Allergy and Infectious Diseases (NIAID), April 23, 2015.

What Is Anaphylaxis

Anaphylaxis is a serious allergic reaction that involves more than
one organ system (for example, skin, respiratory tract, and/or gastrointestinal tract). It can begin very rapidly, and symptoms may be
severe or life-threatening.

Causes

The most common causes of anaphylaxis are reactions to foods
(especially peanuts), medications, and stinging insects. Other potential
triggers include exercise and exposure to latex. Sometimes, anaphylaxis occurs without an identifiable trigger. This is called idiopathic
anaphylaxis.

Symptoms

Anaphylaxis includes a wide range of symptoms that can occur in
many combinations and may be difficult to recognize. Some symptoms
are not life-threatening, but the most severe ones restrict breathing
and blood circulation.

Many of the body's organs can be affected:

- Skin—itching, hives, redness, swelling

- Nose—sneezing, stuffy nose, runny nose

- Mouth—itching, swelling of the lips or tongue

- Throat—itching, tightness, difficulty swallowing, swelling of the
  back of the throat

- Chest—shortness of breath, cough, wheeze, chest pain, tightness

- Heart—weak pulse, passing out, shock

- Gastrointestinal (GI) tract—vomiting, diarrhea, cramps
- Nervous system—dizziness or fainting

How soon after exposure will symptoms occur?

Symptoms can begin within minutes to hours after exposure to the allergen. Sometimes the symptoms go away, only to return anywhere from 8 to 72 hours later. When you begin to experience symptoms, seek immediate medical attention because anaphylaxis can be life-threatening.

How do you know if a person is having an anaphylactic reaction?

Anaphylaxis is likely if a person experiences two or more of the following symptoms within minutes to several hours after exposure to an allergen:

- Hives, itchiness, or redness all over the body and swelling of the lips, tongue, or back of the throat
- Trouble breathing
- Severe GI symptoms such as abdominal cramps, diarrhea, or vomiting
- Dizziness or fainting (signs of a drop in blood pressure)

If you are experiencing symptoms of anaphylaxis, seek immediate treatment and tell your healthcare professional if you have a history of allergic reactions.

Can anaphylaxis be predicted?

Anaphylaxis caused by an allergic reaction is highly unpredictable. The severity of a one attack does not predict the severity of subsequent attacks. Any anaphylactic reaction can become dangerous quickly and must be evaluated immediately by a healthcare professional.

Timing

An anaphylactic reaction can occur as any of the following:

- A single reaction that occurs immediately after exposure to the allergen and gets better with or without treatment within minutes to hours. Symptoms do not recur later in relation to that episode.

- A double reaction. The first reaction occurs within minutes or hours. The initial symptoms seem to go away but later reappear in a second reaction, which typically occurs 8 to 72 hours after the first reaction.

- A single, long-lasting reaction that continues for hours or days.

Treatment

If you or someone you know is having an anaphylactic episode, health experts advise using an auto-injector, if available, to inject epinephrine into the thigh muscle, and calling 9-1-1 if you are not in a hospital. (Epinephrine is a hormone that increases heart rate, constricts the blood vessels, and opens the airways.) If you are in a hospital, summon a resuscitation team.

If epinephrine is not given promptly, rapid decline and death could occur within 30 to 60 minutes. Epinephrine acts immediately but does not last long in the body, so it may be necessary to give repeat doses.

After epinephrine has been given, the patient can be placed in a reclining position with feet elevated to help restore normal blood flow.

A healthcare professional also may give the patient any of the following secondary treatments:

- Medicines to open the airways

- Antihistamines to relieve itching and hives

- Corticosteroids (a class of drugs used to treat inflammatory diseases) to prevent prolonged inflammation and long-lasting reactions

- Additional medicines to constrict blood vessels and increase heart rate

- Supplemental oxygen therapy

- Intravenous fluids

Conditions such as asthma, chronic lung disease, and cardiovascular disease may increase the risk of death from anaphylaxis. Medicines such as those that treat high blood pressure also may worsen symptom severity and limit response to treatment.

Antihistamines should be used only as a secondary treatment. Giving antihistamines instead of epinephrine may increase the risk of a life-threatening allergic reaction.

Management

Before leaving emergency medical care, your healthcare professional should provide the following:

- An epinephrine auto-injector or a prescription for two doses and training on how to use the auto-injector

- A follow-up appointment or an appointment with a clinical specialist such as an allergist or immunologist

- Information on where to get medical identification jewelry or an anaphylaxis wallet card that alerts others of the allergy

- Education about allergen avoidance, recognizing the symptoms of anaphylaxis, and giving epinephrine

- An anaphylaxis emergency action plan

If you or someone you know has a history of severe allergic reactions or anaphylaxis, your healthcare professional should remember to keep you S.A.F.E.

- **Seek support:** Your healthcare professional should tell you the following:

  - Anaphylaxis is a life-threatening condition.

  - The symptoms of the current episode may occur again (sometimes up to three days later).

  - You are at risk for anaphylaxis in the future.

  - At the first sign of symptoms, give yourself epinephrine and then immediately call an ambulance or have someone else take you to the nearest emergency facility.

- **Allergen identification and avoidance:** Before you leave the hospital, your healthcare professional should have done the following:

  - Made efforts to identify the allergen by taking your medical history

  - Explained the importance of getting additional testing to confirm what triggered the reaction, so you can successfully avoid it in the future

- **Follow-up with specialty care:** Your healthcare professional should encourage you to consult a specialist for an allergy evaluation.

- **Epinephrine for emergencies:** Your healthcare professional should give you the following:

  - An epinephrine auto-injector or a prescription and training on how to use an auto-injector

  - Advice to routinely check the expiration date of the auto-injector

Section 13.2

Medical Identification Critical for People with Life-Threatening Allergies

"Medical Identification Critical for People with Life-Threatening Allergies," 2016 © Omnigraphics, Inc. Reviewed November 2015.

In an emergency, making quick decisions with regard to medical treatment may mean the difference between life and death. It is critical for medical response personnel to be aware of any allergies or medical conditions that the patient they are treating might have. But if the patient is unconscious or unable to answer questions, they cannot provide this vital information. As a result, medical care may be delayed, or the treatment provided may be inappropriate for the patient's condition or even dangerous to their health. Wearable medical identification (ID) can play a life-saving role in such emergencies.

An individual with a serious medical condition or a life-threatening allergy can carry the information on a bracelet or necklace that is immediately identifiable. Wearable medical IDs can warn medical responders about the presence of such conditions as Alzheimer's disease, asthma, autism, diabetes, epilepsy, heart disease, high blood pressure, or organ transplant. They can also carry information about allergies to pharmaceutical drugs, foods, insects, or substances such as latex. They also typically display the individual's blood type, along with specific medical treatment requests such as DNR (do not resuscitate), DNI (do not intubate), or organ donation.

Most medical IDs also list any medications the individual takes regularly as well as the names and phone numbers of people to contact in case of emergency. It has become common practice for emergency medical technicians (EMTs) and other first responders to look for medical IDs before proceeding with treatment.

Obtaining a Medical ID

Wearable medical IDs are available from many sources online. They come in a wide variety of attractive styles and are fully customizable for individual needs. Some wearable IDs are designed to inform emergency medical responders of the presence of a more detailed medical alert card. These cards are typically carried in a wallet, purse, or backpack and provide further information about the patient's allergies or other health issues. Patients can consult with their primary-care physicians to obtain guidance in deciding what information to include on their ID.

In addition to people with life-threatening allergies and other health conditions, parents of small children and people who serve as sole caregivers for elderly or disabled individuals should also consider wearing a medical ID bracelet or necklace. If the parent or caregiver is involved in an accident or has another type of medical emergency, the medical ID can provide contact information for alternate care providers to ensure that dependent family members will receive needed assistance and remain safe. Experts also recommend wearable medical IDs for solo travelers, athletes who run or bike alone outdoors over long distances, and people who have undergone recent surgery. At a minimum, these IDs should include contact information in case of emergency.

Reference:

White, Jenna. "Top Ten Reasons People Wear Medical ID Jewelry." Lauren's Hope, February 27, 2013.

Part Three

Foods and Food Additives That Trigger Allergic Reactions

Chapter 14

Food Allergy

What Is Food Allergy?

Food allergy is an abnormal response to a food triggered by the body's **immune system.** There are several types of immune responses to food. This booklet focuses on one type of adverse reaction to food—that in which the body produces a specific type of **antibody** called **immunoglobulin** E (IgE).

The binding of IgE to specific **molecules** present in a food triggers the immune response. The response may be mild or in rare cases it can be associated with the severe and lifethreatening reaction called anaphylaxis, which is described in a later section of this booklet. Therefore, if you have a food allergy, it is extremely important for you to work with your healthcare professional to learn what foods cause your allergic reaction. Sometimes, a reaction to food is not an allergy at all but another type of reaction called food intolerance.

What Is an Allergic Reaction to Food?

A food allergy occurs when the immune system responds to a harmless food as if it were a threat. The first time a person with food allergy is exposed to the food, no symptoms occur; but the first exposure primes

Text in this chapter is excerpted from "Food Allergy," National Institute of Allergy and Infectious Diseases (NIAID), July 2012; and text from from "Supplement B: Care for Children With Food Allergies," U.S. Department of Agriculture (USDA), June 2013.

the body to respond the next time. When the person eats the food again, an allergic response can occur.

What Is a First Exposure to Food?

Usually, the way you are first exposed to a food is when you eat it. But sometimes a first exposure or subsequent exposure can occur without your knowledge.

This may be true in the case of peanut allergy. A person who experiences anaphylaxis on the first known exposure to peanut may have previously

- Touched peanuts
- Used a peanut-containing skin care product
- Breathed in peanut dust in the home or when close to other people eating peanuts

---

The Allergic Reaction Process

An allergic reaction to food is a two-step process.

Step 1: The first time you are exposed to a food **allergen**, your immune system reacts as if the food were harmful and makes specific IgE antibodies to that allergen. The antibodies circulate through your blood and attach to **mast cells** and **basophils**. Mast cells are found in all body **tissues**, especially in areas of your body that are typical sites of allergic reactions. Those sites include your nose, throat, lungs, skin, and **gastrointestinal (GI) tract**. Basophils are found in your blood and also in tissues that have become inflamed due to an allergic reaction.

Step 2: The next time you are exposed to the same food allergen, it binds to the IgE antibodies that are attached to the mast cells and basophils. The binding signals the cells to release massive amounts of chemicals such as **histamine**. Depending on the tissue in which they are released, these chemicals will cause you to have various symptoms of food allergy. The symptoms can range from mild to severe. A severe allergic reaction can include a potentially life-threatening reaction called anaphylaxis.

Generally, you are at greater risk for developing a food allergy if you come from a family in which allergies are common. These allergies are not necessarily food allergies but perhaps other allergic diseases, such as asthma, **eczema** (atopic dermatitis), or allergic rhinitis (hay fever). If you have two parents who have allergies, you are more likely to develop food allergy than someone with one parent who has allergies.

An allergic reaction to food usually takes place within a few minutes to several hours after exposure to the allergen. The process of eating and digesting food and the location of mast cells both affect the timing and location of the reaction.

Symptoms of Food Allergy

If you are allergic to a particular food, you may experience all or some of the following symptoms:

- Itching in your mouth

- Swelling of lips and tongue

- Gastrointestinal (GI) symptoms, such as vomiting, diarrhea, or abdominal cramps and pain

- Hives

- Worsening of eczema

- Tightening of the throat or trouble breathing

- Drop in blood pressure

Eosinophilic Esophagitis

Eosinophilic esophagitis (EoE) is a newly recognized chronic disease that can be associated with food allergies. It is increasingly being diagnosed in children and adults.

Symptoms of EoE include nausea, vomiting, and abdominal pain after eating. A person may also have symptoms that resemble acid reflux from the stomach. In older children and adults, it can cause more severe symptoms, such as difficulty swallowing solid food or solid food sticking in the **esophagus** for more than a few minutes. In infants, this disease may be associated with failure to thrive.

If you are diagnosed with EoE, you will probably be tested for allergies. In some situations, avoiding certain food allergens will be an effective treatment for EoE.

Cross-Reactive Food Allergies

If you have a life-threatening reaction to a certain food, your health-care professional will show you how to avoid similar foods that may trigger this reaction. For example, if you have a history of allergy to shrimp, allergy testing will usually show that you are also allergic to other shellfish, such as crab, lobster, and crayfish. This is called cross-reactivity.

What Is Anaphylaxis?

If you have a food allergy, there is a chance that you may experience a severe form of allergic reaction known as anaphylaxis. Anaphylaxis may begin suddenly and may lead to death if not immediately treated.

Anaphylaxis includes a wide range of symptoms that can occur in many combinations. Some symptoms are not life-threatening, but the most severe restrict breathing and blood circulation.

Many different parts of your body can be affected.

- Skin—itching, hives, redness, swelling
- Nose—sneezing, stuffy nose, runny nose
- Mouth—itching, swelling of lips or tongue
- Throat—itching, tightness, difficulty swallowing, hoarseness
- Chest—shortness of breath, cough, wheeze, chest pain, tightness
- Heart—weak pulse, passing out, shock
- GI tract—vomiting, diarrhea, cramps
- Nervous system—dizziness or fainting

Symptoms may begin within several minutes to several hours after exposure to the food. Sometimes the symptoms go away, only to return 2 to 4 hours later or even as many as 8 hours later. When you begin to experience symptoms, you must seek immediate medical attention because anaphylaxis can be life-threatening.

Anaphylaxis caused by an allergic reaction to a certain food is highly unpredictable. The severity of a given attack does not predict the severity of subsequent attacks. The response will vary depending on several factors, such as

- Your sensitivity to the food
- How much of the food you are exposed to
- How the food enters your body

Any anaphylactic reaction may become dangerous and must be evaluated by a healthcare professional.

Food allergy is the leading cause of anaphylaxis. However, medications, insect stings, and latex can also cause an allergic reaction that leads to anaphylaxis.

How Do You Know If a Person Is Having an Anaphylactic Reaction?

Anaphylaxis is highly likely if at least *one* of the following three conditions occurs:

- Within minutes or several hours of the onset of an illness, a person has skin symptoms (redness, itching, hives) or swollen lips and either
  - Difficulty breathing, or
  - A drop in blood pressure
- A person was exposed to an allergen likely to cause an allergic reaction, and, within minutes or several hours, *two* or *more* of the following symptoms occur:
  - Skin symptoms or swollen lips
  - Difficulty breathing
  - A drop in blood pressure
  - GI symptoms such as vomiting, diarrhea, or cramping
- A person exposed to an allergen previously known to cause an allergic reaction in that person experiences a drop in blood pressure.

Common Food Allergies in Infants, Children, and Adults

In infants and children, the most common foods that cause allergic reactions are

- Egg
- Milk
- Peanut
- Tree nuts such as walnuts
- Soy (primarily in infants)
- Wheat

In adults, the most common foods that cause allergic reactions are

- Shellfish such as shrimp, crayfish, lobster, and crab
- Peanut
- Tree nuts
- Fish such as salmon

Food allergies generally develop early in life but can develop at any age. For example, milk allergy tends to develop early in life, whereas shrimp allergy generally develops later in life.

Children usually outgrow their egg, milk, and soy allergies, but people who develop allergies as adults usually have their allergies for life. Children generally do not outgrow their allergy to peanut.

Finally, foods that are eaten routinely increase the likelihood that a person will develop allergies to that food. In Japan, for example, rice allergy is more frequent than in the United States, and in Scandinavia, codfish allergy is more common than in the United States.

Milk Allergy in Infants and Children

Allergy to cow's milk is common in infants and young children and can develop within days to months of birth.

In children, allergy to cow's milk can cause abdominal pain, hives, and eczema. These symptoms are typically associated with IgE antibodies to milk. Because abdominal pain is also a symptom of **lactose intolerance**, only your healthcare professional can determine whether your child's symptoms are caused by an allergic reaction to cow's milk.

In other children, cow's milk can lead to a different type of reaction to milk, resulting in colic and sleeplessness, as well as blood in the stool and poor growth. This type of reaction to milk is associated with immune responses that are not related to IgE antibody.

Food Allergy: Pregnancy, Breastfeeding, And Introducing Solid Foods To Your Baby

Healthcare experts still do not have enough conclusive evidence to tell pregnant women, nursing mothers, and mothers of infants how to prevent food allergy from developing in their children. Be sure to talk with your healthcare professional before changing your diet or your baby's diet.

Here is what healthcare experts know now:

Pregnancy

- When you are pregnant, you should eat a balanced diet.

- If you are allergic to a food, you should avoid it.

- If you are not allergic to foods—such as egg, tree nuts, peanut, fish, or cow's milk (all highly allergenic), you should not avoid them because there is no conclusive evidence that avoiding these foods will prevent food allergy from developing in your infant in the future.

Breastfeeding

- Healthcare experts recommend that mothers feed their babies only breast milk for the first 4 months of life because of the health benefits of breastfeeding.

- Mothers who breastfeed do not need to avoid foods that are considered to be highly allergenic because there is no conclusive evidence that avoiding these foods will prevent food allergy from developing in their infants.

Introducing Solid Foods

- Healthcare experts in the United States currently suggest that you do not introduce solid food into your baby's diet until 4 to 6 months of age.

- There is no conclusive evidence to suggest that you should delay the introduction of solid foods beyond 4 to 6 months of age.

- There is no conclusive evidence to suggest that you should delay the introduction of the most common potentially allergenic foods (milk, egg, peanut) beyond 4 to 6 months of age. Delay will not prevent your child from developing an allergy in the future.

Diagnosing Food Allergy

Detailed History

Your healthcare professional will begin by taking a detailed medical history to find out whether your symptoms are caused by an allergy to specific foods, a food intolerance, or other health problems.

A detailed history is the most valuable tool for diagnosing food allergy. Your healthcare professional will ask you several questions and listen to your history of food reactions to decide whether the facts fit a diagnosis of food allergy.

Your healthcare professional is likely to ask some of the following questions:

- Did your reaction come on quickly, usually within minutes to several hours after eating the food?
- Is your reaction always associated with a certain food?
- How much of this potentially allergenic food did you eat before you had a reaction?
- Have you eaten this food before and had a reaction?
- Did anyone else who ate the same food get sick?
- Did you take allergy medicines, and if so, did they help? (Antihistamines should relieve hives, for example.)

Diet Diary

Sometimes your healthcare professional can't make a diagnosis based only on your history. In that case, you may be asked to keep a record of what you eat and whether you have a reaction. This diet diary contains more details about the foods you eat than your history. From the diary, you and your healthcare professional may be able to identify a consistent pattern in your reactions.

Elimination Diet

The next step some healthcare professionals use is a limited elimination diet, in which the food that is suspected of causing an allergic reaction is removed from your diet. For example, if you suspect you are allergic to egg, your healthcare professional will instruct you to eliminate this one food from your diet. The limited elimination diet is done under the direction of your healthcare professional.

Skin Prick Test

If your history, diet diary, or elimination diet suggests a specific food allergy is likely, then an allergist will use the skin prick test to confirm the diagnosis.

With a skin prick test, your healthcare professional uses a needle to place a tiny amount of food extract just below the surface of the skin on your lower arm or back. If you are allergic, there will be swelling or redness at the test site. This is a positive result. It means that there are IgE molecules on the skin's mast cells that are specific to the food being tested.

The skin prick test is simple and relatively safe, and results are ready in minutes.

You can have a positive skin prick test to a food, however, without having an allergic reaction to that food. A healthcare professional often makes a diagnosis of food allergy when someone has *both* a positive skin prick test to a specific food *and* a history of reactions that suggests an allergy to the same food.

Blood Test

Instead of the skin prick test, your healthcare professional can take a blood sample to measure the levels of food-specific IgE antibodies.

As with skin prick testing, positive blood tests do not necessarily mean that you have a food allergy. Your healthcare professional must combine these test results with information about your history of reactions to food to make an accurate diagnosis of food allergy.

Oral Food Challenge

Caution: Because oral food challenges can cause a severe allergic reaction, they should always be conducted by a healthcare professional who has experience performing them.

An oral food challenge is the final method healthcare professionals use to diagnose food allergy. This method includes the following steps:

- Your healthcare professional gives you individual doses of various foods (masked so you do not know what food is present), some of which are suspected of starting an allergic reaction.

- Initially, the dose of food is very small, but the amount is gradually increased during the challenge.

- You swallow the individual dose.

- Your healthcare professional watches you to see whether a reaction occurs.

To prevent bias, oral food challenges are often done double blinded. In a true double-blind challenge, neither you nor your healthcare professional knows whether the substance you eat contains the likely allergen. Another medical professional has made up the individual doses. In a single-blind challenge, your healthcare professional knows what you are eating but you do not.

A reaction only to suspected foods and not to the other foods tested confirms the diagnosis of a food allergy.

Preventing and Treating Food Allergy

Prevention

There is currently no cure for food allergies. You can only prevent the symptoms of food allergy by avoiding the allergenic food. After you and your healthcare professional have identified the food(s) to which you are sensitive, you must remove them from your diet.

Read food labels

You must read the list of ingredients on the label of each prepared food that you are considering eating. Many allergens, such as peanut, egg, and milk, appear in prepared foods you normally would not associate with those foods.

Since 2006, U.S. food manufacturers have been required by law to list the ingredients of prepared foods. In addition, food manufacturers must use plain language to disclose whether their products contain any of the top eight allergenic foods—egg, milk, peanut, tree nuts, soy, wheat, shellfish, and fish. Be aware that some labels say "may contain." For the most current food labeling information, visit www.fda.gov.

Keep clean

Simple measures of cleanliness can remove most allergens from the environment of a person with food allergy. For example, simply washing your hands with soap and water will remove peanut allergens, and most household cleaners will remove allergens from surfaces.

Treatment of a Food Allergy Reaction

Unintentional exposure

When you have food allergies, you must be prepared to treat an unintentional exposure. Talk to your healthcare professional and develop a plan to protect yourself in case of an unintentional exposure to the food. For example, you should

- Wear a medical alert bracelet or necklace

- Carry an auto-injector device containing epinephrine (adrenaline)

- Seek medical help immediately

Mild symptoms

Talk to your healthcare professional to find out what medicines may relieve mild food allergy symptoms that are *not part of an anaphylactic reaction*. However, be aware that it is very hard for you to know which reactions are mild and which may lead to anaphylaxis.

Exercise-Induced Food Allergy

Exercise-induced food allergy is a rare situation that requires more than simply eating food to start a reaction. This type of reaction occurs after someone eats a specific food *before* exercising. As exercise increases and body temperature rises

- Itching and light-headedness start

- Hives may appear

- Anaphylaxis may develop

Some people have this reaction from many foods, and others have it only after eating a specific food.

Treating exercised-induced food allergy is simple—avoid eating for a couple of hours before exercising.

Crustacean shellfish, alcohol, tomatoes, cheese, and celery are common causes of exercise-induced food allergy reactions.

Caring for Children with Food Allergies

Some children in your care may have food allergies, so it is important to be aware of the ingredients in all foods before serving. Watch children carefully when serving foods that may cause an allergic reaction.

Food allergy symptoms usually develop within a few minutes to a few hours after eating the offending food. Food allergies can even occur the first time a food is eaten.

No medication can be taken to prevent food allergies. The only way to prevent an allergic reaction is to strictly avoid the food that can cause a reaction. Epinephrine, a medication prescribed by a doctor, is used to control symptoms of an allergic reaction after they occur.

Emergency treatment is critical for someone having a severe allergic reaction, called anaphylaxis.* Contact emergency medical services, or call 911, if a child is having a severe allergic reaction. If untreated, anaphylaxis can cause coma or death.

A written care plan, signed by the child's doctor, should be in place so child care providers know what steps to follow if there is an allergic reaction.

Anaphylaxis is a severe allergic reaction that happens quickly and may cause death. It may cause a child to stop breathing or experience a dangerous drop in blood pressure. If a child is having an anaphylactic reaction, administer epinephrine as soon as possible to improve the child's chances of survival and quick recovery.

What are the most common foods that might cause an allergic reaction?

More than 170 foods are known to cause an allergic reaction in some people. There are eight foods that most commonly trigger an allergic reaction. These foods, and any ingredients made from them, are known as "the top eight allergens" and should be identified as allergens on food labels. These foods include:

1. **Cow's Milk** – Anything made from cow's milk, such as yogurt, cheese, cottage cheese, ice cream, pudding, custard, butter, margarine, cream, sour cream, cream cheese, artificial butter flavor, buttermilk, evaporated milk, nonfat dry milk, nondairy whipped topping, lactose-free milk, and milk based formulas. Goat's milk should also be avoided if someone is allergic to cow's milk. Ingredients made from cow's milk include whey, casein, and caseinates.

2. **Eggs** – Anything made from egg whites, yolks, powdered eggs, dried eggs, egg solids, egg substitutes, meringue, or lecithin. Many foods can have eggs in them—like baked foods, soups, and mayonnaise. Foods that may contain egg ingredients include marshmallows, surimi, pasta, and noodles.

3. **Peanuts** – Peanuts, peanut butter, peanut flour, and hydro-lyzed protein. Peanuts are sometimes found in baked goods, tree nuts, chili, egg rolls, enchilada sauce, mole sauce, and candy. Check with the child's doctor or review the signed medical statement and care plan on file to determine if peanut oil also needs to be avoided.

4. **Tree nuts** – Include, but are not limited to, walnuts, almonds, pecans, hazelnuts, cashews, pistachios, Brazil nuts, nut butters, and nut oils. Tree nuts are sometimes found in baked goods, peanuts, and candy. Check with the child's doctor or review the signed medical statement and care plan on file to determine if coconuts or coconut oil also need to be avoided.

5. **Fish** – Fish sticks, salmon, tuna, cod, tilapia, pollock, halibut, fish sauce, fish paste, and fish broth are some examples. Foods that may contain fish ingredients include Caesar salad dressing, Worcestershire sauce, barbeque sauce, bouillabaisse, imitation fish or shellfish, and surimi.

6. **Shellfish** – Crab, lobster, crawfish, prawns, and shrimp are some examples. Mollusks, such as clams, mussels, oysters, scallops, and squid, are not required to be listed specifically on a food label. Ingredients made from shellfish may include surimi, fish stock, fish sauce, and seafood flavoring.

7. **Soy** – Anything made from soybeans, soy protein, and soy flour. Foods commonly made from soy or that may contain soy ingredients include tofu, edamame, soy nuts, soy nut butter, textured vegetable protein, soy milk, soy yogurt, soy ice cream, and soy sauce. Soy can also be found in processed chicken and meat products. Check with the child's doctor or review the signed medical statement and care plan on file to determine if soybean oil or soy lecithin also needs to be avoided.

8. **Wheat** – Anything made from wheat, such as bread, pasta, cereal, crackers, flour, semolina, durum, and couscous. Wheat is sometimes found in spaghetti sauce, cheese sauce, gravy, lunch meats, processed meats, surimi, imitation crabmeat, starch, and soy sauce.

While these eight allergens are the most common, a child may have a severe, life-threatening allergy to a different food. A child may be allergic to more than one food. Cross-contamination from any of these

Figure 14.1. *The Top Eight Allergens*

allergens on cooking surfaces, utensils, or cooking equipment can also trigger an allergic reaction in someone who has food allergies.

> Many of the foods that have the top eight food allergens are good sources of vitamins and minerals, and should be served only to children without allergies to those foods.

What are some nonfood items that might trigger an allergic reaction?

Food allergens can be found in nonfood items too. If you care for a child with a food allergy, you should avoid using food and nonfood items that contain allergens in your program activities, arts and crafts projects, counting exercises, or cooking activities. Read labels carefully or contact the manufacturer to determine if food and nonfood items contain allergens. Find alternatives to nonfood items that contain allergens and use the safer versions instead. Food allergens can be found in these items:

- **Soaps** (may contain milk, wheat, soy, or nut extracts)
- **Dried pasta** (contains wheat and may contain egg)
- **Crayons** (may contain soy)
- **Finger paints** (may contain milk or egg whites)
- **Modeling clay** (may contain wheat)

What should I do if a child has a food allergy or food intolerance?

Children could have their first allergic reaction while in your care, so you must be prepared to react quickly and effectively. Everyone involved in planning, preparing, and serving food should be extremely aware of food allergy risks and be prepared. Trained providers, proper documentation, clear communication with families, and careful planning for the possibility of an emergency, will ensure a safe environment for children with food allergies.

- **Participate in a food allergy training** conducted by a child care health consultant, a health care provider, or other qualified child care trainer with expertise in young children's health and food allergies.

  - Food allergy training is recommended for all child care providers, even if a program has no enrolled children with known food allergies.

  - Training topics should include information about preventing exposure to specific food allergens, recognizing the symptoms of allergic reactions, and responding to allergic reactions.

  - Contact your State agency or sponsoring organization for more information or for assistance in finding or arranging a training session.

  - Invite the parents of children with food allergies to be involved in the training or education. They can share their knowledge about their experiences with food allergies.

- **Inform all child care providers, including substitutes,** about the children in your care who have food allergies.

- **Talk to the child's parents or guardians about the child's food allergies or food intolerances.** Learn about the child's care plan, as well as what the child knows about what he or she can and cannot eat. The child may not be able to tell the child care provider when he or she is having an allergic reaction to food, so it is important to know the possible symptoms of a reaction.

- **Know where emergency medications, such as epinephrine,** are stored and how they should be used in case a child has an allergic reaction while in your care. More than one person should be trained on how to use epinephrine.

- **Be aware of what is in foods before serving.** Read all food ingredient lists and labels, and check food allergen content statements on packages. Food companies are required to identify the top eight food allergens in products by either: 1) listing allergens in bold type on the ingredient list, or 2) listing the allergens immediately following the ingredient list. If a food product contains any of the top eight allergens, it should have a "Contains" statement on the label. For example, "Contains wheat, milk, and soy ingredients."

  - Although companies are required to identify the top eight food allergens in products, they may not always do so. Be sure to read the ingredient list carefully.

  - Some labels may include a statement about being produced on the "same equipment as" or "made in the same facility as" products that contain the specific allergen the child is allergic to—those food products should also be avoided. For example, "Made on the same equipmentas products containing peanuts." It is important to know that food companies are not required to have these statements on their label.

  - Some food companies may list allergens other than the top eight, but they are not required to do so.

- **Always actively supervise children while they are eating.** Discourage food sharing among children. Pay particular attention during special events such as picnics, field trips, or parties.

- **Follow the regular menu whenever possible.** Provide menus to parents and caregivers. If children in your care have food allergies or intolerances, make sure the menu highlights foods that may cause a reaction in their child.

How can children tell the care provider that they are having an allergic reaction?

- **If having an allergic reaction, a child may try to tell you in his or her own words.** If you hear phrases such as these, the child may be trying to describe that he or she is having an allergic reaction.

  - "This food is too spicy."
  - "My tongue is hot."
  - "My tongue feels like there is hair on it."
  - "There's a frog in my throat."
  - "My lips feel tight."
  - "My mouth feels funny."
  - "My mouth itches."
  - "It feels like something is stuck in my throat."
  - "It feels like there are bugs in my ear."

- "It feels like there is a bump in the back of my throat."**A child may not always be able to tell you in words that he or she is having an allergic reaction.** If you see the child doing some of these behaviors, he or she may be having an allergic reaction.

  - If a child is pulling or scratching at his or her tongue, he or she may be having an allergic reaction.
  - Some children's voices may become hoarse or squeaky if they are having an allergic reaction.
  - The child's words may become slurred if his or her mouth is beginning to swell from an allergic reaction.

How do I reduce the risk of children in my care with either food allergies or food intolerances from having a reaction to food?

Cross-contamination occurs when an allergen is accidentally transferred from one food or surface to another. This transfer may occur from food to food, from hands to food, from kitchen equipment to food, or from a food contact surface to hands or food. Cross-contamination can be prevented through handwashing, cleaning, and proper food handling and storage. Take these steps to reduce the risk of a child having a reaction to food.

- **Wash your hands before and after preparing and serving foods** for the food-allergic child. Soap should be used, not anti-bacterial gel sanitizers.

- **Make sure all children wash their hands** *before* **and** *after* **they eat** so they do not spread food allergens to other areas. The children's faces may need to be wiped clean as well.

- **Wipe down counters and tables** with common household cleaners *before* and *after* meals and snacks.

- **Mop up spills properly** to prevent spreading the allergen to other surfaces.

- **Thoroughly clean handwashing sinks including faucets.** Food allergens, which the food-allergic child should not come into contact with, may get on the sink from dirty hands or dis-carded foods.

- **Establish a regular cleaning routine.** Children can be encouraged to clean-up after themselves and throw away trash, but you should make sure that surfaces and handwashing sinks are cleaned properly.

- **Organize kitchen space** to keep foods for food-allergic chil-dren separate from other foods. For example, label pantry and refrigerator shelves that hold foods that are "safe" for the child. Then, let others know how the kitchen is organized or post infor-mation in the pantry.

- **Prepare foods for the food allergic child first** to prevent spreading food allergens from one surface or utensil to another. Label the foods, and keep them separate from other foods.

- **Be careful to use separate utensils** when preparing and serv-ing food to the food-allergic child. Cross-contamination from food allergens on cooking surfaces, utensils, or cooking equipment can trigger an allergic reaction in a child who has food allergies.

Chapter 15

Food Allergy or Food Intolerance: How Do You Tell the Difference?

Is It Food Allergy or Food Intolerance?

Food allergy is sometimes confused with food intolerance. To find out the difference between food allergy and food intolerance, your healthcare professional will go through a list of possible causes for your symptoms.

Types of Food Intolerance

Lactose Intolerance

Lactose is a sugar found in milk and most milk products. **Lactase** is an **enzyme** in the lining of the gut that breaks down or digests lactose. Lactose intolerance occurs when lactase is missing. Instead of the enzyme breaking down the sugar, **bacteria** in the gut break it down, which forms gas, which in turn causes symptoms of bloating, abdominal pain, and sometimes diarrhea.

Lactose intolerance is uncommon in babies and young children under the age of 5 years. Because lactase levels decline as people get

Text in this chapter is excerpted from "Is It Food Allergy or Food Intolerance?" National Institute of Allergy and Infectious Diseases (NIAID), July 2012.

older, lactose intolerance becomes more common with age. Lactose intolerance also varies widely based on racial and ethnic background.

Your healthcare professional can use laboratory tests to find out whether your body can digest lactose.

Food Additives

Another type of food intolerance is a reaction to certain products that are added to food to enhance taste, add color, or protect against the growth of microbes. Several compounds such as monosodium glutamate (MSG) and sulfites are tied to reactions that can be confused with food allergy.

- MSG is a flavor enhancer. When taken in large amounts, it can cause some of the following:

    - Flushing

    - Sensations of warmth

    - Headache

    - Chest discomfort

    These passing reactions occur rapidly after eating large amounts of food to which MSG has been added.

- Sulfites are found in food for several reasons:

    - They have been added to increase crispness or prevent mold growth.

    - They occur naturally in the food.

    - They have been generated during the winemaking process.

Sulfites can cause breathing problems in people with asthma.

The U.S. Food and Drug Administration (FDA) has banned sulfites as spray-on preservatives for fresh fruits and vegetables. When sulfites are present in foods, they are listed on ingredient labels.

Gluten Intolerance

Gluten is a part of wheat, barley, and rye. Gluten intolerance is associated with celiac disease, also called gluten-sensitive enteropathy. This disease develops when the immune system responds abnormally to gluten. This abnormal response does not involve IgE antibody and is not considered a food allergy.

Food Poisoning

Some of the symptoms of food allergy, such as abdominal cramping, are common to food poisoning. However, food poisoning is caused by microbes, such as bacteria, and bacterial products, such as toxins, that can contaminate meats and dairy products.

Histamine Toxicity

Fish, such as tuna and mackerel that are not refrigerated properly and become contaminated by bacteria, may contain very high levels of histamine. A person who eats such fish may show symptoms that are similar to food allergy. However, this reaction is not a true allergic reaction. Instead, the reaction is called histamine toxicity or scombroid food poisoning.

Other

Several other conditions, such as ulcers and cancers of the gastro-intestinal (GI) tract, cause some of the same symptoms as food allergy. These symptoms, which include vomiting, diarrhea, and cramping abdominal pain, become worse when you eat.

Chapter 16

Milk Allergy

Chapter Contents

Section 16.1

Understanding Milk Allergy

"Understanding Milk Allergy," © 2016 Omnigraphics, Inc.
Reviewed November 2015.

Understanding Milk Allergy

Milk allergy is the most common type of food allergy, particularly among infants and children. Up to 3 percent of infants develop an allergy to milk and dairy products. While most milk allergies pertain to cow's milk, they may also include adverse reactions to milk from other mammals, like goats, sheep, or buffalo. A milk allergy is primarily caused by an abnormal response of the body's immune system to milk protein. The body produces immunoglobulin E (IgE) antibodies to neutralize the protein allergen. These antibodies trigger the release of histamines and other chemicals that produce allergic reactions.

Milk allergy, for the most part, is seen more frequently in infants than in adults. An allergy to milk can develop all of a sudden, even though the food has been well tolerated in the past. While the exact causes of milk allergy are still unclear, certain risk factors have been recognized that increase a person's likelihood of developing a milk or dairy allergy. One of the most significant factors is the existence of milk allergy or any other type of allergy in either or both parents. Besides family history, the presence of other allergic conditions, like atopic dermatitis, also raises the risk of developing milk allergy, particularly in infants.

Most milk allergies manifest within the first year of life. Although 20 percent of children outgrow their allergy by age four and 80 percent by age sixteen, some remain allergic to the food all through life. Milk allergy can manifest in both breastfed and formula-fed babies. Babies who are fed formula can develop allergy symptoms through direct ingestion of milk products. Those who are breastfed can also develop milk allergy, however, through exposure to traces of cow's milk protein that pass into the breast milk from dairy products consumed by the mother. Infants who appear to be allergic to human milk are usually reacting to foods that pass through the breast milk rather than to the breast milk itself.

Symptoms and Diagnosis

In some people, allergic reactions to milk can occur quickly, with symptoms appearing within a few minutes of ingestion of a small amount of milk. In others, the symptoms may appear gradually after a few hours, or even days. A mild allergy to milk might involve such symptoms as hives or skin rashes around the mouth. More severe reactions might include respiratory and gastrointestinal symptoms such as wheezing, flatulence, diarrhea, vomiting, blood or mucous in stools, and infantile colic.

If a milk allergy is suspected, the first step would be to consult a doctor or an allergist. After taking the patient's history, the doctor may administer a skin prick test (SPT). In this procedure, a small amount of milk or a milk protein extract is introduced under the skin with the help of a small, sterile probe. A localized allergic response in the skin, such as a red bump or flare, can indicate an allergy to milk protein. The skin prick test is usually followed up with a blood test, which gives a numerical value for IgE antibodies in blood. These antibodies are responsible for the immediate allergic responses to milk.

An oral food challenge (OFC) is recommended when the doctor is unable to make a definitive diagnosis with SPT and serum antibody levels. In this procedure, the patient ingests measured doses of food containing milk or a milk powder to check for a possible allergic reaction. It is essential that the food challenge be carried out under medical supervision with access to emergency treatment in case the test precipitates a severe allergic reaction.

Milk allergy that is characterized by a delayed onset of mostly gastrointestinal symptoms usually involves T-cells (a type of white blood cell) rather than IgE antibodies. The mechanism for non-IgE-mediated milk allergy remains largely unclear and there are no validated tests for its diagnosis. If a non-IgE-mediated allergy is suspected, the allergist may recommend an extended period of avoidance of all milk products, followed by a phased reintroduction.

Both types of milk allergy are different from lactose intolerance, which is not an allergy. Instead, it occurs when people are unable to digest lactose, the sugar found in milk, because their body does not produce sufficient quantities of lactase, the enzyme needed to metabolize lactose. Although it is not related to milk allergy, people with lactose intolerance often experience similar symptoms after ingesting milk, such as abdominal cramps, bloating, and diarrhea.

Prevention and Treatment

As is the case for all food allergies, the only way to prevent an allergic reaction to milk is to avoid milk proteins completely. The Federal Food Allergen Labeling and Consumer Protection Act (FALCPA) of 2004 established guidelines for labeling packaged food to warn consumers about the potential presence of eight major food allergens, including milk. Therefore, people with food allergies should read product labels and ingredient statements carefully before purchasing or consuming packaged food. Milk and milk derivatives can be found in a wide range of food products, including butter, cheese, chocolate, cream, custard, pudding, and yogurt.

Mild allergic reactions to milk can be treated with antihistamines, but a severe anaphylactic reaction requires immediate medical attention. An injection of epinephrine (adrenaline) is usually given to treat anaphylaxis, and those with severe milk allergy are generally advised to carry an epinephrine auto-injector with them at all times. Following treatment with epinephrine, the patient needs to be placed in an emergency setting for further evaluation and treatment in order to prevent a recurrence of symptoms.

References:

1. "Milk Allergy." Food Allergy Research and Education, 2015.

2. "Milk and Dairy Allergy." American College of Allergy, Asthma, and Immunology, 2014.

3. "Milk: One of the Ten Priority Food Allergens." Health Canada, December 4, 2012.

Section 16.2

Lactose Intolerance Is Not Milk Allergy

Text in this section is excerpted from "Lactose Intolerance: Condition Information," Eunice Kennedy Shriver National Institute of Child Health and Human Development (NICHD), November 30, 2012.

What Is Lactose Intolerance?

People who are lactose intolerant have trouble digesting lactose, the natural sugar found in milk and milk products. They have this condition because their bodies do not make enough lactase. Lactase is an enzyme made in the small intestine. Lactase breaks down lactose into simpler forms of sugar, which are easily absorbed into the blood. Undigested lactose can lead to unpleasant digestive symptoms.

People vary in their degree of lactose intolerance. Most people who are lactose intolerant are able to consume some lactose without symptoms. However, many people who think they are lactose intolerant avoid milk products and do not consume enough calcium and vitamin D, which are nutrients important to bone health. Getting enough calcium is especially important for children and teens, who are at the ages when bones grow the most.

What Are the Symptoms of Lactose Intolerance?

Symptoms of lactose intolerance include:

- Bloating

- Diarrhea

- Gas

- Stomach pain or cramps

Symptoms begin about 30 minutes to 2 hours after eating or drinking foods containing lactose. Symptoms can be mild or severe. The severity of the symptoms usually depends on both the amount of lactose consumed and the amount of lactase in a person's body.

How Many People Are Affected or at Risk for Lactose Intolerance?

How Many People Are Lactose Intolerant?

The true number of people with lactose intolerance is not known. Many people who have symptoms of lactose intolerance have not been diagnosed with the condition. Many people who think they are lactose intolerant do not have difficulty digesting lactose. Many people who have difficulty digesting lactose do not get symptoms.

Who Gets Lactose Intolerance and Who Is at Risk for It?

Lactose intolerance can affect anyone. In the United States, it is most common among:

- African Americans
- Asian Americans
- Hispanic Americans
- Native Americans

Lactose intolerance is uncommon in young children because most infants are born with enough lactase. But for many people, the amount of lactase in their bodies decreases over a lifetime.

Preterm infants born before 34 weeks' gestation can have low lactase levels because their digestive tract is not fully developed.

How Is Lactose Intolerance Diagnosed?

Many people think that they or their children are lactose intolerant without being tested or diagnosed. As a result, many people avoid or greatly limit their intake of dairy products, which are rich in calcium and vitamin D. These nutrients help to build strong bones. Most people who are lactose intolerant are able to consume some amount of lactose without symptoms.

It's not always easy to tell based on symptoms alone whether a person has lactose intolerance or another condition. Many common health problems have similar symptoms. For instance, lactose intolerance has many of the same symptoms as irritable bowel syndrome (IBS); however, IBS can also cause constipation.

If lactose intolerance is suspected, the person may be asked to stop eating or drinking foods that contain lactose for a brief time. If the symptoms go away, then this information may be all a health care provider needs for a diagnosis. The following tests also can help diagnose lactose intolerance:

- **Hydrogen breath test.** For this test, a person drinks a beverage that has lactose in it. Then, the hydrogen level in the breath is measured at set time intervals. Hydrogen gas is formed when lactose is not digested, so high breath hydrogen is a likely sign of problems digesting lactose.

- **Lactose intolerance test.** For this test, blood samples are taken before and after a person drinks a beverage that contains lactose. The amount of sugar (glucose) in the blood is measured. Levels that do not change can suggest problems digesting lactose. The hydrogen breath test is preferred over this test.

- **Stool acidity test.** This test is used for infants and young children. The stool is checked for certain acids that form when lactose is not digested. Glucose in the stool also suggests problems digesting lactose.

How Is Lactose Intolerance Managed?

No treatment can change the body's ability to make lactase. But most people who have problems digesting lactose can take steps to minimize symptoms without giving up milk and milk products completely. Studies show that the following strategies can help:

- Drink low-fat milk or fat-free milk in servings of one cup or less.

- Drink low-fat milk or fat-free milk with other food, such as with breakfast cereal, instead of on an empty stomach.

- Eat dairy products other than milk, such as low-fat or fat-free hard cheeses or cottage cheese, or low-fat or fat-free ice cream or yogurt. These foods contain less lactose per serving compared with milk and may cause fewer symptoms.

- Choose reduced-lactose milk and milk products, which have the same amount of calcium as regular milk.

- Use over-the-counter pills or drops that contain lactase enzyme.

With some trial and error, people with lactose intolerance can learn which milk products and how much of them their bodies can handle. Most people should not avoid milk and milk products completely because they provide calcium, vitamin D, and other key nutrients needed for bone and overall health. People who are lactose intolerant should make sure they get enough of these key nutrients from other sources if they don't get them from dairy foods.

What causes lactose intolerance?

Not having enough lactase in the body is the cause of lactose intolerance. The names for the three types of lactose intolerance describe why a person may not have enough lactase.

- **Primary lactose intolerance.** This type develops in people who were once able to fully digest lactose. It is the most common type. Almost all infants make enough lactase to fully digest lactose found in human milk and infant formulas. But at some point after being weaned, most children in the world begin to make less lactase. Most people with primary lactose intolerance can consume some milk products without having symptoms.

- **Secondary lactose intolerance.** This type results from damage to the intestines, such as from severe illness or disease.

- **Congenital lactose intolerance.** Infants born with this rare type make no lactase at all. It is not uncommon for secondary lactose intolerance to be misdiagnosed during the newborn period as congenital lactose intolerance.

Other FAQs

Is lactose intolerance the same as milk allergy?

No. Milk allergy is a reaction by the body's immune system to the protein in milk. Symptoms of milk allergy include hives, skin rash (eczema), and stomach pain. It is a common allergy in infants and children.

Some parents confuse milk allergy and lactose intolerance. Milk allergy usually appears in the first year of life, whereas symptoms of lactose intolerance are uncommon before age 2 or 3 years. Most children outgrow milk allergy.

If milk products seem to be a problem for your child, talk to your child's health care provider. Only a health care provider can tell whether your child's symptoms are caused by an allergy, lactose intolerance, or something else.

Does lactose intolerance affect bone health?

The role of lactose intolerance and lactose-free diets on bone health is not yet clear. Many people who are lactose intolerant, or think they are, avoid dairy products and do not get enough calcium and vitamin D. Dairy products are especially good sources of these nutrients, which are needed for bone health. People who do not get enough calcium over their lifetime are more likely to get osteoporosis (pronounced os-tee-oh-puh-ROH-sis), or thinning bones. Despite these facts, research has yet to clarify whether lactose intolerance increases the risk of osteoporosis.

Still, experts do know how much calcium and vitamin D people need to grow and maintain healthy bones. People who are or think they are lactose intolerant need to be sure they get enough of these important nutrients, whether from dairy or nondairy sources. It's important that children and teens get enough of these nutrients because most bone mass builds up during this time of life. Building bone mass in youth helps keep bones healthy and strong throughout life and prevents osteoporosis later in life.

How can people with lactose intolerance be sure to get enough calcium?

Milk and milk products are especially good sources of calcium and other nutrients, even for those with lactose intolerance. By following strategies to manage lactose intolerance, most affected people can enjoy milk and milk products with few or no symptoms and gain the nutritional benefits they provide. Some nondairy foods are also healthy sources of calcium.

These foods include:

- Fish with soft bones that you eat, such as canned sardines and salmon

- Kale, Chinese cabbage, broccoli

- Orange juice with added calcium

- Some fortified breads and breakfast cereals

- Soy and rice beverages with added calcium

- Tofu (with calcium sulfate)

People who do not get enough calcium through the foods they eat and drink may need a daily calcium supplement. Use the table below to find out how much calcium you need each day.

Table 16.1. Daily Calcium Needs

Life stage	Recommended amount
Birth to 6 months	200 mg
Infants 7–12 months	260 mg
Children 1–3 years	700 mg
Children 4–8 years	1,000 mg
Children 9–13 years	1,300 mg
Teens 14–18 years	1,300 mg
Adults 19–50 years	1,000 mg
Adult men 51–70 years	1,000 mg
Adult women 51–70 years	1,200 mg
Adults 71 years and older	1,200 mg
Pregnant and breastfeeding teens	1,300 mg
Pregnant and breastfeeding adults	1,000 mg

Section 16.3

Dark Chocolate and Milk Allergies

Text in this section is excerpted from "What FDA Learned
About Dark Chocolate and Milk Allergies," U.S. Food and Drug
Administration (FDA), May 21, 2015.

If you're allergic to milk and you love dark chocolate, how do you know whether you can indulge in a candy bar without having an allergic reaction? That's what the U.S. Food and Drug Administration (FDA) wanted to learn, especially after receiving reports that consumers had harmful reactions after eating dark chocolate.

Milk is a permitted ingredient in dark chocolate, but it is also one of eight major food allergens (substances that can cause reactions that are sometimes dangerous). The U.S. law requires manufacturers to label food products that are major allergens, as well as food products that contain major allergenic ingredients or proteins. Allergens contained in a food product but not named on the label are a leading cause of FDA requests for food recalls, and undeclared milk is the most frequently cited allergen. Chocolates are one of the most common sources of undeclared milk associated with consumer reactions.

FDA tested nearly 100 dark chocolate bars for the presence of milk. Earlier this year, the agency issued preliminary findings, and is now releasing more information about its research. The bars tested by FDA were obtained from different parts of the U.S., and each bar was unique in terms of product line and/or manufacturer. Bars were divided into categories based on the statements on the labels.

The bottom line? Unfortunately, you can't always tell if dark chocolate contains milk by reading the ingredients list. FDA researchers found that of 94 dark chocolate bars tested, only six listed milk as an ingredient. When testing the remaining 88 bars that did not list milk as an ingredient, FDA found that 51 of them actually did contain milk. In fact, the FDA study found milk in 61 percent of all bars tested.

In part, that's because milk can get into a dark chocolate product even when it is not added as an ingredient. Most dark chocolate is produced on equipment that is also used to produce milk chocolate. In these cases, it is possible that traces of milk may inadvertently wind up in the dark chocolate.

Read 'May' as 'Likely'

To inform consumers that dark chocolate products may contain milk even if not intentionally added, many chocolate manufacturers print "advisory" messages on the label. There's quite a variety of advisory messages, such as:

- "may contain milk"
- "may contain dairy"
- "may contain traces of milk"
- "made on equipment shared with milk"
- "processed in a plant that processes dairy"
- "manufactured in a facility that uses milk"

FDA found that milk was present in 3 out of every 4 dark chocolate products with one of these advisory statements. Some products had milk levels as high as those found in products that declared the presence of milk.

When the National Confectioners Association (NCA) was asked for its advice, a spokesperson said that "consumers with milk allergies should not consume dark chocolate products that come with advisory statements, since these products may indeed contain milk proteins."

Another problem is that advisory messages may appear to be conflicting if they are accompanied by dairy-free or vegan statements. "Even a consumer who carefully reads the label may be confused by a statement such as "vegan" (which implies that no animal-derived products were used) along with an advisory—or "may contain" statement—referring to the presence of milk," says Stefano Luccioli, M.D., a senior medical advisor at FDA.

Not Quite 'Dairy Free'

In addition to these advisory statements, labels for chocolate bars may make other claims. Some say "dairy-free" or "lactose free," but FDA found milk in 15% of the dark chocolates with this label. And 25% of dark chocolate products labeled only "vegan" were found to contain milk.

No Message Doesn't Mean No Milk

You shouldn't assume that dark chocolate contains no milk if the label does not mention it at all. "Milk-allergic consumers should be aware that 33% of the dark chocolates with no mention of milk anywhere on the label were, in fact, found to contain milk," says Luccioli.

What Consumers Can Do

- Consumers who are sensitive or allergic to milk should know that dark chocolate products are a high-risk food if you're highly milk-allergic.

- Start by checking the ingredients list to see if it includes milk.

- Read all the label statements on dark chocolate products and avoid those with an advisory statement for milk, even if these products feature also other (and conflicting) statements, such as "dairy-free" or "vegan."

- View even products with dairy-free claims or without any mention of milk with caution, unless the manufacturer is a trusted source and/or uses dedicated equipment for making milk-free chocolate products.

"The chocolate industry will continue to make every effort to understand the needs of allergic consumers and communicate the potential presence of milk allergens in dark chocolate through advisory labeling," says Laura Shumow,Director of Scientific and Regulatory Affairs at NCA.

FDA is evaluating the study findings and considering options for addressing the issues identified in the study. Further, allergen contamination is included in the preventive and risk-based controls mandated by the FDA Food Safety Modernization Act (FSMA). Under the proposed Preventive Controls for Human Food rule that is scheduled to become final this fall, food manufacturers would be required to implement a food safety plan that identifies safeguards in place to prevent or significantly reduce such hazards as food allergens.

The proposed rule includes provisions to prevent unintended cross-contact between foods that contain allergens and those not intended to contain them. Firms covered by the final rule would have from one to three years after the rule becomes final to comply, depending on the size of the firm.

Table 16.2. Milk Detected in Individual Dark Chocolate Products

Label/Package Statement	Total number of dark chocolate products	Number and percent (%) of dark chocolate products testing positive for milk
Milk (or milk-derived component1)	6	6 (100%)
Advisory Statements2 (alone or combined)	59	44 (75%)
Dairy-free or lactose-free3statements alone	13	2 (15%)
Vegan statement alone	4	1 (25%)
No statement regarding milk	12	4 (33%)
TOTAL	94	57 (61%)

- Some examples of milk components include cream, milk fat, and sodium caseinate.

- Advisory statements refers to statements regarding the possible presence of milk, such as "may contain milk (or dairy)," "made on equipment shared with milk," "processed in a plant that processes dairy", or "manufactured in a facility that uses milk." This category also includes "may contain traces" statements, as well as advisory statements combined with either a vegan or dairy-free or lactose statement.

- Lactose-free chocolates are grouped with dairy-free products although the statement "lactose-free" does not necessarily indicate that the product is free from milk. This is because lactose is a "milk sugar," and its removal does not mean that milk proteins are removed as well.

Section 16.4

Baked Milk May Help Kids Outgrow Milk Allergy Faster

Text in this section is excerpted from "Baked Milk May Help Kids Outgrow Milk Allergy Faster," National Institute of Allergy and Infectious Diseases (NIAID), June 17, 2011. Reviewed November 2015.

Background

Allergy to cow's milk is one of the most common food allergies found in the United States. It cannot be prevented, and the only way to manage the condition is to avoid milk and treat symptoms as they arise.

Investigators led by Hugh A. Sampson, M.D., professor of pediatrics, dean for translational research, and director of the Jaffe Food Allergy Institute at Mount Sinai School of Medicine in New York, were working to enable patients to tolerate milk without having allergic reactions by having them consume—rather than avoid—allergenic foods. To help some people outgrow their allergies, Dr. Sampson's team used a form of oral immunotherapy in which a person eats increasing amounts of an allergenic food that has been baked to break down (denature) the proteins causing the allergy.

Previously, members of Dr. Sampson's team observed that children who are allergic to milk fell into two groups: some children were able to eat products that contained baked milk without having an allergic reaction, whereas other children did have an allergic reaction. But the long-term clinical effects of incorporating baked milk into a child's diet were unknown.

Results of Study

Dr. Sampson's group studied 88 children, ages 2 to 17 years old, with diagnosed milk allergy over a period of four to five years. The researchers initially gave the children a plain muffin containing baked milk. Among the 88 children, 65 ate the muffin without experiencing any allergic reactions. Parents of children who passed the muffin test were given guidance on how to incorporate baked milk into their children's diet. Children who reacted to the muffin continued avoiding foods containing milk.

For the next 6 to 12 months, the children who passed the initial muffin test ate food containing baked milk, such as muffins, cookies, or cake, following specific guidance from dieticians on Dr. Sampson's team. These children returned to the clinic for a second food test and at that point were given cheese pizza to determine if they could tolerate baked cheese. Fifty-seven of the 65 children ate the pizza without having an allergic reaction and were then able to begin incorporating baked cheese along with baked milk into their diets.

Children who could eat muffins and pizza were given regular amounts of food containing baked milk over an average of about three years. The children were then tested again, this time to determine if they could tolerate cold skim milk, yogurt, or ice cream. Of the children who passed the initial muffin test, 60 percent were able to consume these additional foods without having an allergic reaction. In addition, controlled exposure to the baked milk products appeared to accelerate the rate at which allergic children outgrew their allergies to milk in uncooked forms.

Significance

The results of this study indicate that if a child with a known milk allergy passes a baked milk challenge, he or she may outgrow the milk allergy much more rapidly than a child who does not pass the test.

Milk allergy is one of the food allergies that children outgrow as they age. Although many children can tolerate milk by age 5, milk allergy can last until age 16. Findings made by Dr. Sampson's team indicate that eating baked milk can reduce the time it takes to outgrow milk allergy.

Dr. Sampson strongly cautions that this type of food challenge should not be performed without strict guidance from a trained health specialist. The investigators observed that children who do not pass a baked milk test often experience much more severe allergic reactions than children who do, and it is nearly impossible to predict which children will have such a reaction.

Participants in this clinical study also received very specific instructions regarding what products could be eaten at home.

Next Steps

The take-home message from the study is that children with milk allergy should see their healthcare professional and be given a baked milk test to determine if they are likely to outgrow milk allergy and are able to safely follow a baked milk diet similar to the one developed by Dr. Sampson's team.

Chapter 17

Egg Allergy

Chapter Contents

Section 17.1

Understanding Egg Allergy

"Understanding Egg Allergy," © 2016 Omnigraphics, Inc.
Reviewed November 2015.

Egg allergy is caused by an inappropriate response of the immune system to the protein component in egg. Egg allergy is one of the most common food allergies, second only to cow's milk allergy, and estimates suggest that it affects around 2 percent of children in the United States. In most cases, the hypersensitivity to the protein present in the albumen (egg white) or the yolk begins in infancy. Although 70 percent of egg allergies disappear by age sixteen, some people may remain allergic to eggs throughout their lives. Egg white allergy is more common than yolk allergy. While some people are allergic to semi-cooked or raw eggs but can tolerate cooked eggs well, there are those who show intolerance to the food whether it is cooked or raw, and whether it includes egg white or yolk.

The mechanism of egg allergy is much the same as in other types of food allergies. An allergic reaction occurs when immunoglobulin E (IgE), a type of antibody used by the body's immune system to fight pathogens, mistakenly recognizes a harmless food component as a harmful invader. The IgE antibodies bind to the egg protein, triggering the release of histamines and other inflammatory chemicals that can set off a series of adverse reactions. The IgE-mediated allergic reaction is rapid and occurs within half an hour of ingesting the food. Non IgE-mediated reactions typically take longer to manifest and their exact mechanism is unclear, although studies have shown that their pathways may involve T-cells, a type of lymphocyte.

Symptoms of egg allergy can vary depending on the degree of sensitivity to the protein. Mild sensitivity may present skin reactions like rashes and hives. In some people, the hypersensitivity may cause respiratory symptoms like wheezing, nasal congestion, or sneezing, as well as gastrointestinal symptoms such as vomiting, diarrhea, and abdominal cramping. In a few cases, egg allergy can cause severe, life-threatening anaphylactic reactions, resulting in a drop in blood pressure, increased heart rate, and loss of consciousness. This type of allergic reaction requires immediate administration of the drug epinephrine and emergency care.

Testing for Egg Allergy

The first step in diagnosing an egg allergy involves reviewing the patient's history of symptoms. The allergist may also order a Skin Prick Test (SPT), in which a measured dose of egg protein in a liquid is placed under the skin using a sterile probe. The appearance of a reddish patch or a small swelling (called a "wheal") within the first 20 minutes of administration of the protein indicates an allergic response. The allergist evaluates the degree of sensitivity to egg protein on the basis of the size of the wheal. If the diagnosis is inconclusive, the doctor may ask for a blood test to evaluate the level of allergen-specific serum IgE.

In some cases, however, egg allergy may be difficult to confirm using these initial tests. For instance, the SPT may yield a negative response even though the patient experiences allergy symptoms after ingesting egg. This problem may arise from differences in quality and stability of the allergen extracts used. Likewise, a blood test may indicate the presence of food-specific IgE despite the absence of any allergy symptoms. In such cases, allergists may resort to an oral challenge test that involves a series of trial-and-error procedures. Often recognized as the "gold standard" for food allergy diagnosis, this test involves a period of egg-free diet followed by gradual reintroduction of the suspect food in measured doses. This test has to be done under medical supervision, particularly in patients who have a history of adverse reactions to the food.

Preventing and Treating Egg Allergy

Although many children outgrow it naturally, there is no cure for egg allergy or any other type of food allergy. The only way to prevent allergic reactions to egg products is to completely avoid egg or egg derivatives. This requires a lot of diligence as egg is a versatile ingredient used in a large number of processed foods, including baked foods, desserts, soups, and pasta. People with egg allergy should be vigilant about reading labels and ingredient lists when they shop for food. They must also be careful to check whether there is a possibility that other food may have come in contact with egg during preparation. At restaurants, it may help to tell the waiter about any food sensitivities, as many restaurants today offer allergy-friendly dining.

As with other food allergies, mild to moderate symptoms of egg allergy are usually treated with antihistamines, bronchodilators, or steroids. Severe, anaphylactic reactions are treated with epinephrine, which can reverse symptoms that can be fatal if left untreated. Some vaccines contain egg protein. People with extreme sensitivity to egg protein are advised to take their shots under the supervision of an allergist or in a medical office equipped to deal with any adverse effects.

Eggs are a major source of dietary protein. A registered dietitian can suggest alternatives to egg to ensure that a person on an egg-free diet gets sufficient protein. They can also suggest egg substitutes that can be incorporated into recipes. Some commonly used substitutes in egg-free recipes include: a mix of baking powder, oil, and water; unflavored gelatin; or yeast dissolved in warm water.

References:

1. "Egg Allergy." Food Allergy Research and Education, 2015.

2. "Types of Food Allergy: Egg Allergy." American College of Allergy, Asthma, and Immunology, 2013.

Section 17.2

Hope for Beating Egg Allergy

Text in this section is excerpted from "Hope for Beating Egg Allergy,"
National Institutes of Health (NIH), July 30, 2012.

Giving small daily doses of egg powder to children with egg allergy could pave the way to letting them eat the food safely, a study finds. This would make life easier on kids whose only current option is to stay away from all foods that contain eggs.

Egg allergy is one of the most common food allergies in children. There's no treatment other than completely avoiding the food. That's tough for children, parents and caregivers; eggs can lurk in everything from marshmallows to salad dressing. And the stakes are high. Children who are allergic to eggs can have reactions ranging from hives to anaphylaxis, a life-threatening condition with symptoms that include throat swelling, a sudden drop in blood pressure, trouble breathing and dizziness.

One possible way to help people with food allergies is oral immunotherapy. In this still-experimental approach, patients eat gradually increasing amounts of the food they're allergic to. A research team led by Dr. A. Wesley Burks at the University of North Carolina and Dr. Stacie M. Jones at the University of Arkansas for Medical Sciences tested oral immunotherapy for children who are allergic to eggs. The study was funded by NIH's National Institute of Allergy and Infectious Disease (NIAID), National Center for Research Resources (NCRR) and the National Center for Advancing Translational Sciences (NCATS).

The researchers recruited 55 children, ages 5 to 18, who were allergic to eggs. Forty of the participants ate daily doses of raw egg-white powder. The others received cornstarch as a placebo. Researchers increased the dose every 2 weeks until the children on oral immunotherapy were eating the equivalent of about one-third of an egg every day.

At 10 months, the participants went into the clinic, where they were "challenged" with increasing doses of egg-white powder and watched closely for symptoms. As reported in the July 19, 2012, issue of the New England Journal of Medicine, more than half of the children who had been eating egg powder daily passed the challenge, with no allergic reaction or only minor symptoms. A year later, 30 children passed a challenge with an even larger dose of egg powder. In contrast, none of the children in the placebo group passed the challenge.

Those 30 children stopped oral immunotherapy and were told to avoid all eggs for 4 to 6 weeks. Then they faced another challenge: a dose of egg powder and a whole cooked egg. Most kids had allergic reactions, but 11 passed the test and were allowed to eat as many eggs or egg-containing foods as they wanted in their normal diets. A year later, those children reported they still had no problems eating eggs.

The study suggests 2 ways that egg oral immunotherapy could help children. First, while they were eating the daily dose of egg powder, most of the children could safely eat eggs. Second, a small group of children—about 1 in 4—were able to eat eggs even after the daily oral immunotherapy ended.

"Although these results indicate that oral immunotherapy may help resolve certain food allergies, this type of therapy is still in its early experimental stages and more research is needed," says Dr. Daniel Rotrosen, director of NIAID's Division of Allergy, Immunology and Transplantation. "We want to emphasize that food oral immunotherapy and oral food challenges should not be tried at home because of the risk of severe allergic reactions."

Section 17.3

Influenza Vaccine and Egg Allergy

This section includes excerpts from "Vaccination: Who Should Do It, Who Should Not and Who Should Take Precautions," Centers for Disease Control and Prevention (CDC), November 4, 2015; and text from "Prevention and Control of Influenza with Vaccines: Recommendations of the Advisory Committee on Immunization Practices, United States, 2015–16 Influenza Season," Centers for Disease Control and Prevention (CDC), August 7, 2015.

The Flu Shot

People who can get the flu shot

- Different flu shots are approved for people of different ages, (see Note), but there are flu shots that are approved for use in people as young as 6 months of age and up. Flu shots are approved for use in pregnant women and people with chronic health conditions.

People who can't get the flu shot

- Children younger than 6 months are too young to get a flu shot

- People with severe, life-threatening allergies to flu vaccine or any ingredient in the vaccine. This might include gelatin, antibiotics, or other ingredients. See Special Considerations Regarding Egg Allergy for more information about egg allergies and flu vaccine.

Note: There are certain flu shots that have different age indications. For example people younger than 65 years of age should not get the high-dose flu shot and people who are younger than 18 years old or older than 64 years old should not get the intradermal flu shot.

People who should talk to their doctor before getting the flu shot

- If you have an allergy to eggs or any of the ingredients in the vaccine. Talk to your doctor about your allergy. See Special Considerations Regarding Egg Allergy for more information about egg allergies and flu vaccine.

- If you ever had Guillain-Barré Syndrome (a severe paralyzing illness, also called GBS). Some people with a history of GBS should not get this vaccine. Talk to your doctor about your GBS history.

- If you are not feeling well. Talk to your doctor about your symptoms.

Special Consideration Regarding Egg Allergy

People who have ever had a severe allergic reaction to eggs can get recombinant flu vaccine if they are 18 years and older or they should get the regular flu shot (IIV) given by a medical doctor with experience in management of severe allergic conditions. People who have had a mild reaction to egg—that is, one which only involved hives—may get a flu shot with additional safety measures. Recombinant flu vaccines also are an option for people if they are 18 years and older and they do not have any contraindications to that vaccine. Make sure your doctor or health care professional knows about any allergic reactions. Most, but not all, types of flu vaccine contain a small amount of egg.

Advisory Committee on Immunization Practices (ACIP) recommends the following:

1. All persons aged ≥6 months should receive influenza vaccine annually. Influenza vaccination should not be delayed to

procure a specific vaccine preparation if an appropriate one is already available.

2. For healthy children aged 2 through 8 years who have no contraindications or precautions, either live attenuated influenza vaccine (LAIV) or IIV is an appropriate option. No preference is expressed for LAIV or IIV for any person aged 2 through 49 years for whom either vaccine is appropriate. An age-appropriate formulation of vaccine should be used.

3. LAIV should not be used in the following populations:

   - Persons aged <2 years or >49 years;

   - Persons with contraindications listed in the package insert:

     - Children aged 2 through 17 years who are receiving aspirin or aspirin-containing products;

     - Persons who have experienced severe allergic reactions to the vaccine or any of its components, or to a previous dose of any influenza vaccine;

   - Pregnant women;

   - Immunocompromised persons (see also "Vaccine Selection and Timing of Vaccination for Immunocompromised Persons");

   - Persons with a history of egg allergy;

   - Children aged 2 through 4 years who have asthma or who have had a wheezing episode noted in the medical record within the past 12 months, or for whom parents report that a health care provider stated that they had wheezing or asthma within the last 12 months. For persons aged ≥5 years with asthma, recommendations are described in item 4 of this list;

   - Persons who have taken influenza antiviral medications within the previous 48 hours.

4. In addition to the groups for whom LAIV is not recommended above, the "Warnings and Precautions" section of the LAIV package insert indicates that persons of any age with asthma might be at increased risk for wheezing after administration of LAIV. The package insert also notes that the safety of LAIV in persons with other underlying medical conditions that might

predispose them to complications after wild-type influenza virus infection (e.g., chronic pulmonary, cardiovascular [except isolated hypertension], renal, hepatic, neurologic, hematologic, or metabolic disorders [including diabetes mellitus]) (2), has not been established. These conditions, in addition to asthma in persons aged ≥5 years, should be considered precautions for the use of LAIV.

5. Persons who care for severely immunosuppressed persons who require a protective environment should not receive LAIV, or should avoid contact with such persons for 7 days after receipt, given the theoretical risk for transmission of the live attenuated vaccine virus to close contacts.

Chapter 18

Seafood Allergy

A seafood allergy is an abnormal reaction of the human body when it is exposed to proteins found in fish or shellfish. Finned fish and shellfish come from unrelated families of food, so being allergic to fish does not necessarily mean a person will also be allergic to shellfish. The fish family includes an estimated 20,000 species characterized by fins, scales, and bones, such as tuna, salmon, cod, and halibut. The shellfish family is divided into two main types of marine invertebrates: crustaceans (such as shrimp, crab, and lobster); and molluscs (including clams, mussels, oysters, and squid).

Shellfish allergies affect approximately 1 percent of people, making them twice as common as fish allergies, which affect approximately .5 percent of people. Unlike some other types of food allergies, seafood allergies usually develop in adulthood. An estimated 60 percent of people with shellfish allergies and 40 percent of people with fish allergies experience their first reaction as an adult. Seafood allergies tend to be lifelong, and the reactions are likely to be more severe than those associated with most other types of food allergies.

Diagnosing Seafood Allergies

In someone is allergic to fish or shellfish, the body's immune system mistakenly recognizes proteins from these species as harmful and generates antibodies to fight them as it would fight an infection. When proteins from seafood enter the body—whether through eating

---

fish, touching or handling fish, or breathing in vapors of cooking fish—the body overreacts and releases histamines into the bloodstream. These chemicals produce various symptoms of allergic reactions, such as coughing, throat tightness, wheezing, watery eyes, skin rashes, stomachaches, diarrhea, or vomiting. A more serious manifestation of a seafood allergy is anaphylaxis, in which the person may experience significant difficulty breathing, a drop in blood pressure, lightheadedness, and loss of consciousness. If the person does not receive medical treatment immediately, an anaphylactic reaction can be life threatening.

Anyone who experiences an allergic reaction to seafood should seek medical advice from an allergist/immunologist—a physician specializing in diagnosing and treating allergies. The allergist will conduct a thorough history and physical examination and perform a skin-prick test or a blood test to isolate and identify the type of allergy. Once diagnosed, the patient will receive instructions on how to avoid allergens and what to do if they have an allergic reaction. The allergist may also provide a referral to a dietitian—a medical professional who specializes in dietetics and nutrition—who can offer additional guidance about which foods to avoid and which foods are safe to consume.

Avoiding Seafood

The best treatment for a seafood allergy is to avoid all forms of the allergenic food, whether it is fish or shellfish. For prepared and packaged foods, be sure to read labels thoroughly to avoid buying foods that may contain fish, even if it is not the main ingredient. The U.S. Food and Drug Administration (FDA) has made it mandatory for manufacturers to mention "fish" on the label of foods that contain fish in any form under the Food Allergen Labeling and Consumer Protection Act of 2004. It is important to note that fish proteins may be present in a wide variety of foods, such as Worcestershire sauce, Caesar salad dressing, and some pasta sauces, dips, and even crackers or biscuits.

At home, make sure all surfaces that were used to prepare fish—utensils, cutting boards, countertops, etc.—are thoroughly cleaned before preparing food for an allergic family member. People with a seafood allergy should also stay away from smoke or steam from cooking fish or shellfish as they carry the protein that may cause an allergic reaction.

Avoid going to restaurants that serve seafood. Cross-contamination is a serious possibility in these establishments, so it is best to choose restaurants that do not serve seafood at all. Chinese, Vietnamese, or Thai food preparations have a risk of cross-contamination due to the predominance of fish in these cuisines. Stay away from fish markets and other places where fish is present. Even if an allergist permits a patient to eat certain types of fish or shellfish, it is important to make sure the allowable foods have not been contaminated with allergens from other types of seafood.

Some dietary supplements, like glucosamine—a supplement often prescribed for people with osteoarthritis—may be obtained from the outer coating of crustaceans. As a result, it may provoke a reaction in people allergic to shellfish. Chondroitin sulfate obtained from shark cartilage is another supplement that should be avoided by people with seafood allergies.

For people who experience severe allergic reactions to seafood, a physician may prescribe emergency allergy medication, such as an epinephrine auto-injector, to alleviate symptoms in case of an allergy attack. This medication should be carried at all times and administered at the very first sign of an allergic reaction to avoid life-threatening anaphylaxis.

References:

1. "Fish/Seafood Allergy." Allergy UK, March 2012.

2. "Seafood Allergy." Asthma and Allergy Foundation of America, 2005.

Chapter 19

Peanut and Tree Nut Allergy

Chapter Contents

Section 19.1

Understanding Peanut and Tree Nut Allergies

"Peanut and Tree Nut Allergies," © 2016 Omnigraphics, Inc.
Reviewed November 2015.

Peanut and Tree Nut Allergies

Peanut allergy is one of the most common food allergies, and its prevalence appears to be increasing. One study indicated that the number of children with peanut allergies tripled between 1997 and 2008 in the United States. Siblings of children who are allergic to peanuts are at a higher risk of developing peanut allergies. Although most peanut allergies last a lifetime, an estimated 20 percent of children outgrow them by the age of six.

Peanuts belong to the legumes family, which also includes soybeans, peas, and lentils. They are different from nuts that grow on trees, such as almonds, walnuts, hazelnuts, cashews, Brazil nuts, and pistachios. However, an estimated 25 to 40 percent of people who are allergic to peanuts are also allergic to tree nuts. As a result, many experts suggest that people who are allergic to peanuts also abstain from eating foods containing tree nuts and seeds.

Peanuts and tree nuts contain structurally similar proteins. In an estimated 1 percent of children and 0.5 percent of adults, exposure to these proteins causes the immune system to overreact and release histamine into the bloodstream, which can trigger a severe, whole-body allergic response called anaphylaxis. The symptoms of anaphylaxis can include:

- Hives

- Swelling and rashes

- Itching

- Swelling of the lips and tongue

- Constriction of the throat

- Difficulty breathing and swallowing

- Vomiting

- Diarrhea

- Dizziness and fainting

- Drop in blood pressure

Generally, people who are allergic to nuts will develop a reaction within a few minutes of exposure. Anyone who experiences these symptoms should seek medical attention. For mild allergic reactions, the health care provider may prescribe antihistamines to subdue the immune response. Severe reactions require immediate treatment with epinephrine (adrenaline), typically administered in an auto-injector. Left untreated, anaphylaxis can be fatal.

Diagnosis and Treatment

Peanut and tree nut allergies can be difficult to diagnose through skin tests or blood tests. When these types of allergies are suspected, the allergist may ask the patient to avoid the food in question for two to four weeks. If the patient's symptoms improve as a result of the food-elimination diet, they are most likely allergic to that specific food. When the results are inconclusive, the allergist may request an oral food challenge. During this test, the patient consumes tiny amounts of peanuts or tree nuts in a controlled environment, with emergency medication and equipment on hand in case they have a severe allergic reaction.

The primary form of treatment for peanut and tree nut allergies is strict avoidance of these foods. Eating foods that contain peanuts or tree nuts is the most common cause of severe allergic reactions. Casual contact with the skin is less likely to trigger a severe reaction, unless the residue is transferred from the skin to the eyes, nose, or mouth. Inhaling peanut fumes does not cause an allergic reaction in most people.

People who are allergic to peanuts and tree nuts should always read food labels carefully to ensure that they do not eat products that contain even trace amounts of nuts. Under U.S. law, food manufacturers are required to note whether their products contain nuts. Many companies also voluntarily note whether products were processed in a facility or with equipment that also handles nuts.

People with peanut and tree nut allergies must also be aware of hidden or unexpected sources of nuts. Some common products that often contain peanuts or tree nuts include baked goods, candy, nougat, pralines, egg rolls, chili sauce, enchilada sauce, and mole sauce. Certain types of food establishments are considered dangerous for individuals with peanut allergies due to the risk of cross-contamination, including bakeries, ice cream shops, and African, Asian, or Mexican restaurants.

The primary form of treatment for peanut and tree nut allergies is strict avoidance of these foods. Eating foods that contain peanuts or tree nuts is the most common cause of severe allergic reactions. Casual contact with the skin is less likely to trigger a severe reaction, unless the residue is transferred from the skin to the eyes, nose, or mouth. Inhaling peanut fumes does not cause an allergic reaction in most people.

People who are allergic to peanuts and tree nuts should always read food labels carefully to ensure that they do not eat products that contain even trace amounts of nuts. Under U.S. law, food manufacturers are required to note whether their products contain nuts. Many companies also voluntarily note whether products were processed in a facility or with equipment that also handles nuts.

People with peanut and tree nut allergies must also be aware of hidden or unexpected sources of nuts. Some common products that often contain peanuts or tree nuts include baked goods, candy, nougat, pralines, egg rolls, chili sauce, enchilada sauce, and mole sauce. Certain types of food establishments are considered dangerous for individuals with peanut allergies due to the risk of cross-contamination, including bakeries, ice cream shops, and African, Asian, or Mexican restaurants.

References:

1. American College of Allergy, Asthma, and Immunology. "Peanut Allergy," 2014.

2. Food Allergy Research and Education. "Peanut Allergy," 2015.

Section 19.2

Cracking Nut-Allergy Mechanisms

Text in this section is excerpted from "Cracking Nut-Allergy
Mechanisms," U.S. Department of Agriculture (USDA),
October 2013.

Food allergy is an immune response to eating foods that contain
specific components called "allergens." An increase in food allergy of
18 percent was seen between 1997 and 2007, according to a study
released by the Centers for Disease Control and Prevention. Just eight
foods account for most allergic reactions. Although not all allergies are
lifelongpeople who have allergic reactions to peanuts and tree nuts are
often considered to have them throughout life.

The mechanisms underlying food allergies are not completely
understood. But researchers at the Agricultural Research Service's
Food Processing and Sensory Quality Research Unit in New Orleans,
Louisiana, are studying allergen immune system interactions involved
in nut allergies.

Common Peptides Are Key

People affected by nut allergy experience wide variation in the
breadth and intensity of their allergic reactions. For example, among
people who are allergic to a specific tree nut, one individual may be
five times more allergic than another.

Tree nuts can be members of several plant families. Though thought
of as nuts, peanuts are not nuts. They are members of the Legumino-
sae family and grow underground. Still, both nuts and legumes have
commonalities: They both consist of a dry fruit contained inside a shell.
Some, but not all, people who have allergies to certain nuts can still
eat peanuts, and vice versa.

In New Orleans, ARS chemist Soheila Maleki has worked with
university collaborators on key components of a Structural Database
of Allergenic Proteins (SDAP). The computational database was developed by Catherine Schein and colleagues at the University of Texas
Medical Branch, in Galveston, Texas. The team is in the process of

validating SDAP's ability to help predict when an individual will react to two or more different types of nuts. This condition is called "cross-reactivity."

Foods, including peanuts and tree nuts, contain proteins, which are digested into smaller fragments called "peptides." A peptide is called an "epitope" when it is recognized by antibodies—immune system components in the bloodstream. Immunoglobulin E (IgE) is an antibody that is elevated in allergic individuals. When IgE binds to the epitopes, the food is recognized as foreign by the immune system, and an allergic reaction occurs.

The proteins between cross-reactive nuts are thought to have similar IgE antibody-recognition sites. The researchers took known IgE binding sites (epitope sequences) from peanut and nut proteins and ran those through the SDAP database in order to predict cross-reactive epitopes in other nuts.

"The database provides other sequences that are likely to be allergenic based on the known sequence," says Maleki.

The computer-generated binding sequences were then made into synthetic epitopes for testing purposes. "We needed to know if the computer predicted the novel binding sites correctly," says Maleki. "So we tested those synthesized sequences using serum from people allergic to peanut and tree nuts."

Food-allergen studies commonly involve use of blood serum from allergic individuals because their serum's IgE recognizes allergenic epitopes. The serum, which was provided by cooperators at the University of California Davis, allowed the team to match previously unknown epitopes within the major allergenic proteins known to be common to a variety of nut and peanut allergies.

The authors found that similar immunoglobulin epitopes on allergenic proteins, as defined by SDAP, could account for some of the cross-reactivity between peanuts and tree nuts. The finding indicates that SDAP can be useful for predicting previously unidentified cross-reactive epitopes, based on their similarity to known IgE epitopes.

"The novel sequences we found and validated using the database are similar, but not identical, to the sequences we fed into the software," says Maleki. "We were able to confirm sites that the immune system sees and binds but that we could not have predicted otherwise."

The study was funded by the U.S. Environmental Protection Agency and the National Institutes of Health and was published in Allergy in 2011.

Increasing Diagnostic Reliability

Previously, Maleki had assessed the diagnostic reliability of standard peanut-allergy tests. She found that while people generally eat peanuts that have been heat treated (via roasting or boiling), the extracts that are commonly used to diagnose peanut allergies are from raw peanuts. She and colleagues hypothesized that raw peanut proteins undergo specific changes during roasting that may contribute to increases in allergenic properties.

Since then, Maleki and colleagues have published a series of studies that shed light on the molecular differences between raw and heat-treated nuts in terms of their inherent peptides that trigger human allergic reactions.

The major allergenic proteins (or allergens) of peanut are known as "Ara h 1," "Ara h 2," and "Ara h 3." For one study, Maleki looked into how the peanut-roasting process alters how well an allergic individual's immunoglobulins bind to peanut allergens. The team compared the reaction by human IgE antibody to the heated and unheated forms of Ara h 1. The study showed that roasting-induced side reactions, such as browning, increased the amount of IgE that recognizes and binds to Ara h 1—when compared to the amount that binds to Ara h 1 from raw peanuts.

"This result partly accounts for the increased allergenic properties observed in processed, roasted peanuts," says Maleki.

In another study, Maleki and colleagues in Spain showed that a combination treatment of heat and high pressure (autoclaving) applied to peanuts significantly reduced allergic reaction. Autoclaving involves a higher moisture environment, similar to steaming or boiling, than roasting. As result, autoclaving does not initiate the browning effect that comes with roasting. The less allergenic reaction to the combination-treated peanuts was confirmed by skin-prick tests applied to volunteers known to have peanut allergies.

Section 19.3

Peanut Consumption in Infancy Lowers Risk of Peanut Allergy

Text in this section is excerpted from "Peanut Consumption in
Infancy Lowers Peanut Allergy," National Institutes of Health (NIH),
March 9, 2015.

At a Glance

• Infants who regularly consumed peanut-containing foods from
infancy to age 5 were less likely to become allergic to peanuts.

• The study is the first to show that early consumption of peanut
products may prevent peanut allergy.

A food allergy occurs when the immune system reacts to a harmless
food as if it were a threat. Symptoms can range from upset stomach
and diarrhea, to hives and itching, to tightening of the throat and
trouble breathing. Peanuts are one of the most common foods that
cause allergic reactions. Peanut allergy develops early in life, is rarely
outgrown, and is the leading cause of death due to food allergy in the
United States.

Clinical guidelines previously recommended that infants at high
risk for allergy avoid allergenic foods, such as peanuts. Studies showed,
however, that food elimination doesn't prevent the development of
food allergies, and the American Academy of Pediatrics withdrew this
recommendation in 2008.

A research team led by Dr. Gideon Lack of King's College London
observed that the risk of developing peanut allergy was 10 times higher
among Jewish children in the United Kingdom than in Israeli children of similar ancestry. In the U.K., peanut-based foods are typically
avoided in the first year of life. But in Israel, foods containing peanuts are often introduced at around 7 months of age. The researchers
hypothesized that regular exposure to peanuts in the diet might help
protect against the development of peanut allergy.

To test this theory, the researchers followed more than 600 infants
beginning at 4 to 11 months of age. All were considered at high risk of

developing peanut allergy because they already had egg allergy and/ or severe eczema, an allergic skin disorder.

The infants were randomly assigned to either avoid peanut entirely or to regularly eat at least 6 grams of peanut protein per week (provided in the form of a snack food or as smooth peanut butter). The regimen was closely monitored with recurring clinic visits and telephone calls until participants were 5 years old. The study was funded primarily by NIH's National Institute of Allergy and Infectious Diseases (NIAID). Results appeared on February 26, 2015, in New England Journal of Medicine.

The researchers tested the participants for peanut allergy at age 5. They found that peanut allergy was present in 17.2% of children who had avoided peanuts, but in only 3.2% of the children who had consumed peanuts. This represented an 81% reduction of peanut allergy in children who regularly ate peanut products beginning in infancy.

"Food allergies are a growing concern, not just in the United States but around the world," NIAID Director Dr. Anthony S. Fauci says. "For a study to show a benefit of this magnitude in the prevention of peanut allergy is without precedent. The results have the potential to transform how we approach food allergy prevention."

The researchers will continue to follow the children to determine if protection against peanut allergy remains once children stop consuming peanut products. "Because there are risks, parents of infants and young children with eczema or egg allergy should consult with an allergist, pediatrician, or their general practitioner prior to feeding them peanut products," Lack notes.

Section 19.4

Sublingual Immunotherapy Shows Promise for Peanut Allergy

Text in this section is excerpted from "Therapy Shows Promise for Peanut Allergy," National Institutes of Health (NIH), February 2013.

An experimental therapy may one day make life easier for people with peanut allergy, who now need to avoid all foods containing peanuts.

Food allergies are caused by your immune system, which normally protects your body from harmful germs. When you're allergic, the immune system responds to a harmless substance as if it were a threat. Symptoms can range from hives and itching to a life-threatening reaction called anaphylaxis.

Peanuts are one of the most common foods to cause allergic reactions in both children and adults. The only way to prevent symptoms is to completely avoid peanuts and all products made with them. But that's not easy to do.

An NIH-funded research team tested an approach called sublingual immunotherapy to treat peanut allergy. The therapy involves placing a small amount of liquid under the tongue and then swallowing it.

The researchers enrolled 40 people (ages 12 to 37) who had peanut allergy. They were randomly assigned to receive either sublingual immunotherapy or an inactive placebo.

After 44 weeks, 14 of the 20 treated patients (70%) could safely swallow at least 10 times more peanut powder than they could at the start of the study. Only 3 of the 20 (15%) taking placebo could similarly increase their dose safely. After 68 weeks of therapy, patients could swallow even more peanut powder.

"Immunotherapy continues to show promise for treating food allergies, but it is not yet ready for widespread use," says study co-leader Dr. David Fleischer of National Jewish Health in Denver. "This is an experimental treatment—promising, but with potentially serious side effects." The researchers are now working to improve the technique.

Several other trials are testing oral immunotherapy for food allergy. But if you're allergic, don't try any type of immunotherapy on your own. You could have a dangerous reaction.

Section 19.5

Allergies to a Legume Called Lupin: What You Need to Know

Text in this section is excerpted from "Allergies to a Legume Called Lupin: What You Need to Know," U.S. Food and Drug Administration (FDA), August 15, 2014.

What is Lupin?

Lupin (sometimes called "lupine") is a legume belonging to the same plant family as peanuts. "For many people, eating lupin or a lupin-derived ingredient, such as a flour, is safe," says Stefano Luccioli, M.D., a senior medical advisor at the Food and Drug Administration (FDA). "But there are reports in the medical literature of allergic reactions to lupin, some of which can be severe."

Reactions can include anaphylaxis (a severe response to an allergen that can include shock), which is life-threatening and can occur very quickly. Allergens are substances, such as lupin, that can cause allergic reactions.

As with most food allergens, people can develop an allergy to lupin over time. However, for people who have an existing legume allergy, eating lupin could cause an allergic reaction on first exposure. Studies show that people who are allergic to peanuts, in particular, appear to have a greater chance of being allergic to lupin. "While many parents know to look for and avoid peanut ingredients in the diet of their peanut-allergic child, they may have no idea what lupin is or whether it is an ingredient that could cause their child harm," Luccioli says.

Although lupin is a food staple for many Europeans—who may be more aware of its allergenic properties and are accustomed to seeing it listed as a food ingredient—it is relatively new to the U.S. market. Some Americans may not have heard of this legume, which can be found in the form of lupini beans at Italian and other ethnic specialty stores, as well as in packaged food products.

Often Found in Gluten-Free Products

But lupin is likely to become more popular, especially because lupin-derived ingredients are good substitutes for gluten-containing flours and are frequently being used in gluten-free products.

"We're seeing more gluten-free products on the grocery aisles these days," Luccioli says, and increasingly, consumers are more aware of gluten and are buying these products. Therefore, it's increasingly important that they recognize that lupin is a potential allergen.

Read the Label

The law requires that food labels list the product's ingredients. When lupin is present in a food, it is therefore required to be listed on the label. So, consumers wishing to avoid lupin — and those with peanut allergies, who need to be particularly careful — can identify its presence by looking for "lupin" or "lupine" on the label.

What should you do if you believe you are having an allergic reaction caused by lupin or a lupin-derived ingredient? (Symptoms of a possible allergic reaction include hives, swelling of the lips, vomiting and breathing difficulties). "Stop eating the product and seek immediate medical care or advice," Luccioli says.

FDA is actively monitoring complaints of lupin allergies by U.S. consumers, he adds. You or your health care professional can help by reporting lupin-related adverse events (possible reactions from eating it) to FDA in the following ways:

- By phone at 240-402-2405

- By email at CAERS@cfsan.fda.gov

- By mail at: FDA, CAERS, HFS-700, 2A-012/CPK1, 5100 Paint Branch Parkway, College Park, MD 20740

Chapter 20

Wheat Allergy

Chapter Contents

Section 20.1

What Is Wheat Allergy?

"What Is Wheat Allergy?" © 2016 Omnigraphics, Inc.
Reviewed November 2015.

There are four proteins found in wheat: albumin, globulin, gliadin, and glutenin (also known as gluten). In an individual with a wheat allergy, the immune system develops IgE (immunoglobulin E) antibodies to one or more of these proteins. When the person consumes wheat, the antibodies attack the protein, causing abnormal clinical reactions. These reactions may range from a mild skin rash or runny nose to a severe asthma attack or life-threatening anaphylaxis. Other possible symptoms of wheat allergy include bloated stomach, nausea, vomiting, and diarrhea.

A wheat allergy is different from gluten sensitivity and celiac disease. The majority of wheat allergies involve albumin and globulin. People with gluten sensitivity cannot tolerate gluten, which can be found in grains such as rye and barley in addition to wheat. Celiac disease is a severe form of gluten sensitivity in which the immune system reacts to gluten by producing IgG (immunoglobulin G) antibodies, which cause inflammation in the lining of the small intestine. This inflammation can cause permanent damage to the small intestine and prevent it from absorbing nutrients. For people with celiac disease, the symptoms are generally confined to the abdomen and get worse over time.

Diagnosis and Treatment

Wheat allergy is usually diagnosed by a pinprick skin test or an immunoglobulin blood test. Doctors may also ask the patient to keep a food diary, noting symptoms experienced after eating or eliminating certain foods from their diet. Wheat allergies are most commonly found in infants and toddlers. In the majority of these cases, the child outgrows the allergy within a few years and wheat can gradually be reintroduced to their diet. A family history of allergies is considered a risk factor for developing a wheat allergy.

Avoidance of wheat-based products is the best treatment for a wheat allergy. Wheat proteins are present in many food items, such as bread, pasta, breakfast cereals, crackers, pretzels, cakes, and some sauces. Wheat proteins are also found in beer, root beer, and gravy. Monosodium glutamate (MSG), used as a flavor enhancer in many foods, is another product in which wheat proteins can be found. The FDA has made it mandatory for food manufacturers to mention "wheat" on the product label if wheat is present in any form. People with wheat allergies must read food labels carefully. It is also important to be aware of cross contamination of food during preparation and clean all surfaces thoroughly.

Wheat products are a staple in many American households. Fortunately, there are a variety of alternative foods that can replace wheat, such as maize, corn, rice, potato, soy, chickpea, tapioca, oats, millets, and quinoa. Wheat-free noodles, crackers, cereals, and other products have become widely available in recent years due to rising demand by people with gluten sensitivity. A dietitian with expertise in food allergies can help people choose among the alternatives.

References:

1. Nordqvist, Christian. "What Is Wheat Allergy?" Medical News Today, November 12, 2013.

2. "Wheat Allergy and Sensitivity." Sandwell and West Birmingham Hospitals NHS Trust, July 2014.

Section 20.2

Celiac Disease and Gluten Sensitivity

Text in this section is excerpted from "Celiac Disease and Gluten Sensitivity," Office of Women's Health (OWH), November 5, 2013.

People who have celiac disease can't eat something called gluten, which is in foods made with wheat, rye, and barley. When the person eats gluten, a couple of things happen. First, the immune system, which usually fights off germs, starts to harm the digestive system. And because the digestive system isn't working right, the person can't get the nutrients the body needs to be healthy and strong.

The only way to deal with celiac disease is to avoid gluten. That may sound pretty hard, but there are lots of healthy—and yummy—options. Keep reading to learn more about celiac disease, including:

- Celiac symptoms
- Diagnosing celiac disease
- Living with celiac
- Gluten sensitivity

Celiac Symptoms

Symptoms of celiac disease include:

- Gas
- Diarrhea or constipation
- Stomach pain
- Feeling very tired
- Becoming irritable or depressed
- Losing weight
- A very itchy skin rash with blisters

If a person with celiac disease keeps eating gluten, there could be some other serious effects. For example, there could be long-term bone problems, and it could be hard for a woman to get pregnant. Someone who thinks she may have celiac disease should see a doctor.

Diagnosing Celiac Disease

It can be hard to diagnose celiac disease because other diseases have similar symptoms. You may have to go through several steps to get a diagnosis. Your doctor may ask you if anyone else in your family has celiac disease, because that increases the chances that you may have it. Your doctor also likely will do a blood test. You may also have a test called an endoscopy, in which a tube is placed down your throat and into your digestive system. It may feel uncomfortable, but it shouldn't hurt.

Living with Celiac Disease

At first, it can seem hard to give up all the foods that are made with gluten. From pizza to pasta and cakes to couscous, lots of foods have gluten. But several tips can help:

- **Learn about ingredients.** You might be surprised by which foods have gluten, such as packaged rice mixes, lunchmeats, canned soups, and instant cocoa. Get a list of which items to avoid. You can ask your doctor or a celiac disease organization.

- **Look for alternatives.** Gluten-free breads, cakes, pastas, and many other products are available. Look in health food stores and some supermarkets.

- **Work with friends and family.** Make sure people keep anything with gluten away from your food. Even a small amount of gluten can hurt your digestive system.

- **Read labels.** Remember that "wheat-free" doesn't mean "gluten-free."

- **Join a support group.** Other people with celiac will have helpful advice and can really understand what you are going through. Ask your doctor if there is a group in your area.

- **See a dietitian.** A dietitian can help you figure out a healthy eating plan.

If you have celiac disease, remember that it can take time to adjust to the changes you're facing.

Gluten Sensitivity

Sometimes a person may not have celiac disease but still have problems with gluten. This may be called gluten sensitivity or gluten intolerance. It also may be called non-celiac gluten sensitivity.

Gluten sensitivity can cause similar symptoms to celiac disease, such as tiredness and stomachaches. It can cause other symptoms too, including muscle cramps and leg numbness. Gluten sensitivity doesn't harm a person's digestive system the same way celiac does, and it affects your body differently from a wheat allergy.

Researchers are still learning more about gluten sensitivity. If your doctor thinks you have this problem, he or she may suggest that you avoid eating gluten to see if your symptoms go away. However, before starting to avoid gluten, you should be tested to rule out celiac disease, which is a serious disorder.

Section 20.3

"Gluten-Free" Now Means What It Says

Text in this section is excerpted from "'Gluten-Free' Now Means
What It Says," U.S. Food and Drug Administration (FDA),
August 5, 2014.

In August 2013, the U.S. Food and Drug Administration (FDA) issued a final rule that defined what characteristics a food has to have to bear a label that proclaims it "gluten-free." The rule also holds foods labeled "without gluten," "free of gluten," and "no gluten" to the same standard.

Manufacturers had one year to bring their labels into compliance. As of August 5, 2014, any food product bearing a gluten-free claim labeled on or after this date must meet the rule's requirements.

This rule was welcomed by advocates for people with celiac disease, who face potentially life-threatening illnesses if they eat the gluten found in breads, cakes, cereals, pastas and many other foods.

Andrea Levario, executive director of the American Celiac Disease Alliance, notes that there is no cure for celiac disease and the only way to manage the disease is dietary—not eating gluten. Without a standardized definition of "gluten-free," these consumers could never really be sure if their body would tolerate a food with that label, she adds.

As one of the criteria for using the claim "gluten-free," FDA set a gluten limit of less than 20 ppm (parts per million) in foods that carry this label. This is the lowest level that can be consistently detected in foods using valid scientific analytical tools. Also, most people with celiac disease can tolerate foods with very small amounts of gluten. This level is consistent with those set by other countries and international bodies that set food safety standards.

"This standard 'gluten-free' definition eliminates uncertainty about how food producers label their products. People with celiac disease can rest assured that foods labeled 'gluten-free' meet a clear standard established and enforced by FDA," says Felicia Billingslea, director of FDA's division of food labeling and standards.

What Is Gluten?

Gluten is a mixture of proteins that occur naturally in wheat, rye, barley and crossbreeds of these grains.

As many as 3 million people in the United States have celiac disease. It occurs when the body's natural defense system reacts to gluten by attacking the lining of the small intestine. Without a healthy intestinal lining, the body cannot absorb the nutrients it needs. Delayed growth and nutrient deficiencies can result and may lead to conditions such as anemia (a lower than normal number of red blood cells) and osteoporosis, a disease in which bones become fragile and more likely to break. Other serious health problems may include diabetes, autoimmune thyroid disease and intestinal cancers.

Before the rule there were no federal standards or definitions for the food industry to use in labeling products "gluten-free." An estimated 5 percent of foods formerly labeled "gluten-free" contained 20 ppm or more of gluten.

How Does FDA Define 'Gluten-Free'?

In addition to limiting the unavoidable presence of gluten to less than 20 ppm, FDA now allows manufacturers to label a food "gluten-free" if the food does not contain any of the following:

- an ingredient that is any type of wheat, rye, barley, or crossbreeds of these grains

- an ingredient derived from these grains and that has not been processed to remove gluten

- an ingredient derived from these grains and that has been processed to remove gluten, if it results in the food containing 20 or more parts per million (ppm) gluten

Foods such as bottled spring water, fruits and vegetables, and eggs can also be labeled "gluten-free" if they inherently don't have any gluten.

Under the final rule, a food label that bears the claim "gluten-free," as well as the claims "free of gluten," "without gluten," and "no gluten," but fails to meet the requirements of the rule is considered misbranded and subject to regulatory action by FDA.

According to Felicia Billingslea, director of FDA's division of food labeling and standards, consumers should know that some foods labeled "gluten free" that are in the marketplace may have been labeled before the rule's compliance date of August 5.

Some of these foods, like pasta, have a longer shelf life and may legally remain on the shelves a little bit longer. Therefore, it is possible that stores may still be selling some foods that are labeled "gluten-free" produced before the compliance date of the final rule.

If consumers have any doubts about a product's ingredients and whether or not the product is gluten-free, they should contact the manufacturer or check its website for more information.

What About in Restaurants?

Some restaurants use the term "gluten-free" in their menus. The gluten-free final rule applies to packaged foods, which may be sold in some retail and food-service establishments such as some carry-out restaurants. However, given the public health significance of "gluten-free" labeling, restaurants making a gluten-free claim on their menus should be consistent with FDA's definition.

State and local governments play an important role in oversight of restaurants. FDA will work with partners in state and local governments with respect to gluten-free labeling in restaurants.

Billingslea suggests that consumers who are concerned about gluten-free claims in restaurants ask the following questions when ordering foods described as gluten-free:

- What does the restaurant mean by the term "gluten free?"

- What ingredients are used in this item?

- How is the item prepared?

"With the new FDA gluten-free regulations now being enforced, restaurants will be well-served to ensure they are meeting the FDA-defined claim," said Joy Dubost, Ph.D., R.D., Senior Director of Nutrition, National Restaurant Association. "We will continue to work with restaurant operators and chefs to assist and ensure a favorable dining experience for consumers."

Chapter 21

Soy Allergy

Introduction

Soy is a plant in the pea family. Although it has been a staple in Asian diets for centuries, it has gained popularity in the United States in recent years. Soybeans, the high-protein seeds of the soy plant, contain chemical compounds called isoflavones that have a variety of uses in traditional or folk medicine. Since isoflavones are similar to the female hormone estrogen, soy products have long been used to treat such women's health concerns as menopausal symptoms, osteoporosis, and breast cancer, as well as conditions like high blood pressure, high cholesterol levels, memory loss, and prostate cancer.

Soy is available in the form of dietary supplements. In addition, soybeans can be cooked and eaten or used to make tofu, soymilk, and other foods. Soy is also commonly used as an additive in a wide variety of processed foods, including baked goods, cheese, and pasta.

Symptoms and Diagnosis

Despite its potential health benefits, soy is a fairly common food allergen. Soy allergy occurs when the human immune system overreacts to the protein in soy, causing the body to produce immunoglobulin E (IgE) antibodies. The IgE antibodies get attached to mast cells when some allergens such as soy proteins are consumed. They cross link with

"Understanding Soy Allergy," © 2016 Omnigraphics, Inc. Reviewed November 2015.

Common soy containing foods in the U.S.

Edamame (green soybeans), miso (soybean pastes), soy nuts, soy milk, soy protein, soy apricot, tamari, and tempeh (fermented soybean products) are some of the soy containing food products. As per U.S. Food and Drug Administration (FDA) regulations under Food Allergen Labeling and Consumer Protection Act (FALCPA), the major eight food allergens which includes soy, should be mentioned in the label of food products in plain language.

the IgE molecules, causing the release of Histamine and other chemicals that are typically involved in an allergic response. Soy allergy affects approximately 0.4 percent of children in the United States. A majority of children outgrow soy allergy by the age of three or years. It is relatively less common in adults.

Reactions to soy or its derivatives may involve a range of allergic symptoms, tingling in the mouth, hives, itching or eczema, swelling of the hips, face, tongue, and throat or other parts of the body, wheezing and abdominal cramps. Anaphylaxis—a severe, life-threatening whole-body allergic response—may occur in some people with soy allergy, but it is rather rare. The most common symptoms of a soy allergy are pruritus (itching) around the lips, mouth, face, or other parts of the body; allergic rhinitis (nasal congestion, sneezing, and watery eyes); and nausea, vomiting, and diarrhea.

How the allergy is diagnosed

A soy allergy is initially diagnosed with a skin prick test (SPT), wherein a measured dose of a liquid containing soy protein extract is introduced into the top layer of the skin with a sterile probe. The appearance of a red bump or flare on the skin indicates a sensitivity to soy and helps the allergist make a diagnosis. A blood test may also be done to measure the amount of IgE antibody in the blood.

Avoiding Soy Products

There is no cure for soy allergy. The only way to prevent symptoms from occurring is to exclude soy products from the diet and avoid foods containing soy in any form. Soy is one of the eight common allergens covered under the federal Food Allergen Labeling and Consumer Protection Act. As a result, food manufacturers are required to state on the label whether a product contains soy or has been manufactured in a facility or with equipment that also produces soy-containing products. People with soy allergy should read food labels carefully and avoid ingesting products that contain even traces of soy. If the information on the label is insufficient, they should contact the manufacturer for clarification.

Soy is widely used as an ingredient in commercial foods. In fact, it is estimated that soy plays a role in the production of 20,000 to 30,000 food products, either directly as an ingredient or indirectly as animal feed. Soy fat and oils are used in foods like margarine and mayonnaise. Soy isolates find use in meat products, soups, sauces, and imitation dairy products. Tofu, which is clotted soymilk, is a popular ingredient in many savory and sweet dishes. Soy meals and soy flour are part of many types of cereals, breads, and pasta. Lecithin, a derivative of soy, is a common additive in a variety of baked food, chocolates, and confections. Most individuals who are allergic to soy can safely tolerate refined soybean oil and lecithin, but they should check with their allergist before consuming these ingredients Child nutrition staff should always carefully read labels to make sure the food is free from soy.

Research on a Hypoallergenic Strain of Soy

To address growing concerns about food allergies all over the world, scientists have worked to produce a genetically modified (GM) variety of soybean that eliminates P34, the protein in soybeans that is responsible for causing food allergy. They hope to create a "hypoallergenic soy" that will not trigger allergic reactions. Animal studies using the hypoallergenic variety are underway and will serve as a springboard for human trials. Commercial use of this new form of soy is a long way off, however, pending regulatory approvals in countries that are wary of using GM food technology.

References:

1. Agricultural Research Service. "Allergic to Certain Foods?" U.S. Department of Agriculture, February 13, 2009.

2. National Food Service Management Institute. "Food Allergy Fact Sheet: Soy Allergies." University of Mississippi, 2012.

Chapter 22

Ingredients and Food Additives That Trigger Reactions

Chapter Contents

Section 22.1

Food Additives and Intolerance

Text in this section is excerpted from "Food Ingredients of Public
Health Concern," U.S. Department of Agriculture (USDA),
June 11, 2015.

Food Intolerance

Some individuals may be intolerant of certain food additives and
color additives. Food intolerances are often confused with allergic
reactions, but the adverse effects of food intolerances do not involve
the same immunological mechanisms as an allergic reaction. Food
intolerances generally do not result in life-threatening reactions like
food allergies; however, they are still of public health significance, and
FSIS is equally concerned about all food ingredients that may cause
adverse health effects.

Some people experience gastrointestinal disturbance when they
drink milk. Often, the gastrointestinal disturbance is not an allergic
reaction to milk proteins but intolerance to **lactose**, a sugar molecule
in milk and milk products. People intolerant to lactose are generally
deficient in lactase, the enzyme that breaks down lactose in the intestinal tract. As people get older, their lactase levels tend to decline. In
individuals with insufficient levels of lactase, bacteria in the intestine
break down lactose, which produces gas, bloating, cramping, and sometimes diarrhea. It is not just whole milk that is the problem for these
individuals, as a variety of food products may contain milk derivatives
that contain lactose.

Sulfites, including sulfur dioxide, sodium sulfite, sodium bisulfite,
potassium bisulfite, sodium metabisulfite, and potassium metabisulfite, have been used as food preservatives. One of the main uses of
sulfiting agents is to prevent browning of processed fruits, vegetables,
and shellfish. Sulfites are not used directly on meat or poultry products, but other ingredients added to meat or poultry products may
contain sulfites.

People who have an intolerance to sulfites can experience symptoms including chest tightness, hives, stomach cramps, diarrhea, and

breathing problems. The underlying mechanisms for sulfite intolerance are not completely understood. For some individuals, though, the sensitivity to sulfites may be an allergic type of response. People with asthma appear to be at an increased risk of having asthma symptoms following exposure to sulfites.

The presence of sulfiting agents must be declared on the label if their concentration in the finished meat or poultry food product is 10 ppm or higher. However, some finished meat and poultry food products may be comprised of multiple separate components, e.g., potatoes or apple cobbler in a frozen dinner. For these products, if a separate component contains 10 ppm or more sulfiting agents, the sulfiting agents must be declared even though the total product contains less than 10 ppm of sulfiting agents. When sulfiting agents are required to be declared on a label, they must be (1) declared by their specific name or as "sulfiting agents," and (2) listed in the ingredients statement in order of predominance or at the end of the ingredients statement with the statement,

"This Product Contains Sulfiting Agents" (or the specific name of the sulfite compound).

Federal Food, Drug, and Cosmetic Act (FD&C) Yellow No. 5, or **tartrazine**, has been used as a color additive in a variety of food products. Some consumers appear to have an intolerance to tartrazine. In these consumers, tartrazine may cause symptoms similar to an allergic reaction, i.e., hives and swelling, but the reaction is not considered a true allergy. Tartrazine was also thought to be associated with the onset of asthma attacks, but more recent scientific evidence indicated tartrazine was an unlikely cause of asthma symptoms. To help protect people who may be intolerant to tartrazine, the FDA requires that any food for human use that contains Yellow No. 5 must specifically declare it as an ingredient.

Monosodium Glutamate (MSG) is included as a flavor enhancer in a number of meat and poultry products. Some individuals have reported headaches, chest tightness, nausea, diarrhea, and sweating following consumption of products containing MSG. There is scientific debate over whether MSG causes adverse health effects in individuals. Nonetheless, given the significant consumer concern about this ingredient, FSIS urges companies to ensure that its use is properly declared in labeling.

Gluten is the protein found in cereal grains, including wheat, barley, rye, and oats. It is what helps give dough its elasticity. Some individuals have a condition known as celiac disease, which is basically intolerance to gluten. Although it is not an allergic reaction, it does involve immunological mechanisms that result in inflammation and damage to the lining of the small intestine. Persons with celiac disease experience fatigue, bloating, cramping, chronic diarrhea, and nutrient malabsorption. FSIS permits statements highlighting the presence of certain gluten containing ingredients. If an establishment wishes to make a special claim that a meat or poultry product is gluten-free, then it must be able to support that special claim.

Nitrate and **nitrites** are different compounds, both of which are composed of nitrogen and oxygen. They are used as curing agents in many meat and poultry products, including hotdogs, bologna, salami and other processed meats. These compounds contribute to the characteristic cured flavor and reddish-pink color of cured products. They are also important in inhibiting the growth of Clostridium spp. These compounds may cause headaches and hives in some people. In excessive amounts, nitrate or nitrite can be toxic. In addition to labeling requirements, the amount of nitrite or nitrate added to a product is restricted by regulation.

Some products that traditionally include nitrite or nitrate can be manufactured without the use of added nitrite or nitrate. Such products are formulated to only include naturally occurring sources of nitrite or nitrate, such as celery juice powder, parsley, cherry powder, beet powder, spinach, or sea salt. Such products must be labeled appropriately. For example, an "uncured" bacon product should include a declaration such as "Uncured Bacon, No Nitrates or Nitrites added except those naturally occurring in___" on the product label. In addition, such products generally must bear the statement "Not Preserved, Keep Refrigerated Below 40°F At All Times," as the naturally occurring sources of nitrite or nitrate do not inhibit the outgrowth of Clostridium spp. to the same extent as the highly purified chemical forms. Exceptions to this refrigeration handling statement would be finished products that have been dried according to other requirements or that contain a sufficient amount of salt to achieve an internal brine concentration of 10% or more.

> **NOTE:** FD&C coloring agents, like Red No. 3 and Red No. 40, are often added to cure mixes as a tint to distinguish nitrite from salt. FSIS policy has always been that since the coloring agent does not function as a color additive in the meat or poultry product, it is considered to be incidental and does not require declaration on the product label.

Section 22.2

Histamine Intolerance

Text in this section is excerpted from "Bad Bug Book—Handbook of Foodborne Pathogenic Microorganisms and Natural Toxins," U.S. Food and Drug Administration (FDA), October 7, 2014.

Scombrotoxin is a combination of substances, histamine prominent among them. Histamine is produced during decomposition of fish, when decarboxylase enzymes made by bacteria that inhabit (but do not sicken) the fish interact with the fish's naturally occurring histidine, resulting in histamine formation. Other vasoactive biogenic amines resulting from decomposition of the fish, such as putrescine and cadaverine, also are thought to be components of scombrotoxin. Time / temperature abuse of scombrotoxin-forming fish (e.g., tuna and mahi-mahi) create conditions that promote formation of the toxin. Scombrotoxin poisoning is closely linked to the accumulation of histamine in these fish.

FDA has established regulatory guidelines that consider fish containing histamine at 50 ppm or greater to be in a state of decomposition and fish containing histamine at 500 ppm or greater to be a public health hazard. The European Union issued Council Directive (91/493/EEC) in 1991, which states that when 9 samples taken from a lot of fish are analyzed for histamine, the mean value must not exceed 100 ppm; two samples may have a value of more than 100 ppm, but less than 200 ppm; and no sample may have a value exceeding 200 ppm.

Disease

The disease caused by scombrotoxin is called scombrotoxin poisoning or histamine poisoning. Treatment with antihistamine drugs is warranted when scombrotoxin poisoning is suspected.

- **Mortality:** No deaths have been confirmed to have resulted from scombrotoxin poisoning.

- **Dose:** In most cases, histamine levels in illness-causing (scombrotoxic) fish have exceeded 200 ppm, often above 500 ppm. However, there is some evidence that other biogenic amines also may play a role in the illness.

- **Onset:** The onset of intoxication symptoms is rapid, ranging from minutes to a few hours after consumption.

- **Disease / Complications:** Severe reactions (e.g., cardiac and respiratory complications) occur rarely, but people with pre-existing conditions may be susceptible. People on certain medications, including the anti-tuberculosis drug isoniazid, are at increased risk for severe reactions.

- **Symptoms:** Symptoms of scombrotoxin poisoning include tingling or burning in or around the mouth or throat, rash or hives, drop in blood pressure, headache, dizziness, itching of the skin, nausea, vomiting, diarrhea, asthmatic-like constriction of air passage, heart palpitation, and respiratory distress.

- **Duration:** The duration of the illness is relatively short, with symptoms commonly lasting several hours, but, in some cases, adverse effects may persist for several days.

- **Route of entry:** Oral.

- **Pathway:** In humans, histamine exerts its effects on the cardiovascular system by causing blood-vessel dilation, which results in flushing, headache, and hypotension. It increases heart rate and contraction strength, leading to heart palpitations, and induces intestinal smooth-muscle contraction, causing abdominal cramps, vomiting, and diarrhea. Histamine also stimulates motor and sensory neurons, which may account for burning sensations and itching associated with scombrotoxin poisoning. Other biogenic amines, such as putrescine and cadaverine, may potentiate scombrotoxin poisoning by interfering with the enzymes necessary to metabolize histamine in the human body.

Frequency

Scombrotoxin poisoning is one of the most common forms of fish poisoning in the United States. From 1990 to 2007, outbreaks of scombrotoxin poisoning numbered 379 and involved 1,726 people, per reports to the Centers for Disease Control and Prevention (CDC). However, the actual number of outbreaks is believed to be far greater than that reported.

Sources

Fishery products that have been implicated in scombrotoxin poisoning include tuna, mahi-mahi, bluefish, sardines, mackerel, amberjack, anchovies, and others. Scombrotoxin-forming fish are commonly distributed as fresh, frozen, or processed products and may be consumed in a myriad of product forms. Distribution of the toxin within an individual fish or between cans in a case lot can be uneven, with some sections of a product capable of causing illnesses and others not.

Cooking, canning, and freezing do not reduce the toxic effects. Common sensory examination by the consumer cannot ensure the absence or presence of the toxin. Chemical analysis is a reliable test for evaluating a suspect fishery product. Histamine also may be produced in other foods, such as cheese and sauerkraut, which also has resulted in toxic effects in humans.

Diagnosis

Diagnosis of the illness is usually based on the patient's symptoms, time of onset, and the effect of treatment with antihistamine medication. The suspected food should be collected; rapidly chilled or, preferably, frozen; and transported to the appropriate laboratory for histamine analyses. Elevated levels of histamine in food suspected of causing scombrotoxin poisoning aid in confirming a diagnosis.

Target Populations

All humans are susceptible to scombrotoxin poisoning; however, as noted, the commonly mild symptoms can be more severe for individuals taking some medications, such as the antituberculosis drug isoniazid. Because of the worldwide network for harvesting, processing, and distributing fishery products, the impact of the problem is not limited to specific geographic areas or consumption patterns.

Chapter 23

Other Health Problems Related to Food Allergic Reactions

Chapter Contents

Section 23.1

Food Protein-Induced Enterocolitis Syndrome (FPIES)

Text in this section is excerpted from "Food Protein Induced
Enterocolitis Syndrome (FPIES)," Centers for Disease Control and
Prevention (CDC), September 19, 2012.

Food Protein-Induced Enterocolitis Syndrome (FPIES) is a gastro-intestinal food allergy, which causes symptoms of vomiting usually within 1 to 3 hours after eating the causative food. There often may also be diarrhea within 5 to 8 hours, which may be bloody. Vomiting and diarrhea may be so severe as to cause dehydration, and even shock; lethargy and pallor may also occur. It usually occurs in infants, with onset most often before 3 months, but up to 1 year, and usually it resolves by about 3 years of age. It most often is due to milk or soy proteins, but may also be due to rice, or other food proteins.

FPIES has also been described in adults, particularly due to shell-fish. The symptoms of vomiting and diarrhea with FPIES generally resolve quickly with elimination of the causative food from the diet. In chronic cases, there may be weight loss and failure to thrive. Definitive diagnosis of FPIES may require physician-supervised oral food challenges to be done in an inpatient setting, to demonstrate the response.

Food protein-induced proctocolitis is another distinct gastrointestinal food allergy, which causes blood-streaked stools, and usually presents in the first months of life. It can cause anemia. It has been called by different terms, including allergic proctocolitis, food-induced eosinophilic proctocolitis, milk protein-induced proctocolitis, and eosinophilic colitis.

While many allergies are IgE mediated (e.g., anaphylactic shock), FPIES and food protein induced proctocolitis are not IgE mediated. They are thought to be cell mediated. In some cases of FPIES, IgE may also be present, but would not be considered to be related.

Another non-IgE mediated food allergy is food protein-induced enteropathy. It also occurs in young infants, and causes chronic diarrhea, weight loss, and failure to thrive. It is also treated by strict dietary elimination of the allergen, and is usually outgrown by age 2 or 3 years.

Oral allergy syndrome involves symptoms of itching, swelling, or tingling of the lips, mouth, or throat, in response to a food, often to raw fruits or vegetables. This is considered a gastrointestinal allergy, which is IgE mediated, and may also be considered an adverse food reaction.

Section 23.2

Oral Allergy Syndrome and Exercise-Induced Food Allergy

Text in this chapter is excerpted from "Oral Allergy Syndrome
and Exercise-Induced Food Allergy," National Institute of
Allergy and Infectious Diseases (NIAID), February 8, 2012.
Reviewed November 2015.

Oral Allergy Syndrome

Oral allergy syndrome (OAS) is an allergy to certain raw fruits and vegetables, such as apples, cherries, kiwis, celery, tomatoes, and green peppers. OAS occurs mostly in people with hay fever, especially spring hay fever due to birch pollen and late summer hay fever due to ragweed pollen.

Eating the raw food causes an itchy, tingling sensation in the mouth, lips, and throat. It can also cause swelling of the lips, tongue, and throat; watery, itchy eyes; runny nose; and sneezing. Just handling the raw fruit or vegetable may cause a rash, itching, or swelling where the juice touches the skin.

Cooking or processing easily breaks down the proteins in the fruits and vegetables that cause OAS. Therefore, OAS typically does not occur with cooked or baked fruits and vegetables or processed fruits, such as applesauce.

Exercise-Induced Food Allergy

Exercise-induced food allergy requires more than simply eating food to start a reaction. This type of reaction occurs after someone eats a specific food *before* exercising. As exercise increases and body temperature rises, itching and light-headedness start, hives may appear, and even anaphylaxis may develop. Some people have this reaction from many foods, and others have it only after eating a specific food.

Treating exercised-induced food allergy is simple—avoid eating for a couple of hours before exercising.

Crustacean shellfish, alcohol, tomatoes, cheese, and celery are common causes of exercise-induced food allergy reactions.

Section 23.3

Esonophilic Esophagitis and Food Allergy

This chapter includes excerpts from "Eosinophilic Esophagitis and Food Allergy," National Institute of Allergy and Infectious Diseases (NIAID), November 18, 2015; and text from "Eosinophilic Gastrointestinal Disorders," National Institute of Allergy and Infectious Diseases (NIAID), April 23, 2014.

Eosinophilic esophagitis (EoE) is a newly recognized chronic disease that can be associated with food allergies. It is increasingly being diagnosed in children and adults. EoE is characterized by inflammation and accumulation of a specific type of immune cell, called an eosinophil, in the esophagus. This is the most common type of Eosinophilic gastrointestinal disorders (EGID).

Symptoms of EoE include nausea, vomiting, and abdominal pain after eating. A person may also have symptoms that resemble acid reflux from the stomach. In older children and adults, it can cause more severe symptoms, such as difficulty swallowing solid food or solid food sticking in the esophagus for more than a few minutes. In infants, this disease may be associated with failure to thrive.

If you are diagnosed with EoE, you will probably be tested for allergies. In some situations, avoiding certain food allergens will be an effective treatment for EoE.

In healthy people, small numbers of eosinophils may be found in all areas of the gastrointestinal tract except the esophagus. However, people with EGIDs have high eosinophil counts in the gastrointestinal tract.

The diagnosis of EGIDs, particularly EoE, is increasing in both adults and children. Health experts believe that this increase reflects changes in diagnostic practice as well as an actual increase in the number of cases. According to the Registry for Eosinophilic Gastrointestinal Disorders, EoE may affect up to one in 1,000 people.

For most patients, EGIDs are life-long conditions. Early treatment and continued followup are important to decrease the long-term effects of these diseases.

Cause

Health experts are working to understand the factors that influence development of EGIDs. These disorders sometimes run in families, and scientists have identified several genetic variations associated with EoE.

Symptoms

Symptoms of EGIDs vary from person to person and depend on where in the gastrointestinal system eosinophils accumulate. Many signs of EGIDs closely resemble those of other gastrointestinal disorders, such as inflammatory bowel diseases.

Common EGID symptoms include

- Trouble swallowing

- A feeling that food is stuck in the throat or chest

- Chest or abdominal pain

- Heartburn or acid reflux that does not improve after taking appropriate medicine

- Nausea

- Vomiting

- Poor appetite

- Bloating

Diagnosis

Currently, the only clear-cut way for doctors to diagnose an EGID is by conducting an endoscopy with biopsy. In this procedure, a doctor uses an endoscope—a thin tube with a camera and light on the end—to look at the gastrointestinal tract and take small tissue samples called biopsies. A pathologist reviews the biopsies, looking for high levels of eosinophils and signs of tissue damage.

Treatment

Treatment with diet changes and/or medicines can alleviate EGID symptoms and prevent further damage to the gastrointestinal tract. Treatment options vary depending on the location of eosinophils and the severity of symptoms.

Diet changes

Many people with EoE respond well to diet changes, and dietary restrictions also may be helpful in treating those with other forms of EGID.

Sometimes, doctors will advise a "six food elimination diet," in which patients avoid all common allergenic foods, including milk, eggs, wheat, soy, peanuts and other nuts, and fish and shellfish.

Some people with EoE require a stricter diet called an elemental diet, which does not contain any whole or partial proteins for the immune system to recognize and respond to. People on an elemental diet consume prescription liquid formulas that contain amino acids (the building blocks of proteins), fats, sugars, vitamins, and minerals. Some people find it difficult to drink enough of the formula to maintain proper nutrition and may require tube feedings directly into the stomach.

Once EGID symptoms are under control, certain foods may be slowly added back into the diet under the guidance of a doctor and dietician.

Medicines

Because dietary management of EGIDs can be challenging, some patients choose medicines to treat their EGID. The Food and Drug Administration has not yet approved any medications for the treatment of EGIDs, but doctors may use certain drugs "off-label" to treat these disorders. Corticosteroids used to control asthma, such as fluticasone propionate or budesonide, may help suppress inflammation in people with EoE. While people with asthma typically take these medicines with an inhaler or nebulizer, those with EoE swallow the drugs so that the medicine comes in direct contact with the esophagus.

Studies have shown that these drugs can resolve symptoms completely in some people with EoE, although symptoms return when medicine is stopped.

People with other types of EGIDs may take corticosteroids designed for delivery to specific parts of the gastrointestinal tract. In more severe cases, doctors may prescribe oral corticosteroids, such as prednisone, which deliver medicine to the whole body.

Chapter 24

Advice for Consumers about Food Labels

Chapter Contents

Section 24.1

Questions and Answers about Food Labels

Text in this section is excerpted from "Food Allergen Labeling And
Consumer Protection Act Questions and Answers," U.S. Food and
Drug Administration (FDA), December 16, 2014.

General

*What is the Food Allergen Labeling and Consumer Protection Act
(FALCPA)?*

FALCPA is an amendment to the Federal Food, Drug, and Cosmetic
Act and requires that the label of a food that contains an ingredient
that is or contains protein from a "major food allergen" declare the
presence of the allergen in the manner described by the law.

Why did Congress pass this Act?

Congress passed this Act to make it easier for food allergic consumers and their caregivers to identify and avoid foods that contain major
food allergens. In fact, in a review of the foods of randomly selected
manufacturers of baked goods, ice cream, and candy in Minnesota and
Wisconsin in 1999, FDA found that 25 percent of sampled foods failed
to list peanuts or eggs as ingredients on the food labels although the
foods contained these allergens.

When does FALCPA become effective?

FALCPA applies to food products that are labeled on or after January 1, 2006.

What is a "major food allergen?"

FALCPA identifies eight foods or food groups as the major food
allergens. They are milk, eggs, fish (e.g., bass, flounder, cod), Crustacean shellfish (e.g., crab, lobster, shrimp), tree nuts (e.g., almonds,
walnuts, pecans), peanuts, wheat, and soybeans.

FALCPA identifies only 8 allergens. Aren't there more foods consumers are allergic to?

Yes. More than 160 foods have been identified to cause food allergies in sensitive individuals. However, the eight major food allergens identified by FALCPA account for over 90 percent of all documented food allergies in the U.S. and represent the foods most likely to result in severe or life-threatening reactions.

How serious are food allergies?

It is estimated that 2 percent of adults and about 5 percent of infants and young children in the U.S. suffer from food allergies. Approximately 30,000 consumers require emergency room treatment and 150 Americans die each year because of allergic reactions to food.

Does FALCPA apply to imported foods as well?

FALCPA applies to both domestically manufactured and imported packaged foods that are subject to FDA regulation.

FDA held public meetings on allergens and gluten; what were the outcomes of those meetings?

FDA held two meetings. The first meeting, a Food Advisory Committee Meeting held in June 2005, evaluated FDA's draft report, "Approaches to Establish Thresholds for Major Food Allergens and for Gluten in Food." See Approaches to Establish Thresholds for Major Food Allergens and for Gluten in Food (Draft Report). This draft report was written to help develop FDA's policy on food allergens and to implement FALCPA.

FDA held a second public meeting in August 2005 to obtain expert comment and consultation from stakeholders to help FDA develop a regulation to define and permit the voluntary use on food labeling of the term "gluten-free" (Public Meeting On: Gluten-Free Food Labeling). The meeting focused on food manufacturing, analytical methods, and consumer issues related to reduced levels of gluten in food. Information presented during and following the meeting provided FDA important and relevant data regarding current industry practices in the production of foods marketed as "gluten-free," challenges faced by manufacturers of "gluten-free" foods, and consumer perceptions and expectations of what "gluten-free" means to them. FDA used this information to develop its proposal on the use of the term "gluten-free."

Will FDA establish a threshold level for any allergen?

FDA may consider a threshold level for one or more food allergens.

Labeling

How food labels changed as a result of FALCPA?

FALCPA requires food manufacturers to label food products that contain an ingredient that is or contains protein from a major food allergen in one of two ways.

The first option for food manufacturers is to include the name of the food source in parenthesis following the common or usual name of the major food allergen in the list of ingredients in instances when the name of the food source of the major allergen does not appear elsewhere in the ingredient statement. For example:

Ingredients: Enriched flour (wheat flour, malted barley, niacin, reduced iron, thiamin mononitrate, riboflavin, folic acid), sugar, partially hydrogenated soybean oil, and/or cottonseed oil, high fructose corn syrup, whey (milk), eggs, vanilla, natural and artificial flavoring) salt, leavening (sodium acid pyrophosphate, monocalcium phosphate), lecithin (soy), mono-and diglycerides (emulsifier)

The second option is to place the word "Contains" followed by the name of the food source from which the major food allergen is derived, immediately after or adjacent to the list of ingredients, in type size that is no smaller than the type size used for the list of ingredients. For example: *Contains Wheat, Milk, Egg, and Soy*

Is the ingredient list specific about what type of tree nut, fish, or shellfish is in the product?

FALCPA requires the type of tree nut (e.g., almonds, pecans, walnuts); the type of fish (e.g., bass, flounder, cod); and the type of Crustacean shellfish (e.g., crab, lobster, shrimp) to be declared.

After January 1, 2006, do I still find products on the supermarket or grocery shelf without the improved labeling?

Yes. FALCPA does not require food manufacturers or retailers to remove or relabel products from supermarket shelves that do not reflect the additional allergen labeling so long as the products were labeled before January 1, 2006. Therefore, FDA advises consumers with allergies to always read a product's ingredient statement in conjunction with any "contains" statement.

Does FALCPA require the use of a "may contain" statement in any circumstance?

No. Advisory statements are not required by FALCPA.

Are flavors, colors, and food additives subject to the allergen labeling requirements?

Yes. FALCPA requires that food manufacturers label food products that contain ingredients, including a flavoring, coloring, or incidental additive that are, or contain, a major food allergen using plain English to identify the allergens.

Are there any foods exempt from the labeling requirements?

Yes. Under FALCPA, raw agricultural commodities (generally fresh fruits and vegetables) are exempt as are highly refined oils derived from one of the eight major food allergens and any ingredient derived from such highly refined oil.

What does FDA require in order for a product to be exempt?

FALCPA states that any person can petition the Secretary of Health and Human Services for an exemption either through a petition process or a notification process.

The petition process requires scientific evidence (including the analytical method used to produce the evidence) that demonstrates that such food ingredient, as derived by the method specified in the petition, does not cause an allergic response that poses a risk to human health.

The notification process must include scientific evidence (including the analytical method used) that demonstrates that the food ingredient (as derived by the production method specified in the notification) does not contain allergenic protein.

If either the petition or the notification is granted by the Secretary, the result is that the ingredient in question is not considered a "major food allergen" and is not subject to the labeling requirements.

How will FDA make sure food manufacturers adhere to the new labeling regulations?

As a part of its routine regulatory functions, FDA inspects a variety of packaged foods to ensure that they are properly labeled.

What is cross-contact?

Cross-contact is the inadvertent introduction of an allergen into a product. It is generally the result of environmental exposure during processing or handling, which may occur when multiple foods are produced in the same facility. It may occur due to use of the same processing line, through the misuse of rework, as the result of ineffective cleaning, or from the generation of dust or aerosols containing an allergen.

Are mislabeled food products removed from the market?

Yes. A food product that contains an undeclared allergen may be subject to recall. In addition, a food product that is not properly labeled may be misbranded and subject to seizure and removed from the market place.

The number of recalls due to undeclared allergens (8 of the most common allergens only) remained steady between 1999 and 2001. In 2002, recall actions nearly doubled, rising from 68 to 116. This rise may be attributed to the increased awareness of food allergies among consumers and manufacturers and increased attention from FDA inspectors to issues related to food allergy in manufacturing plants.

Gluten

Why is there a concern about gluten?

Gluten describes a group of proteins found in certain grains (wheat, barley, and rye.) It is of concern because people with celiac disease cannot tolerate it. Celiac disease (also known as celiac sprue) is a chronic digestive disease that damages the small intestine and interferes with absorption of nutrients from food. Recent findings estimate that 2 million people in the U.S. have celiac disease or about 1 in 133 people.

What does FALCPA require with regard to gluten?

FALCPA requires FDA to issue a proposed rule that will define and permit the voluntary use of the term "gluten free" on the labeling of foods by August 2006 and a final rule no later than August 2008.

What has FDA done in response to the FALCPA mandate?

FDA held a public meeting in August 2005 to obtain expert comment and consultation from stakeholders to help FDA develop a regulation to define and permit the voluntary use on food labeling of the term "gluten-free" (Public Meeting On: Gluten-Free Food Labeling). The meeting focused on food manufacturing, analytical methods, and consumer issues related to reduced levels of gluten in food.

Advice for Consumers

How can I avoid foods to which I'm allergic?

FDA advises consumers to work with health care providers to find out what food(s) can cause an allergic reaction. In addition, consumers who are allergic to major food allergens should read the ingredient statement on food products to determine if products contain a major allergen. A "Contains _____ " statement, if present on a label, can also be used to determine if the food contains a major food allergen.

But I don't understand what some of the terms mean. How will I know what they are?

FALCPA was designed to improve food labeling information so that consumers who suffer from food allergies—especially children and their caregivers—will be able to recognize the presence of an ingredient that they must avoid. For example, if a product contains the milk-derived protein casein, the product's label would have to use the term "milk" in addition to the term "casein" so that those with milk allergies would clearly understand the presence of an allergen they need to avoid.

What about food prepared in restaurants? How will I know that the food I ordered does not contain an ingredient to which I am allergic?

FALCPA only applies to packaged FDA-regulated foods. However, FDA advises consumers who are allergic to particular foods to ask questions about ingredients and preparation when eating at restaurants or any place outside the consumer's home.

How will FALCPA apply to foods purchased at bakeries, food kiosks at the mall, and carry out restaurants?

FALCPA's labeling requirements extend to retail and food-service establishments that package, label, and offer products for human consumption. However, FALCPA's labeling requirements do not apply to foods that are placed in a wrapper or container in response to a consumer's order—such as the paper or box used to provide a sandwich ordered by a consumer.

Section 24.2

Finding Food Allergens Where They Shouldn't Be

Text in this section is excerpted from "Finding Food Allergens Where They Shouldn't Be," U.S. Food and Drug Administration (FDA), October 23, 2014.

If you're allergic to a food ingredient, you probably look for it on the food product's label. But some labels may not be as reliable as they should be. In fact, allergens not listed on the label, referred to as "undeclared allergens," are the leading cause of food recalls requested by the U.S. Food and Drug Administration (FDA).

FDA is working on three fronts to reduce the number of such recalls: by researching the causes of these errors; working with industry on best practices; and developing new ways to test for the presence of allergens.

Federal law requires that labels of FDA-regulated foods marketed in the U.S. identify major food allergens. In some people, these allergens—milk, eggs, fish, crustacean shellfish, tree nuts, wheat, peanuts, and soybeans—can cause potentially life-threatening reactions. A food product with a label that omits required allergen information is misbranded and can be seized by FDA. However, firms generally recall such food products from the marketplace voluntarily.

Help Report Food-Allergic Reactions

The first step is learning more about the problem. Steven Gendel, Ph.D., FDA food allergen coordinator, emphasizes that consumers can help by reporting food-allergic reactions to the FDA consumer complaint coordinator in their district. "We look at every complaint to determine the appropriate course of action," he says.

"What we're trying to learn," Gendel explains, "is what foods are most affected, what allergens are most involved, and how labeling errors might have happened. Those answers will help us to reduce the number of recalls for undeclared allergens."

Recalled Foods and the Allergens Involved

Looking for these answers, Gendel has sifted through FDA-collected recall data and found some clear trends.

For example, from September 2009 to September 2012, about one-third of foods reported to FDA as serious health risks involved undeclared allergens. The five food types most often involved in food allergen recalls were bakery products; snack foods; candy; dairy products and dressings (such as salad dressings, sauces and gravies).

The allergens most often involved in recalls were milk, wheat and soy. Consumers can find out what products have been recalled recently at FDA's website and at the Food Allergy Research and Education (FARE) website, as well as from the companies that make the products.

Within the candy category, there were many reports of undeclared milk in products containing dark chocolate. For example undeclared milk led to several recalls for chocolate-coated snack bars with labels that the products were "dairy-free" or "vegan." "This represented a significant risk for milk-allergic consumers," says Gendel.

The Source of the Problem

Recall data show that such labeling errors occur most commonly because of the use of the wrong label. This may happen when similar products made with different ingredients, including allergens, are sold in look-alike packages.

Gendel also found mistakes associated with the use of new technologies, such as computerization and the ability to print labels directly on packaging. This can save costs but also create new opportunities for errors.

The data suggest that food allergen recalls can be reduced through improved industry awareness and simple changes in the way packages, labels and ingredients are handled and tracked within production facilities.

FDA Exploring New Ways to Test for Allergens

Of course, keeping unwanted allergens out of food requires good methods for detecting them.

The most common test used worldwide is the enzyme-linked immunosorbent assay (ELISA), which uses antibodies (parts of the immune system that help neutralize viruses and bacteria) and spectroscopic detection to test for allergens.

Mark Ross, Ph.D., an FDA chemist, says ELISA is the standard test because it is easy to use, relatively low-cost, and has been improved by scientists over time. But ELISA, like similar tests used in medicine, can produce false positive results, so backup methods are needed. In addition, some allergens are so similar that scientists need another test besides ELISA to tell them apart.

Ross is working with other FDA researchers to develop methods for analyzing allergens based on mass spectrometry, a technology that more effectively determines the allergen protein content of a complex mixture of proteins, fats, sugars, and chemicals in a food.

Chapter 25

Tips on Avoiding Food Allergy Reactions

Chapter Contents

Section 25.1

A Food Diary Can Reduce Risk of Reactions

"A Food Diary Can Reduce Risk of
Reactions," © 2016 Omnigraphics, Inc.
Reviewed November 2015.

Food allergies have emerged as a growing health crisis. They affect 15 million people in the United States, including 4 percent of adults and 8 percent of children, and account for 200,000 emergency room visits per year. When someone develops a food allergy, the body's immune system overreacts to the allergenic food by releasing histamines and other chemicals into the bloodstream. This process can cause a number of different symptoms to occur, such as hives, rashes, nasal congestion, breathing difficulties, diarrhea, nausea, and vomiting. Although some people experience only minor symptoms, food allergies can also trigger anaphylaxis, a severe, whole-body allergic reaction that is potentially fatal.

It is not always easy to identify which food can trigger an allergic reaction. For some people the symptoms could be obviously related to a particular food, and for others the symptoms could appear mysteriously, making the allergen difficult to pinpoint. Not even diagnostic tests conducted by experts can precisely recognize food allergens in all cases. To help people identify the cause and manage their food allergy on an everyday basis, one of the best methods is to keep a written record of everything they eat.

Keeping a Food Diary

A food journal should be maintained on an everyday basis and record the details of every meal, beverage, snack, and dietary supplement. In addition, each entry should include any noticeable symptoms after a meal, even just a general feeling of indigestion or fatigue. The details that should be noted in the food diary include the symptoms experienced, whether they were mild or severe, and their duration. Other information that could be included in the journal include any medications taken; any exposure to environmental allergens such as pollen, dust mites, mold, perfumes, latex, or animal dander; any other illnesses or conditions experienced, such as the common cold, hepatitis, and insect bites; and any symptoms that were a result of physical stimuli, such as heat, cold, pressure, exercise, and extreme sun exposure.

It is important to note that a food item may contain a number of ingredients. Any kind of ingredient may cause an allergic reaction, which could range from mild to severe. If the symptoms occur while eating in a place other than home—for instance, at a restaurant—it would be helpful to talk to the chef and ask for a list of all the ingredients used in the food consumed.

If the allergic reaction is due to processed or pre-packaged food, the label should be saved and the quantity consumed should be noted.

All the information noted in the food diary can help an allergist make an informed diagnosis of the cause of allergy symptoms and determine the best course of treatment. A number of helpful food journal applications are available for mobile phone and tablet users to keep track of their allergies. Identifying and avoiding food culprits can help people maintain their health wisely and enjoy a better quality of life.

Reference:

"Identifying Your Food Intolerances." Allergy UK, October 2012.

Section 25.2

Working with a Dietitian if Your Child Has Food Allergies

"Working with a Dietitian if Your Child Has Food
Allergies," © 2016 Omnigraphics, Inc.
Reviewed November 2015.

Learning that a child has food allergies can be frightening for parents. Once an allergist has diagnosed food allergies, many parents feel overwhelmed by the challenge of eliminating allergenic foods while also providing their child with healthy, nutritious meals. Without proper meal planning and supplementation, the dietary restrictions caused by food allergies can affect nutrient intake and potentially harm a child's growth, development, and future health.

Up to 90 percent of food-related allergic reactions in the United States can be traced to eight foods: cow's milk, eggs, wheat, soy, peanuts, tree nuts, fish, and shellfish. Yet these foods are high in vitamins, minerals, and other important nutrients. Nuts, for instance, are rich in vitamin E, niacin, manganese, magnesium, and chromium. As a result, at least 25 percent of children with food allergies experience vitamin and mineral deficiencies.

When certain foods must be eliminated from a child's diet, parents need to find ways to replace the nutrients that they provide. Many parents find it helpful to work with a registered dietitian in order to create meal plans that are appetizing and nutritious while also eliminating allergens. Dietitians can help ease parental anxiety by providing individualized education about how to avoid certain foods and substitute safe alternatives. They can also help families ensure that the child with food allergies receives adequate nutrition to promote growth and development. Finally, a registered dietitian can devise an action plan to help families cope with situations in which the child might encounter allergens.

Choosing a Qualified Dietitian

Training for dietitians in the United States includes four years of college to obtain a bachelor's degree in nutrition and dietetics, followed by a stipulated period of internship or professional practice. Dietitians are also required to pass a registration examination conducted by the Commission on Dietetic Registration before they can become a Registered Dietitian (RD). Many dietitians specialize in certain areas by working under other professional dietitians. They also keep abreast with the latest developments in the field by attending seminars and workshops regularly.

Parents of children with food allergies who are interested in working with a dietitian should first assess the person's qualifications and experience. Experts advise asking prospective dietitians about their education, training, and professional memberships. It may also be helpful to know how long they have treated patients with food allergies and what specialized training they have undertaken to gain proficiency in treating food allergies. The *American Dietetic Association* maintains a searchable list of registered dietitians on its Web site, www.eatright.org.

How the Dietitian Can Help

During the initial consultation with parents of a child with food allergies, a dietitian is likely to ask what the child eats on a regular basis, what foods have been identified as allergens, and what symptoms the child has experienced. This information will help the dietitian develop a meal plan for the child that includes safe alternative foods and provides all the nutrients the child needs to grow and thrive. The dietitian's goal is to provide suggestions for healthy, nutritious meals that offer a variety of food choices that the child will enjoy.

The dietitian can also provide parents with expert advice on how to avoid allergenic foods, from reading product labels to recognizing places where cross-contamination or accidental exposure could occur—such as school classrooms, restaurants, movie theaters, or airplanes. The dietitian can also give parents an extensive list of safe alternatives that they can substitute for allergy-inducing foods in meals or recipes.

Many dietitians ask families to keep a diary of the child's daily meals—noting any allergy symptoms observed—in order to facilitate meal planning. The dietitian will also monitor the child's growth and development through regular follow-up sessions and suggest dietary changes over time to meet their nutritional needs. Since children often outgrow allergies to certain foods, the dietitian can watch for these changes and help parents reintroduce the foods in a gradual and safe manner.

References:

1. Bowers, Elizabeth Shimer. "Can a Dietitian Help with Children's Food Allergies?" Everyday Health, May 27, 2015.

2. Feuling, Mary Beth. "The Balancing Act: Nutrition and Food Allergy." Children's Hospital of Wisconsin, October 2015.

Part Four

Airborne, Chemical, and Other Environmental Allergy Triggers

Chapter 26

Environmental Allergies

An allergic reaction is a specific response of the body's immune system to a normally harmless substance called an allergen. A variety of environmental allergens, such as pollen and animal dander, can trigger allergic reactions in the nose (allergic rhinitis, or hay fever) and in the lung (asthma). Not all reasons for susceptibility to environmental allergies are understood, although a family history of allergies is an important risk factor. National Institute of Allergy and Infectious Diseases (NIAID) supports and conducts research aimed at understanding how allergic rhinitis and asthma develop and identifying new strategies to diagnose, treat, and prevent environmental allergies.

Understanding Environmental Allergies

Causes of Environmental Allergies

Both genetic and environmental factors can contribute to the development of allergies. Allergic rhinitis (hay fever) and asthma are triggered by exposure to airborne allergens. Sources of allergens include pollens, animal dander, house dust mites, molds, cockroaches, and rodents.

Text in this chapter is excerpted from "Environmental Allergies," National Institute of Allergy and Infectious Diseases (NIAID), April 22, 2015.

Pollen

Each spring, summer, and fall, plants release tiny pollen grains to fertilize other plants of the same species.

People with allergic rhinitis or asthma aggravated by pollen have symptoms only for the period or season when the pollen grains to which they are allergic are in the air. For example, in most parts of the United States, grass pollen is present during the spring. Allergic rhinitis caused by pollen, also called "seasonal allergic rhinitis," affects approximately 7 percent of adults and 9 percent of children in the United States. However, not all seasonal symptoms are due to pollen. Rhinovirus, the cause of the common cold, causes runny noses and triggers asthma attacks in the fall and spring. It is not always easy to figure out whether allergy or a common cold is the cause of these symptoms, although some clues can help tell the two apart. For example, a fever suggests a cold rather than an allergy, and symptoms lasting more than two weeks suggest allergies rather than a cold.

Most of the pollens that generate allergic reactions come from trees, weeds, and grasses. These plants make small, light, and dry pollen grains that are carried by wind. Among North American plants, grasses are the most common cause of allergy. Ragweed is a main culprit among the weeds, but other major sources of weed pollen include sagebrush, pigweed, lamb's quarters, and tumbleweed. Certain species of trees, including birch, cedar, and oak, also produce highly allergenic pollen. Plants that are pollinated with the help of insects, such as roses and ornamental flowering trees like cherry and pear trees, usually do not cause allergic rhinitis or asthma.

A pollen count, often reported by local weather broadcasts or allergy websites, is a measure of how much pollen is in the air. Pollen counts tend to be highest early in the morning on warm, dry, breezy days and lowest during chilly, wet periods. Although pollen counts reflect the past 24 hours, they are useful as a general guide for when it may be wise to stay indoors with windows closed to avoid contact with a certain pollen.

Mold

Molds are found both indoors and outdoors. Outdoor molds are carried by the wind, like pollens. There are many different types of molds, but only some seem to cause health problems. High levels of the mold *Alternaria* have been associated with severe asthma in the late summer in the upper Midwest of the United States. *Aspergillus*, another type of mold, is associated with a severe and chronic form of asthma.

Indoor molds may cause allergy as well as other health effects. Some people report not feeling well when living in a moldy or damp environment, even if they do not have allergies. However, there has been little research examining the health effects of indoor molds.

Other Indoor Allergens

Allergic rhinitis and asthma also can be triggered by exposure to house dust, for example, during household chores such as vacuuming or sweeping. Dust is a mixture of substances and may contain allergens from house dust mites, pets, mold, cockroaches, and rodents. Cockroach and mouse allergy are common in low-income, urban areas and are key causes of asthma-related illness among children, as NIAID-funded research has shown. For example, NIAID-supported scientists reported that the combination of cockroach allergy and exposure to the insects is an important cause of asthma-related illness and hospitalizations among inner-city children.

While exposure to animals like cats and dogs can cause symptoms of allergic rhinitis and asthma in sensitive people, exposure in early life may have a protective effect. NIAID-funded scientists found that exposure to dust from homes with dogs may protect against allergies and asthma.

Symptoms of Environmental Allergies

Symptoms of allergic rhinitis and asthma include the following:

- Runny nose and mucus production
- Sneezing
- Itchy nose, eyes, ears, and mouth
- Stuffy nose
- Red and watery eyes
- Swelling around the eyes
- Coughing
- Wheezing
- Chest tightness
- Shortness of breath

Diagnosis of Environmental Allergies

A healthcare professional may perform skin, blood, or allergy component tests to help diagnose environmental allergies.

Skin Tests

A skin prick test can detect if a person is sensitive to a specific allergen. Being "sensitive" means that the immune system produces a type of antibody called IgE against that allergen. IgE attaches to specialized cells called mast cells. This happens throughout the body, including the lining of the nose and the airways, as well as the skin.

During a skin prick test, a healthcare professional uses a piece of plastic to prick the skin on the arm or back and place a tiny amount of allergen extract just below the skin's surface. In sensitive people, the allergen binds to IgE on mast cells in the skin and causes them to release histamine and other chemicals that produce itching, redness, and minor swelling.

A positive skin test to a particular allergen does not necessarily indicate that a person has allergic rhinitis or asthma caused by that allergen. Up to 50 percent of the U.S. population may have at least one positive skin test to a common allergen, but less than half of those people have allergic rhinitis or asthma. Therefore, healthcare professionals often will try to match skin test results with the kind of allergen exposures person may have had.

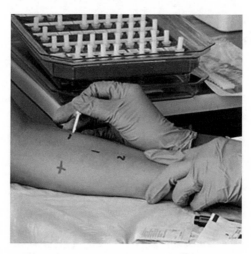

Figure 26.1. *Skin Prick Test*

A person receiving a skin prick test. A number of allergens can be tested with a skin prick test, including those from cockroach, cat, and ragweed and grass pollens.

Blood Tests

Instead of performing a skin test, doctors may take a blood sample to measure levels of allergen-specific IgE antibodies. Most people who are sensitive to a particular allergen will have IgE antibodies detectable by both skin and blood tests.

As with skin testing, a positive blood test to an allergen does not necessarily mean that a person's symptoms are caused by that allergen.

Allergy Component Tests

One reason why a positive skin or blood test does not always indicate that a person's symptoms are caused by a particular allergen is that allergens comprise many different components, some of which are more likely to cause symptoms than others. For example, birch tree pollen contains proteins, sugars, and fats. IgE antibodies to birch pollen proteins are likely to cause allergic reactions, but IgE antibodies to the sugars in birch pollen, although common, are less likely to cause allergic reactions. Allergy component tests are blood tests that can determine exactly which component of an allergen the IgE in a person's blood recognizes. This can help a health professional determine whether the allergen is likely to cause symptoms.

Treatments for Environmental Allergies

A variety of medications can help control allergic rhinitis and asthma symptoms. Some people with environmental allergies receive immunotherapy, a long-term treatment that aims to change the course of allergic disease by modifying the body's immune response to allergens.

Medications To Treat Allergic Rhinitis

Certain over-the-counter and prescription medicines may help reduce the severity of allergic rhinitis symptoms.

Antihistamines

Antihistamines, which are taken by mouth or as a nasal spray, can relieve sneezing and itching in the nose and eyes. They reduce runny nose and, to a lesser extent, nasal stuffiness. Some older antihistamines can cause side effects such as drowsiness and loss of alertness and coordination. Effective, newer antihistamines cause fewer or no side effects.

Nasal Corticosteroids

Nasal corticosteroid sprays are anti-inflammatory medicines that help block allergic reactions. They are widely considered the most effective medication for allergic rhinitis and can reduce all symptoms, including nasal congestion. Unlike corticosteroids taken by mouth or as an injection, nasal corticosteroids have few side effects. Combining a nasal antihistamine with a nasal corticosteroid appears to be more effective than either of the sprays alone. However, it is not clear that taking an oral antihistamine with a nasal corticosteroid is helpful.

Decongestants

Oral and nasal decongestants help shrink the lining of the nasal passages, relieving nasal stuffiness. Decongestant nose drops and sprays are intended for short-term use. When used for more than a few days, these medicines may lead to even more congestion and swelling inside the nose. Doctors may recommend using decongestants along with an antihistamine because antihistamines do not have a strong decongestant effect.

Leukotriene Receptor Antagonists

Leukotriene receptor antagonists, such as the prescription drug montelukast, block the action of leukotrienes, chemical messengers involved in allergic reactions.

Cromolyn Sodium

Cromolyn sodium is a nasal spray that blocks the release of chemicals that cause allergy symptoms. The drug causes few side effects but must be taken four times a day.

Medications to Treat Asthma

Asthma medications are divided into two categories: relievers and controllers. Relievers are used for asthma attacks and not for long-term treatment of the disease. Controllers are used to prevent asthma symptoms. For controllers to work properly, people with asthma have to use them consistently, even when feeling well.

Relievers

Short-Acting Beta-Adrenergic Agonists

Short-acting beta-agonists (SABAs) such as albuterol can provide immediate symptom relief that lasts four to six hours. They do not decrease allergic inflammation but instead relax the muscles around the airway that tighten when an allergic person is exposed to an allergen or other asthma trigger. For people who rarely experience asthma attacks, SABAs may be used as the only medicine on an as-needed basis. People who are taking controller medicines often use SABAs for symptom relief.

Oral Corticosteroids

Oral corticosteroids such as prednisone, methyl prednisolone, and dexamethasone are typically used to treat severe asthma attacks. People with very severe asthma may use corticosteroids as controller medications, taking them daily or every other day. When used long-term at high doses, oral corticosteroids can cause many side effects, including weight gain, high blood pressure, diabetes, brittle bones, thinning skin, muscle weakness, and cataracts. Doctors who treat people with severe asthma usually will use various combinations of medications to try to reduce the corticosteroid dose.

Controllers

Inhaled Corticosteroids

Inhaled corticosteroids are effective at improving quality of life and preventing severe asthma attacks in people with persistent asthma. These medications can sometimes cause yeast infections in the mouth. If given in very high doses for long periods, they may cause some of the side effects typical of oral corticosteroids, such as brittle bones and an increased risk of cataracts. People with moderate to severe asthma may take inhaled corticosteroids along with other drugs called long-acting beta-adrenergic agonists.

Leukotriene Receptor Antagonists and 5-Lipoxygenase Inhibitors

Leukotriene receptor antagonists (LTRAs) block the action of leukotrienes, chemical messengers involved in allergic reactions. They may be used alone to treat mild asthma or along with an inhaled corticosteroid to treat moderate asthma, as well as to treat allergic rhinitis. People who have both mild asthma and allergic rhinitis can take an LTRA to treat both conditions.

A related medication, called zileuton, prevents leukotriene production by blocking an enzyme called 5-lipoxygenase. Zileuton is only used for severe asthma, and evidence suggests that it may be particularly useful for people with asthma who have reactions to aspirin, a syndrome called aspirin-exacerbated respiratory disease, or AERD.

Long-Acting Beta-Adrenergic Agonists

In combination with an inhaled corticosteroid, long-acting beta-agonists (LABAs) are effective for asthma control. LABAs, the effects of which last for 12 hours, typically are not used alone because some studies have suggested that LABAs can be harmful if used without an inhaled corticosteroid.

Cromolyn Sodium

Doctors may recommend cromolyn sodium to treat mild asthma in young children. Liquid cromolyn sodium is placed in a mist-generating machine called a nebulizer, and children breathe in the mist.

Omalizumab

The U.S. Food and Drug Administration (FDA) has approved the injectable medicine omalizumab to treat allergic asthma. Omalizumab works by binding to IgE, the antibody responsible for allergies, and removing it from the body. Omalizumab can prevent severe episodes of asthma in people whose asthma is not adequately controlled by other medicines.

Chapter 27

Pollen Allergy

Chapter Contents

Section 27.1

What Is Pollen Allergy?

Text in this section is excerpted from "Pollen," National Institute of
Environmental Health Sciences (NIEHS), April 24, 2015.

Ragweed Pollen

Ragweed and other weeds such as curly dock, lambs quarters, pigweed, plantain, sheep sorrel and sagebrush are some of the most pro-
lific producers of pollen allergens.

Although the ragweed pollen season runs from August to November,
ragweed pollen levels usually peak in mid-September in many areas
in the country.

In addition, pollen counts are highest between 5:00 and 10:00 a.m.
and on dry, hot, and windy days.

Preventive Strategies

- Avoid the outdoors between 5:00–10:00 a.m. Save outside activities for late afternoon or after a heavy rain, when pollen levels
  are lower.

- Keep windows in your home and car closed to lower exposure
  to pollen. To keep cool, use air conditioners and avoid using
  window and attic fans.

- Be aware that pollen can also be transported indoors on people
  and pets.

- Dry your clothes in an automatic dryer rather than hanging
  them outside. Otherwise pollen can collect on clothing and be
  carried indoors.

Grass Pollen

As with tree pollen, grass pollen is regional as well as seasonal. In
addition, grass pollen levels can be affected by temperature, time of
day and rain.

Of the 1,200 species of grass that grow in North America, only a small percentage of these cause allergies. The most common grasses that can cause allergies are:

- Bermuda grass
- Johnson grass
- Kentucky bluegrass
- Orchard grass
- Sweet vernal grass
- Timothy grass

Preventive Strategies

- If you have a grass lawn, have someone else do the mowing. If you must mow the lawn yourself, wear a mask.
- Keep grass cut short.
- Choose ground covers that don't produce much pollen, such as Irish moss, bunch, and dichondra.
- Avoid the outdoors between 5:00–10:00 a.m. Save outside activities for late afternoon or after a heavy rain, when pollen levels are lower.
- Keep windows in your home and car closed to lower exposure to pollen. To keep cool, use air conditioners and avoid using window and attic fans.
- Be aware that pollen can also be transported indoors on people and pets.
- Dry your clothes in an automatic dryer rather than hanging them outside. Otherwise pollen can collect on clothing and be carried indoors.

Tree Pollen

Trees can aggravate your allergy whether or not they are on your property, since trees release large amounts of pollen that can be distributed miles away from the original source.

Trees are the earliest pollen producers, releasing their pollen as early as January in the Southern states and as late as May or June in the Northern states.

Most allergies are specific to one type of tree such as:

- catalpa
- elm
- hickory
- olive
- pecan
- sycamore
- walnut

or to the male cultivar of certain trees. The female of these species are totally pollen-free:

- ash
- box elder
- cottonwood
- date palm
- maple (red)
- maple (silver)
- Phoenix palm
- poplar
- willow

Some people, though, do show cross-reactivity among trees in the alder, beech, birch and oak family, and the juniper and cedar family.

Preventive Strategies

- If you buy trees for your yard, look for species that do not aggravate allergies such as crape myrtle, dogwood, fig, fir, palm, pear, plum, redbud and redwood trees or the female cultivars of ash, box elder, cottonwood, maple, palm, poplar or willow trees.

- Avoid the outdoors between 5:00–10:00 a.m. Save outside activities for late afternoon or after a heavy rain, when pollen levels are lower.

- Keep windows in your home and car closed to lower exposure to pollen. To keep cool, use air conditioners and avoid using window and attic fans.

- Be aware that pollen can also be transported indoors on people and pets.

- Dry your clothes in an automatic dryer rather than hanging them outside. Otherwise pollen can collect on clothing and be carried indoors.

Section 27.2

Ragweed Allergy: The Most Common Type of Pollen Allergy

Text in this section is excerpted from "Ragweed Pollen Season," U.S. Environmental Protection Agency (EPA), May 2014.

Background

Allergies are a major public health concern, with hay fever (congestion, runny nose, itchy eyes) accounting for more than 13 million visits to physicians' offices and other medical facilities every year. One of the most common environmental allergens is ragweed, which can cause hay fever and trigger asthma attacks, especially in children and the elderly. An estimated 26 percent of all Americans are sensitive to ragweed.

Ragweed plants mature in mid-summer and produce small flowers that generate pollen. Ragweed pollen season usually peaks in late summer and early fall, but these plants often continue to produce pollen until the first frost. A single ragweed plant can produce up to a billion pollen grains in one season, and these grains can be carried long distances by the wind.

Climate change can affect pollen allergies in several ways. Warmer spring temperatures cause some plants to start producing pollen earlier, while warmer fall temperatures extend the growing season for other plants, such as ragweed. Warmer temperatures and increased carbon dioxide concentrations also enable ragweed and other plants to produce more pollen. This means that many locations could experience longer allergy seasons and higher pollen counts as a result of climate change.

About the Indicator

The indicator (Figure 27.1) shows changes in the length of the ragweed pollen season in 11 cities in the central United States and Canada. These locations were selected as part of a study that looked at trends in pollen season at sites similar in elevation, but across a

253

range of latitudes from south to north. At each location, air samples have been collected and examined since at least the 1990s as part of a national allergy monitoring network. Pollen spores are counted and identified using microscopes.

Pollen counts from each station have been analyzed to determine the start and end dates of each year's ragweed pollen season. Because the length of ragweed season naturally varies from year to year, statistical techniques have been used to determine the average rate of change over time. This indicator shows the total change in season length from 1995 to 2013, which was determined by multiplying the average annual rate of change by the number of years in the period.

Key Points

- Since 1995, ragweed pollen season has grown longer at 10 of the 11 locations studied (see Figure 27.1).

- The increase in ragweed season length generally becomes more pronounced from south to north. Ragweed season increased by 27 days in Saskatoon, Saskatchewan; 22 days in Winnipeg, Manitoba; 21 days in Minneapolis, Minnesota; and 19 days in Fargo, North Dakota (see Figure 27.1). This trend is consistent with many other observations showing that climate is changing more rapidly at higher latitudes.

- The trends in Figure 27.1 are strongly related to changes in the length of the frost-free season and the timing of the first fall frost. Northern areas have seen fall frosts happening later than they used to, with the delay in first frost closely matching the increase in pollen season. Meanwhile, some southern stations have experienced only a modest change in frost-free season length since 1995.

Indicator Notes

This indicator is based on data from a limited number of cities in the central states and provinces. These cities cover a broad range from north to south, however, which allows researchers to establish a clear connection between pollen season changes and latitude.

Many factors can influence year-to-year changes in pollen season, including typical local and regional variations in temperature and

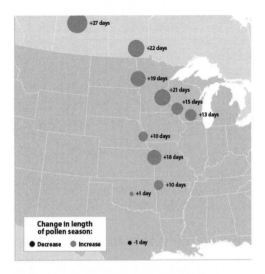

Figure 27.1. *Change in the length of Ragweed Pollen Season, 1995–2013*
This figure shows how the length of ragweed pollen season changed at 11
locations in the central United States and Canada between 1995 and 2013.
Gray circles represent a longer pollen season; the black circle represents a
shorter season. Larger circles indicate larger changes.

Data source: Ziska et al., 2014

precipitation, extreme events such as floods and droughts, and changes
in plant diversity. Adding more years of data would provide a better
picture of long-term trends, but widespread data were not available
prior to 1995.

This indicator does not show how the intensity of ragweed pollen
season (pollen counts) might also be changing.

Section 27.3

Ragweed Therapy Offers Allergy Sufferers Longer Relief

Text in this section is excerpted from "FDA Approves Ragwitek for Short Ragweed Pollen Allergies," U.S. Food and Drug Administration (FDA), April 17, 2014.

Ragwitek approved for short ragweed pollen allergies

The U.S. Food and Drug Administration(FDA) approved Ragwitek, the first allergen extract administered under the tongue (sublingually) to treat short ragweed pollen induced allergic rhinitis (hay fever), with or without conjunctivitis (eye inflammation), in adults 18 years through 65 years of age.

Ragwitek contains an extract from short ragweed (*Ambrosia artemisiifolia*) pollen. It is a tablet that is taken once daily by placing it sublingually, where it rapidly dissolves. Treatment with Ragwitek is started 12 weeks before the start of ragweed pollen season and continued throughout the season. The first dose is taken in a health care professional's office where the patient is to be observed for at least 30 minutes for potential adverse reactions. After the first dose, patients can take Ragwitek at home.

The approval of Ragwitek offers millions of adults living with ragweed pollen allergies in the United States an alternative to allergy shots to help manage their disease.

Individuals with allergic rhinitis with or without conjunctivitis may experience a runny nose, repetitive sneezing, nasal itching, nasal congestion, and itchy and watery eyes. Short ragweed pollen is one of the most common seasonal allergens and is prevalent during the late summer and early fall months in most of the United States. Short ragweed pollen induced allergies are generally managed by avoiding the allergen, medications to relieve symptoms, or with allergy shots.

The safety and effectiveness of Ragwitek was evaluated in studies conducted in the United States and internationally. Safety was assessed in approximately 1,700 adults. The most commonly reported adverse reactions by patients treated with Ragwitek were itching in the mouth and ears and throat irritation. Of the 1,700 adults, about 760 were evaluated to determine effectiveness. Some patients received Ragwitek; others received an inactive substitute (placebo). The patients reported their symptoms and additional medications needed to get through the allergy season. During treatment for one ragweed pollen season, patients who received Ragwitek experienced approximately a 26 percent reduction in symptoms and the need for medications compared to those who received a placebo.

The prescribing information includes a boxed warning to inform that severe allergic reactions, some of which can be life-threatening, can occur. Ragwitek also has a medication guide for distribution to the patient.

Chapter 28

Household Allergens: Animal Dander, Cockroach, Dust Mite, and Mold Allergy

Chapter Contents

Section 28.1

Dust Mite Allergy

Text in this section is excerpted from "Dust Mites," National Institute
of Environmental Health Sciences (NIEHS), May 22, 2014.

Dust Mites

Dust mites are tiny microscopic relatives of the spider and live on
mattresses, bedding, upholstered furniture, carpets, and curtains.

These tiny creatures feed on the flakes of skin that people and pets
shed daily and they thrive in warm and humid environments.

No matter how clean a home is, dust mites cannot be totally eliminated. However, the number of mites can be reduced by following the
suggestions below.

Preventive Strategies

- Use a dehumidifier or air conditioner to maintain relative
  humidity at about 50% or below.

- Encase your mattress and pillows in dust-proof or allergen
  impermeable covers (available from specialty supply mail order
  companies, bedding and some department stores).

- Wash all bedding and blankets once a week in hot water (at
  least 130–140°F) to kill dust mites. Non-washable bedding can
  be frozen overnight to kill dust mites.

- Replace wool or feathered bedding with synthetic materials and
  traditional stuffed animals with washable ones.

- If possible, replace wall-to-wall carpets in bedrooms with bare
  floors (linoleum, tile or wood) and remove fabric curtains and
  upholstered furniture.

- Use a damp mop or rag to remove dust. Never use a dry cloth
  since this just stirs up mite allergens.

- Use a vacuum cleaner with either a double-layered microfilter bag or a HEPA filter to trap allergens that pass through a vacuum's exhaust.

- Wear a mask while vacuuming to avoid inhaling allergens, and stay out of the vacuumed area for 20 minutes to allow any dust and allergens to settle after vacuuming.

Section 28.2

Cockroach Allergy

Text in this section is excerpted from "Cockroaches," National Institute of Environmental Health Sciences (NIEHS), May 22, 2014.

Cockroaches

Cockroaches are one of the most common and allergenic of indoor pests.

Recent studies have found a strong association between the presence of cockroaches and increases in the severity of asthma symptoms in individuals who are sensitive to cockroach allergens.

These pests are common even in the cleanest of crowded urban areas and older dwellings. They are found in all types of neighborhoods.

The proteins found in cockroach saliva are particularly allergenic but the body and droppings of cockroaches also contain allergenic proteins.

Preventive Strategies

- Keep food and garbage in closed, tight-lidded containers. Never leave food out in the kitchen.

- Do not leave out pet food or dirty food bowls.

- Eliminate water sources that attract these pests, such as leaky faucets and drain pipes.

- Mop the kitchen floor and wash countertops at least once a week.

- Plug up crevices around the house through which cockroaches can enter.

- Limit the spread of food around the house and especially keep food out of bedrooms.

- Use bait stations and other environmentally safe pesticides to reduce cockroach infestation.

Section 28.3

Animal Dander Allergy

Text in this section is excerpted from "Pets & Animals," National Institute of Environmental Health Sciences (NIEHS), May 22, 2014.

Pets and Animals

Many people think animal allergies are caused by the fur or feathers of their pet. In fact, allergies are actually aggravated by:

- proteins secreted by oil glands and shed as dander

- proteins in saliva (which stick to fur when animals lick themselves)

- aerosolized urine from rodents and guinea pigs

Keep in mind that you can sneeze with and without your pet being present. Although an animal may be out of sight, their allergens are not. This is because pet allergens are carried on very small particles. As a result pet allergens can remain circulating in the air and remain on carpets and furniture for weeks and months after a pet is gone. Allergens may also be present in public buildings, schools, etc. where there are no pets.

Preventive Strategies

- Remove pets from your home if possible.

- If pet removal is not possible, keep them out of bedrooms and confined to areas without carpets or upholstered furniture.

- If possible, bathe pets weekly to reduce the amount of allergens.

- Wear a dust mask and gloves when near rodents.

- After playing with your pet, wash your hands and clean your clothes to remove pet allergens.

- Avoid contact with soiled litter cages.

- Dust often with a damp cloth.

Section 28.4

Mold Allergy

Text in this section is excerpted from "Mold," National Institute of Environmental Health Sciences (NIEHS), May 26, 2015.

Mold

Molds are microscopic organisms that play an important role in the breakdown of plant and animal matter. Outdoors, molds can be found in shady, damp areas, or places where leaves or other vegetation is decomposing. Indoor molds can grow on virtually any surface, as long as moisture, oxygen, and organic material are present. When molds are disturbed, they release tiny cells called spores into the surrounding air.

What Are the Most Common Forms of Mold?

According to the Centers for Disease Control and Prevention, the most common indoor molds are:

- Cladosporium

- Penicillium

- Aspergillus

- Alternaria

- Stachybotrys chartarum (also known as black mold)

What Are Some of the Health Effects Associated with Mold Exposure?

Symptoms stemming from mold spore exposure may include:

- Nasal and sinus congestion
- Eye irritation
- Blurred vision
- Sore throat
- Chronic cough
- Skin rash

After contact with certain molds, individuals with chronic respiratory disease may have difficulty breathing, and people who are immunocompromised may be at increased risk for lung infection. A study conducted by NIEHS-funded scientists shows that mold exposure during the first year of life may increase the risk of childhood asthma.

What Can I Do to Get Rid of Mold in My Home?

According to the U.S. Department of Housing and Urban Development (HUD), residents can do any of the following to prevent, and or get rid of, mold in their homes:

- Keep your house clean and dry.
- Fix water problems, such as roof leaks, wet basements, and leaking pipes or faucets.
- Make sure your home is well ventilated, and always use ventilation fans in bathrooms and kitchens.
- If possible, keep humidity in your house below 50 percent, by using an air conditioner or dehumidifier.
- Avoid using carpeting in areas of the home that may become wet, such as kitchens, bathrooms, and basements.
- Dry floor mats regularly.

Chapter 29

Air Quality

Air pollution comes from many different sources: stationary sources such as factories, power plants, and smelters and smaller sources such as dry cleaners and degreasing operations; mobile sources such as cars, buses, planes, trucks, and trains; and naturally occurring sources such as windblown dust, and volcanic eruptions, all contribute to air pollution. Air Quality can be affected in many ways by the pollution emitted from these sources. These pollution sources can also emit a wide variety of pollutants. The U.S. Environmental Protection Agency (EPA) has these pollutants classified as the six principal pollutants (or "criteria pollutants"–as they are also known). These pollutants are monitored by the EPA, as well as national, state and local organizations.

The Clean Air Act provides the principal framework for national, state, and local efforts to protect air quality. Under the Clean Air Act, EPA's Office of Air Quality Planning and Standards (OAQPS) is responsible for setting standards, also known as national ambient air quality standards (NAAQS), for pollutants which are considered harmful to people and the environment. OAQPS is also responsible

Text in this chapter is excerpted from "Air Quality," U.S. Environmental Protection Agency (EPA), September 24, 2015; text from "About Air Toxics," U.S. Environmental Protection Agency (EPA), September 28, 2015; text from "Pollutants and Sources," U.S. Environmental Protection Agency (EPA), September 10, 2015; and text from "What Are the Six Common Air Pollutants?" U.S. Environmental Protection Agency (EPA), September 19, 2015.

for ensuring that these air quality standards are met, or attained (in cooperation with state, Tribal, and local governments) through national standards and strategies to control pollutant emissions from automobiles, factories, and other sources.

Finding Out if the Air We Breathe Is Clean

OAQPS is responsible for setting the National Ambient Air Quality Standards (NAAQS), which control pollutants harmful to people and the environment. There are two types of standards, primary and secondary. Primary standards protect against adverse health effects; secondary standards protect against welfare effects, such as damage to farm crops and vegetation and damage to buildings. The six criteria pollutants addressed in the NAAQS are Carbon Monoxide, Nitrogen Dioxide, Lead, Ozone (or smog), Particulate Matter, and Sulfur Dioxide. If the levels of these pollutants are higher than what is considered acceptable by U.S. Environmental Protection Agency (EPA), then the area in which the level is too high is called a nonattainment area. OAQPS monitors very closely many areas for criteria pollutants and attainment.

Through various programs, OAQPS monitors for criteria pollutants. One such program is the Ambient Air Monitoring Program. Through this program, air quality samples are collected to judge attainment of ambient air quality standards, to prevent or alleviate air pollution emergencies, to observe pollution trends throughout regions, and to evaluate the effects of urban, land-use, and transportation planning relating to air pollution. There are other important types of pollution monitoring programs; two of which are Enhanced Ozone Monitoring and Air Pollution Monitoring.

The Air Pollution Monitoring program monitors all of the six criteria pollutants. Measurements are taken to assess areas where there may be a problem, and to monitor areas that already have problems. The goal of this program is to control areas where problems exist and to try to keep other areas from becoming problem air pollution areas.

Working to Clean up the Air

In order to work towards attainment, OAQPS requires that each state containing nonattainment areas to develop a written plan for cleaning the air in those areas. The plans developed are called SIPS or state implementation plans. Through these plans, the states outline efforts that they will make to try to correct the levels of air pollution and bring their areas back into attainment.

If an area does not meet attainment, it's designated a nonattainment area. Nonattainment means that the area is not meeting the levels set in the NAAQS (National Ambient Air Quality Standards). OAQPS lists and follows closely those areas listed as nonattainment and requires that they develop plans for reaching attainment.

General Questions

What are toxic air pollutants?

Toxic air pollutants, also known as hazardous air pollutants, are those pollutants that are known or suspected to cause cancer or other serious health effects, such as reproductive effects or birth defects, or adverse environmental effects. EPA is working with state, local, and tribal governments to reduce air toxics releases of 187 pollutants to the environment. Examples of toxic air pollutants include benzene, which is found in gasoline; perchloroethylene, which is emitted from some dry cleaning facilities; and methylene chloride, which is used as a solvent and paint stripper by a number of industries. Examples of other listed air toxics include dioxin, asbestos, toluene, and metals such as cadmium, mercury, chromium, and lead compounds.

What are the health and environmental effects of toxic air pollutants?

People exposed to toxic air pollutants at sufficient concentrations and durations may have an increased chance of getting cancer or experiencing other serious health effects. These health effects can include damage to the immune system, as well as neurological, reproductive (e.g., reduced fertility), developmental, respiratory and other health problems. In addition to exposure from breathing air toxics, some toxic air pollutants such as mercury can deposit onto soils or surface waters, where they are taken up by plants and ingested by animals and are eventually magnified up through the food chain. Like humans, animals may experience health problems if exposed to sufficient quantities of air toxics over time.

Where do toxic air pollutants come from?

Most air toxics originate from human-made sources, including mobile sources (e.g., cars, trucks, buses) and stationary sources (e.g., factories, refineries, power plants), as well as indoor sources (e.g., some building materials and cleaning solvents). Some air toxics are also released from natural sources such as volcanic eruptions and forest fires.

How are people exposed to air toxics?

People are exposed to toxic air pollutants in many ways that can pose health risks, such as by:

- Breathing contaminated air.

- Eating contaminated food products, such as fish from contaminated waters; meat, milk, or eggs from animals that fed on contaminated plants; and fruits and vegetables grown in contaminated soil on which air toxics have been deposited.

- Drinking water contaminated by toxic air pollutants.

- Ingesting contaminated soil. Young children are especially vulnerable because they often ingest soil from their hands or from objects they place in their mouths.

- Touching (making skin contact with) contaminated soil, dust, or water (for example, during recreational use of contaminated water bodies).

Once toxic air pollutants enter the body, some persistent toxic air pollutants accumulate in body tissues. Predators typically accumulate even greater pollutant concentrations than their contaminated prey. As a result, people and other animals at the top of the food chain who eat contaminated fish or meat are exposed to concentrations that are much higher than the concentrations in the water, air, or soil.

Can I find out about the toxics in my community?

National Air Toxics Assessment provides emissions and health risk information on 33 air toxics that present the greatest threat to public health in the largest number of urban areas. Maps and lists are available and can be requested by state or county level.

Toxics Release Inventory includes information for the public about releases of toxic chemicals from manufacturing facilities into the environment through the air, water, and land. You can access the data by typing in your zip code.

What progress has EPA made in reducing toxic emissions?

- **Controls for industrial and commercial sources of toxics**—EPA has issued rules covering over 80 categories of major industrial sources, such as chemical plants, oil refineries, aerospace manufacturers, and steel mills, as well as categories of smaller sources, such as dry cleaners, commercial sterilizers, secondary lead smelters, and chromium electroplating facilities. These standards are projected to reduce annual air toxics emissions by about 1.5 million tons.

- **Controls for cars and trucks** — EPA and state governments (e.g., California) have reduced emissions of benzene, toluene, and other air toxics from mobile sources by requiring the use of reformulated gasoline and placing limits on tailpipe emissions. Important new controls for fuels and vehicles are expected to reduce selected motor vehicle air toxics from 1990 levels by more than 75% by 2020.

- **Indoor air** — EPA, in close cooperation with other Federal agencies and the private sector, is actively involved in efforts to better understand indoor air pollution and to reduce people's exposure to air pollutants in offices, homes, schools, and other indoor environments.

The Pollutants

Hazardous air pollutants, also known as toxic air pollutants or air toxics, are those pollutants that cause or may cause cancer or other serious health effects, such as reproductive effects or birth defects, or adverse environmental and ecological effects. EPA is required to control 187 hazardous air pollutants. Examples of toxic air pollutants include benzene, which is found in gasoline; perchlorethlyene, which is emitted from some dry cleaning facilities; and methylene chloride, which is used as a solvent and paint stripper by a number of industries. Through appropriate rulemaking, the Clean Air Act list can be modified. A current list of modifications (www3.epa.gov/ttn/atw/pollutants/atwsmod.html) is available.

The Sources

Most air toxics originate from human-made sources, including mobile sources (e.g., cars, trucks, buses) and stationary sources (e.g., factories, refineries, power plants), as well as indoor sources (e.g., building materials and activities such as cleaning). There are two types of stationary sources that generate routine emissions of air toxics:

- "Major" sources are defined as sources that emit 10 tons per year of any of the listed toxic air pollutants, or 25 tons per year of a mixture of air toxics. These sources may release air toxics from equipment leaks, when materials are transferred from one

location to another, or during discharge through emission stacks
or vents

- "Area" sources consist of smaller-size facilities that release
lesser quantities of toxic pollutants into the air. Area sources
are defined as sources that emit less than 10 tons per year of a
single air toxic, or less than 25 tons per year of a combination
of air toxics. Though emissions from individual area sources are
often relatively small, collectively their emissions can be of concern–particularly where large numbers of sources are located in
heavily populated areas.

EPA published the initial list of "source categories" in 1992
(57FR31576, July 16, 1992) and since that time has issued several revisions and updates to the list and promulgation schedule.
For each listed source category, EPA indicates whether the sources
are considered to be "major" sources or "area" sources. The 1990
Clean Air Act Amendments direct EPA to set standards for all major
sources of air toxics (and some area sources that are of particular
concern).

What are the six common air pollutants?

The Clean Air Act requires EPA to set National Ambient Air Quality Standards for six common air pollutants. These commonly found
air pollutants (also known as "criteria pollutants") are found all over
the United States. They are particle pollution (often referred to as particulate matter), ground-level ozone, carbon monoxide, sulfur oxides,
nitrogen oxides, and lead. These pollutants can harm your health and
the environment, and cause property damage. Of the six pollutants,
particle pollution and ground-level ozone are the most widespread
health threats. EPA calls these pollutants "criteria" air pollutants
because it regulates them by developing human health-based and/or
environmentally-based criteria (science-based guidelines) for setting
permissible levels. The set of limits based on human health is called
primary standards. Another set of limits intended to prevent environmental and property damage is called secondary standards.

Air Pollution Trends

For each of these pollutants, EPA tracks two kinds of air pollution
trends: air concentrations based on actual measurements of pollutant
concentrations in the ambient (outside) air at selected monitoring sites

throughout the country, and emissions based on engineering estimates of the total tons of pollutants released into the air each year. Despite the progress made in the last 30 years, millions of people live in counties with monitor data showing unhealthy air for one or more of the six common air pollutants.

Health Effects Information

Exposure to these pollutants is associated with numerous effects on human health, including increased respiratory symptoms, hospitalization for heart or lung diseases, and even premature death.

State Implementation Plan Status and Information

EPA must designate areas as meeting (attainment) or not meeting (nonattainment) the standard. The Clean Air Act (CAA) requires states to develop a general plan to attain and maintain the NAAQS in all areas of the country and a specific plan to attain the standards for each area designated nonattainment for a NAAQS. These plans, known as State Implementation Plans, or SIPs, are developed by state and local air quality management agencies and submitted to EPA for approval.

Chapter 30

Tobacco Smoke

Cigarette Smoke

Cigarette smoke contains a number of toxic chemicals and irritants. People with allergies may be more sensitive to cigarette smoke than others and research studies indicate that smoking may aggravate allergies.

Smoking does not just harm smokers but also those around them. Research has shown that children and spouses of smokers tend to have more respiratory infections and asthma than those of non-smokers. In addition, exposure to secondhand smoke can increase the risk of allergic complications such as sinusitis and bronchitis.

Common symptoms of smoke irritation are burning or watery eyes, nasal congestion, coughing, hoarseness and shortness of breath presenting as a wheeze.

Asthma is a chronic disease that affects the airways of the lungs. During an asthma attack, airways (tubes that carry air to your lungs) become swollen, making it hard to breathe. As the walls of the airways swell, they narrow, and less air gets in and out of the lungs. Cells in the airways can make more mucus (a sticky, thick liquid) than usual, which can make breathing even harder.

This chapter includes excerpts from "Cigarette Smoke," National Institute of Environmental Health Sciences (NIEHS), April 23, 2015; and text from "Asthma and Secondhand Smoke," Centers for Disease Control and Prevention (CDC), September 1, 2015.

Symptoms of an asthma attack include:

- Coughing

- Shortness of breath or trouble breathing

- Wheezing

- Tightness or pain in the chest

- Asthma attacks can be mild, moderate, or serious—and even life threatening

How Is Smoking Related to Asthma?

If you have asthma, an asthma attack can occur when something irritates your airways and "triggers" an attack. Your triggers might be different from other people's triggers.

Tobacco smoke is one of the most common asthma triggers. Tobacco smoke—including secondhand smoke—is unhealthy for everyone, especially people with asthma. Secondhand smoke is a mixture of gases and fine particles that includes:

- Smoke from a burning cigarette, cigar, or pipe tip

- Smoke that has been exhaled (breathed out) by someone who smokes

Secondhand smoke contains more than 7,000 chemicals, including hundreds that are toxic and about 70 that can cause cancer.

If you have asthma, it's important that you avoid exposure to secondhand smoke.

If you are among the 21% of U.S. adults who have asthma and smoke, quit smoking.

Preventive Strategies

- Don't smoke and if you do, seek support to quit smoking.
- Seek smoke-free environments in restaurants, theaters and hotel rooms.
- Avoid smoking in closed areas like homes or cars where others may be exposed to secondhand smoke.

Chapter 31

Sensitivity to Environmental Odors

Environmental Odors

What are environmental odors?

Many substances in the environment can produce odors. You typically smell these odors when you are outdoors and sometimes when you are indoors with your windows open. You may smell and react to certain chemicals in the air before they are at harmful levels. Those odors can become a nuisance and bother people, causing temporary symptoms such as headache and nausea. Other odors can be toxic and cause harmful health effects.

Where do environmental odors come from?

Environmental odors can come from many sources:

- **Animals:** Confined animal feeding operations (CAFOs)

- **Human activities:** Compost, sewage, garbage, fires, household cleaning agents

This chapter includes excerpts from "Environmental Odors," Agency for Toxic Substances and Disease Registry (ATSDR), October 23, 2015; and text from "Indoor Environmental Quality," The National Institute for Occupational Safety and Health (NIOSH), January 22, 2015.

- **Industry:** Oil refineries, landfills, paper mills, wastewater treatment plants
- **Nature:** Moist soil, gardens, fires
- **Vehicles:** Diesel exhaust

Can environmental odors make me sick?

Everyone reacts to odors differently. Some people are more sensitive to environmental odors than others. When you are more sensitive to an odor, you may have symptoms even at a low concentration of the odor in air. In general, as concentration levels increase, more people will have symptoms.

What symptoms can I expect?

Symptoms vary based on your sensitivity to the odor. In most cases, symptoms will depend on the type of substance, its concentration in air, how often exposure occurs (frequency), how long exposure lasts (duration), your age, and your state of health.

Young children, the elderly, and pregnant women may be more sensitive to odors. In general, the most common symptoms are the following:

- Headaches
- Nasal congestion
- Eye, nose, and throat irritation
- Hoarseness, sore throat
- Cough
- Chest tightness
- Shortness of breath
- Wheezing
- Heart tremors (palpitations)
- Nausea
- Drowsiness
- Mental depression

These symptoms generally occur at the time of exposure. Their intensity will depend on the concentration of the odor in air, how often you smell it, and how long exposure lasts.

- If the concentration of an odor in air is **below levels of irritation** (levels known to cause eye, nose, or throat irritation in people), the symptoms will pass when you move out of the exposure area.

- If the concentration of an odor in air is **at or above levels of irritation** and the exposure duration is longer, the symptoms may last after moving out of the exposure area.

Are all environmental odors toxic?

No. Toxicity is the degree to which a substance (a toxin) can harm humans or animals. The following factors affect toxicity:

- Toxicity depends on the amount of a substance (concentration) in the air you breathe, how often (frequency) you breathe that air, and how much time (duration) you spend breathing that air.

- If the substance is at the right concentration, frequency, and duration, the odor can be toxic and cause adverse health effects.

- If those conditions do not exist, odors are generally not toxic.

- If you are sensitive to environmental odors, you may react to low concentrations of a substance in air. The length of exposure is important whether you are sensitive or not.

Indoor Environmental Quality(IEQ)

Chemicals and Odors

Chemicals and related odors can be sources of Indoor Environmental Quality (IEQ) problems in buildings. Odors are organic or inorganic compounds and can be both pleasant and unpleasant. Some odors can be health hazards and some are not. While most chemical contaminants originate from within the building, chemicals can be drawn into a building from the outdoors as well.

Reducing exposure to chemicals in the workplace is a preventative action that can lead to improved outcomes for both worker health and to the environment.

Chemical Contaminant Sources

There are a variety of chemical contaminants found in a variety of sources. Volatile organic compounds (VOCs) are common chemical contaminants found in office and home environments and are a source of odors. VOCs are organic (containing carbon) chemicals that can easily evaporate into the air. Many products found in the office environment may have the potential to release VOCs. Examples include:

- Caulks, sealants, and coatings
- Adhesives
- Paints, varnishes and/or stains
- Wall coverings
- Cleaning agents
- Fuels and combustion products
- Carpeting
- Vinyl flooring
- Fabric materials and furnishings
- Air fresheners and other scented products
- Personal products of employees like perfume, shampoos, etc.

If these and other chemical contaminant sources are not controlled, indoor environmental quality problems can arise, even if the building's ventilation system is properly designed and well maintained. Some examples of building related chemicals, odors, and their sources are listed below:

Contaminated Outdoor Air

- General air pollutants (oxides of sulfur and nitrogen, ozone, others)
- General vehicle exhaust (carbon monoxide, oxides of nitrogen)
- Exhaust from gasoline and/or diesel powered vehicles on nearby roads or in parking lots, or garages (carbon monoxide, oxides of nitrogen)
- Odors from dumpsters
- Exhaust from the neighboring buildings (VOCs and odors)
- Unsanitary debris near the building's outdoor air intake (various odors)

Soil Emissions

- Radon (odorless and not visible)
- Leakage from underground fuel tanks (gasoline or solvent odors)

- Contaminants from previous uses of the site (e.g., methane)
- Pesticides

Building Emissions

Indoor

- Bioaerosols from water damage, microbial VOCs (VOCs from fungi)
- Emissions from office equipment (VOCs, ozone)
- Emissions from stored supplies (solvents, toners, ammonia, chlorine)
- Emissions from building carpet, furnishings, and other building components (VOCs including formaldehyde from glues, fabric treatments, stains and varnishes)
- Emissions from special use areas within the building such as laboratories, print shops, art rooms, smoking lounges, beauty salons, food preparation areas, and others (various chemicals and related odors)
- Emissions from indoor construction activities (VOCs from use of paint, caulk, adhesives, and other products)
- Elevator motors and other building mechanical systems (solvents and other chemicals)
- Plumbing problems (sewer odors, improper bathroom ventilation)
- Emissions from housekeeping / cleaning activities (ammonia, chlorine, and other cleaning agents such as detergent, dust residual from carpet shampoo, and disinfectants)
- Use of deodorizers and fragrances
- Emissions from pesticide use inside the building
- Accidental events such as spills inside the building
- Emissions from stored trash inside the building
- Fire damage inside the building (soot, polychlorinated biphenyls from electrical equipment, odors)

Outdoor

- Loading docks (vehicle exhausts, chemical spills)
- Emissions from pesticide use outside the building
- Emissions from outdoor construction activities (VOCs from roofing chemicals, and other products)
- Accidental events such as spills outside the building
- Fire damage outside the building

Emissions from Building Occupants

Potentially hazardous

- Smoking
- Cooking odors
- Cosmetic odors
- Increased levels of carbon dioxide

Unpleasant

- Body odor

Chapter 32

Building Associated Illnesses

The rapid emergence of indoor air quality problems and associated occupant complaints have led to terms which describe illnesses or effects particularly associated buildings. These include:

- Sick Building Syndrome

- Building Related Illness

- Multiple Chemical Sensitivity

Sick Building Syndrome (SBS)

Sick Building Syndrome (SBS) is a catch-all term that refers to a series of acute complaints for which there is no obvious cause and where medical tests reveal no particular abnormalities. The symptoms display when individuals are in the building but disappear when they leave.

Complaints may include such symptoms as:

- irritation of the eyes, nose, and throat

- headache

Text in this chapter is excerpted from "Fundamentals of Indoor Air Quality in Buildings," U.S. Environmental Protection Agency (EPA), October 16, 2015.

281

- stuffy nose

- mental fatigue

- lethargy

- kin irritation

These complaints are often accompanied by non-specific complaints such as the air is stuffy or stale. A single causative agent (e.g., contaminant) is seldom identified and complaints may be resolved when building operational problems and/or occupant activities identified by investigators are corrected. Experience in resolving SBS complaints has led to many of the suggestions for "good practice" found in I-BEAM.

The likely outcomes of SBS problems which are not quickly resolved include:

- increased absenteeism

- reduced work efficiency

- deteriorating employee morale

Building Related Illness (BRI)

Building related illness (BRI) refers to an defined illness with a known causative agent resulting from exposure to the building air. While the causative agent can be chemical (e.g., formaldehyde), it is often biological. Typical sources of biological contaminants are:

- humidification systems

- cooling towers

- drain pans or filters

- other wet surfaces

- water damaged building material

Symptoms may be specific or mimic symptoms commonly associated with the flu, including fever, chills and cough. Serious lung and respiratory conditions can occur. Common examples of building related illness include:

- Legionnaires' disease

- hypersensitivity pneumonitis

- humidifier fever

Multiple Chemical Sensitivity (MCS)

It is generally recognized that some persons can be sensitive to particular agents at levels which do not have an observable affect in the general population. In addition, it is recognized that certain chemicals can be sensitizers in that exposure to the chemical at high levels can result in sensitivity to that chemical at much lower levels.

Some evidence suggests that a subset of the population may be especially sensitive to low levels of a broad range of chemicals at levels common in today's home and working environments. This apparent condition has come to be known as multiple chemical sensitivity (MCS).

Persons reported to have MCS apparently have difficulty being in most buildings. There is significant professional disagreement concerning whether MCS actually exists and what the underlying mechanism might be. Building managers may encounter occupants who have been diagnosed with MCS. Resolution of complaints in such circumstances may or may not be possible with the guidance provided in Indoor Air Quality Building Education and Assessment Model (I-BEAM). Responsibility to accommodate such individuals is subject to negotiation and may involve arrangements to work at home or in a different location.

Chapter 33

Climate Change and Allergies

Health Impacts

Climate change is expected to affect air quality through several pathways, including production and allergenicity of allergens and increase regional concentrations of ozone, fine particles, and dust. Some of these pollutants can directly cause respiratory disease or exacerbate existing conditions in susceptible populations, such as children or the elderly. Some of the impacts that climate change can have on air quality include:

- Increase ground level ozone and fine particle concentrations, which can trigger a variety of reactions including chest pains, coughing, throat irritation, and congestion, as well as reduce lung function and cause inflammation of the lungs.

- Increase carbon dioxide concentrations and temperatures, thereby affecting the timing of aeroallergen distribution and amplifying the allergenicity of pollen and mold spores.

- Increase precipitation in some areas leading to an increase in mold spores.

Text in this chapter is excerpted from "Asthma, Respiratory Allergies and Airway Diseases," National Institute of Environmental Health Sciences (NIEHS), March 28, 2013.

- Increase in rate of ozone formation due to higher temperatures and increased sunlight.

- Increase the frequency of droughts, leading to increased dust and particulate matter.

Adaptation and Mitigation

- Mitigating short-lived contamination species that both air pollutants and green house gases, such as ozone or black carbon. Examples include urban tree covers or rooftop gardens in urban settings.

- Decreasing the use of vehicle miles traveled to reduce ozone precursors.

- Utilizing alternative transportation options, such as walking or biking, which have the co-benefit of reducing emissions while increasing cardiovascular fitness and contributing to weight loss. However, these activities also have the potential to increase exposure to harmful outdoor air pollutants, particularly in urban areas.

- Increasing the use of air conditioning can alleviate the health effects of exposure to chronic or acute heat. However, this can potentially result in higher greenhouse gas emissions depending on the method of power generation.

Research Needs

- Developing and validating real-time remote sensing and other in situ monitoring techniques to evaluate air quality, aeroallergens, aerosolized pathogens, dust burdens, and other climate-sensitive exposures directly linked to asthma and airway diseases.

- Understanding and modeling the impact of climate change on air quality, aeroallergens, and aerosolized marine toxins, and the resulting effects on asthma and airway diseases including in vulnerable populations.

- Identifying and mapping populations and communities at increased risk of climate-related respiratory disease, which will also help to identify populations at risk for other climate-related health impacts as many environmentally mediated diseases share common risk factors.

- Studying the health effects of airborne and indoor dust on asthma exacerbation, including changes in dust composition resulting from climate change.

- Understanding the acute and long-term impacts of wild fires on asthma and other respiratory diseases.

- Examining chemicals used in energy efficient technologies to ensure that they do not contribute to lung sensitization, asthma, or other respiratory diseases.

- Examining the relative risks for respiratory disease based on chemicals with lower global warming potential than existing greenhouse gases.

Chapter 34

Insect Sting Allergy

Overview

Stinging or biting insects include bees, wasps, hornets, and fire ants.

The health effects of stinging or biting insects or scorpions range from mild discomfort or pain to a lethal reaction for those workers allergic to the insect's venom. Anaphylactic shock is the body's severe allergic reaction to a bite or sting and requires immediate emergency care. Thousands of people are stung by insects each year, and as many as 90–100 people in the United States die as a result of allergic reactions. This number may be underreported as deaths may be mistakenly diagnosed as heart attacks or sunstrokes or may be attributed to other causes.

Bees, Wasps, and Hornets

Bees, wasps, and hornets are most abundant in the warmer months. Nests and hives may be found in trees, under roof eaves, or on equipment such as ladders.

U.S. Geographic Region

Bees, wasps, and hornets are found throughout the United States.

Text in this chapter is excerpted from "Insects and Scorpions," National Institute for Occupational Safety and Health (NIOSH), July 30, 2015.

Preventing Insect Stings

People should take the following steps to prevent insect stings:

- Wear light-colored, smooth-finished clothing.
- Avoid perfumed soaps, shampoos, and deodorants.
  - Don't wear cologne or perfume.
  - Avoid bananas and banana-scented toiletries.
- Wear clean clothing and bathe daily. (Sweat may anger bees.)
- Wear clothing to cover as much of the body as possible.
- Avoid flowering plants when possible.
- Keep work areas clean. Social wasps thrive in places where humans discard food.
- Remain calm and still if a single stinging insect is flying around. (Swatting at an insect may cause it to sting.)
- If you are attacked by several stinging insects at once, run to get away from them. (Bees release a chemical when they sting, which may attract other bees.)
  - Go indoors.
  - A shaded area is better than an open area to get away from the insects.
  - If you are able to physically move out of the area, do not to attempt to jump into water. Some insects (particularly Africanized Honey Bees) are known to hover above the water, continuing to sting once you surface for air.
- If a bee comes inside your vehicle, stop the car slowly, and open all the windows.

First Aid

If someone is is stung by a bee, wasp, or hornet:

- Have someone stay with the person to be sure that they do not have an allergic reaction.
- Wash the site with soap and water.
- Remove the stinger using gauze wiped over the area or by scraping a fingernail over the area.
  - Never squeeze the stinger or use tweezers.

- Apply ice to reduce swelling.

- Do not scratch the sting as this may increase swelling, itching, and risk of infection.

Fire Ants

Imported fire ants first came to the United States around 1930. Now there are five times more ants per acre in the United States than in their native South America. The fire ants that came to the United States escaped their natural enemies and thrived in the southern landscape.

Fire ants bite and sting. They are aggressive when stinging and inject venom, which causes a burning sensation. Red bumps form at the sting, and within a day or two they become white fluid-filled pustules.

U.S. Geographic Region

Mostly the Southeastern United States, with limited geographic distribution in New Mexico, Arizona, and California.

Preventing Fire Ant Stings and Bites

- Do not disturb or stand on or near ant mounds.

- Be careful when lifting items (including animal carcasses) off the ground, as they may be covered in ants.

- Fire ants may also be found on trees or in water, so always look over the area before starting to work.

First Aid

One should take the following steps if stung or bitten by fire ants:

- Rub off ants briskly, as they will attach to the skin with their jaws.

- Antihistamines may help.
  - Follow directions on packaging.
  - Drowsiness may occur.

- Take the stung person to an emergency medical facility immediately if a sting causes severe chest pain, nausea, severe sweating, loss of breath, serious swelling, or slurred speech.

Scorpions

Scorpions usually hide during the day and are active at night. They may be hiding under rocks, wood, or anything else lying on the ground. Some species may also burrow into the ground. Most scorpions live in dry, desert areas. However, some species can be found in grasslands, forests, and inside caves.

U.S. Geographic Region

Southern and Southwestern United States.

Symptoms

Symptoms of a scorpion sting may include:

- A stinging or burning sensation at the injection site (very little swelling or inflammation)
- Positive "tap test" (i.e., extreme pain when the sting site is tapped with a finger)
- Restlessness
- Convulsions
- Roving eyes
- Staggering gait
- Thick tongue sensation
- Slurred speech
- Drooling
- Muscle twitches
- Abdominal pain and cramps
- Respiratory depression

These symptoms usually subside within 48 hours, although stings from a bark scorpion can be life-threatening.

Preventing Scorpion Stings

One should take the following steps to prevent scorpion stings:

- Wear long sleeves and pants.
- Shake out clothing or shoes before putting them on.

First Aid

One should take the following steps if stung by a scorpion:

- Contact a qualified health care provider or poison control center for advice and medical instructions.

- Ice may be applied directly to the sting site (never submerge the affected limb in ice water).

- Remain relaxed and calm.

- Do not take any sedatives.

- Capture the scorpion for identification if it is possible to do so safely.

Chapter 35

Latex Allergies

Latex in Medical Products

Latex gloves have proved effective in preventing transmission of many infectious diseases to health care workers. But for some workers, exposures to latex may result in allergic reactions. Reports of such reactions have increased in recent years—especially among health care workers.

What is latex?

The term "latex" refers to natural rubber latex, the product manufactured from a milky fluid derived from the rubber tree, *Hevea brasiliensis*. Several types of synthetic rubber are also referred to as "latex," but these do not release the proteins that cause allergic reactions.

What is latex allergy?

Latex allergy is a reaction to certain proteins in latex rubber. The amount of latex exposure needed to produce sensitization or an allergic reaction is unknown. Increasing the exposure to latex proteins

Text in this chapter is excerpted from "Latex Allergy: A Prevention Guide," he National Institute for Occupational Safety and Health (NIOSH), June 6, 2014; and text from "Researchers Link Protein to Drug Allergies," National Institutes of Health (NIH), January 26, 2015.

increases the risk of developing allergic symptoms. In sensitized persons, symptoms usually begin within minutes of exposure; but they can occur hours later and can be quite varied. Mild reactions to latex involve skin redness, rash, hives, or itching. More severe reactions may involve respiratory symptoms such as runny nose, sneezing, itchy eyes, scratchy throat, and asthma (difficult breathing, coughing spells, and wheezing). Rarely, shock may occur; however, a life-threatening reaction is seldom the first sign of latex allergy.

Who is at risk of developing latex allergy?

Health care workers are at risk of developing latex allergy because they use latex gloves frequently. Workers with less glove use (such as housekeepers, hairdressers, and workers in industries that manufacture latex products) are also at risk.

Is skin contact the only type of latex exposure?

No. Latex proteins become fastened to the lubricant powder used in some gloves. When workers change gloves, the protein/powder particles become airborne and can be inhaled.

How is latex allergy treated?

Detecting symptoms early, reducing exposure to latex, and obtaining medical advice are important to prevent long-term health effects. Once a worker becomes allergic to latex, special precautions are needed to prevent exposures. Certain medications may reduce the allergy symptoms; but complete latex avoidance, though quite difficult, is the most effective approach.

Are there other types of reactions to latex besides latex allergy?

Yes. The most common reaction to latex products is irritant contact dermatitis—the development of dry, itchy, irritated areas on the skin, usually the hands. This reaction is caused by irritation from wearing gloves and by exposure to the powders added to them. Irritant contact dermatitis is not a true allergy. Allergic contact dermatitis (sometimes called chemical sensitivity dermatitis) results from the chemicals added to latex during harvesting, processing, or manufacturing. These chemicals can cause a skin rash similar to that of poison ivy.

How can I protect myself from latex allergy?

Take the following steps to protect yourself from latex exposure and allergy in the workplace:

1. Use nonlatex gloves for activities that are not likely to involve contact with infectious materials (food preparation, routine housekeeping, general maintenance, etc.).

2. Appropriate barrier protection is necessary when handling infectious materials. If you choose latex gloves, use powder-free gloves with reduced protein content.

   - Such gloves reduce exposures to latex protein and thus reduce the risk of latex allergy.

   - So-called hypoallergenic latex gloves do not reduce the risk of latex allergy. However, they may reduce reactions to chemical additives in the latex (allergic contact dermatitis).

3. Use appropriate work practices to reduce the chance of reactions to latex.

   - When wearing latex gloves, do not use oil-based hand creams or lotions (which can cause glove deterioration).

   - After removing latex gloves, wash hands with a mild soap and dry thoroughly.

   - Practice good housekeeping: frequently clean areas and equipment contaminated with latex-containing dust.

4. Take advantage of all latex allergy education and training provided by your employer and become familiar with procedures for preventing latex allergy.

5. Learn to recognize the symptoms of latex allergy: skin rash; hives; flushing; itching; nasal, eye, or sinus symptoms; asthma; and (rarely) shock.

What if I think I have latex allergy?

If you develop symptoms of latex allergy, avoid direct contact with latex gloves and other latex-containing products until you can see a physician experienced in treating latex allergy.

If you have latex allergy, consult your physician regarding the following precautions:

- Avoid contact with latex gloves and products.

- Avoid areas where you might inhale the powder from latex gloves worn by other workers.

- Tell your employer and health care providers (physicians, nurses, dentists, etc.) that you have latex allergy.

- Wear a medical alert bracelet.

Chapter 36

Allergy to Vaccine Components

Allergy To Vaccine Components

Vaccine components can cause allergic reactions in some recipients. These reactions can be local or systemic and can include anaphylaxis or anaphylactic-like responses. The vaccine components responsible can include the vaccine antigen, animal proteins, antibiotics, preservatives (such as thimerosal), or stabilizers (such as gelatin). The most common animal protein allergen is egg protein in vaccines prepared by using embryonated chicken eggs (influenza and yellow fever vaccines).

Generally, people who can eat eggs or egg products safely may receive these vaccines, while those with histories of anaphylactic allergy (swelling of the mouth and throat, difficulty breathing, hypotension, shock) to eggs or egg proteins ordinarily should not. Screening people by asking whether they can eat eggs without adverse effects is a reasonable way to identify those who might be at risk from receiving yellow fever and influenza vaccines.

Protocols have been developed for testing and vaccinating people with anaphylactic reactions to egg ingestion. The available recombinant influenza vaccine, Flublok, is manufactured without the use of eggs and does not carry a contraindication for egg allergy. Therefore,

Text in this chapter is excerpted from "The Pre-Travel Consultation," Centers for Disease Control and Prevention (CDC), July 10, 2015; and text from "Yellow Fever VIS," Centers for Disease Control and Prevention (CDC), June 13, 2014.

Flublok can be administered to people with egg allergy of any severity who are aged 18–49 years and do not have other contraindications.

Recent studies have indicated that other components in vaccines in addition to egg proteins (such as gelatin) may cause allergic reactions, including anaphylaxis in rare instances. Some vaccines contain a preservative or trace amounts of antibiotics to which people might be allergic. Providers administering the vaccines should carefully review the prescribing information before deciding if the rare person with such an allergy should receive the vaccine. No recommended vaccine contains penicillin or penicillin derivatives.

Some vaccines (MMR vaccine, inactivated polio vaccine [IPV], hepatitis A vaccine, some hepatitis B vaccines, some influenza vaccines, rabies vaccine, varicella vaccine, and smallpox vaccine) contain trace amounts of neomycin or other antibiotics; the amount is less than would normally be used for the skin test to determine hypersensitivity. However, people who have experienced anaphylactic reactions to this antibiotic generally should not receive these vaccines. Most often, neomycin allergy is a contact dermatitis—a manifestation of a delayed-type (cell-mediated) immune response rather than anaphylaxis. A history of delayed-type reactions to neomycin is not a contraindication to receiving these vaccines.

Thimerosal, an organic mercurial compound in use since the 1930s, has been added to certain immunobiologic products as a preservative. Thimerosal is present at preservative concentrations in multidose vials of some brands of vaccine. Receiving thimerosal-containing vaccines has been postulated to lead to induction of allergy. However, there is limited scientific evidence for this assertion. Allergy to thimerosal usually consists of local delayed-type hypersensitivity reactions. Thimerosal elicits positive delayed-type hypersensitivity patch tests in 1%–18% of people tested, but these tests have limited or no clinical relevance. Most people do not experience reactions to thimerosal administered as a component of vaccines, even when patch or intradermal tests for thimerosal indicate hypersensitivity. A localized or delayed-type hypersensitivity reaction to thimerosal is not a contraindication to receipt of a vaccine that contains thimerosal.

Since mid-2001, vaccines routinely recommended for infants have been manufactured without thimerosal as a preservative.

Reporting Adverse Events After Immunization

Modern vaccines are extremely safe and effective. Benefits and risks are associated with the use of all immunobiologics—no vaccine is completely effective or completely safe for all recipients. Adverse events after immunization have been reported with all vaccines, ranging from frequent, minor, local reactions to extremely rare, severe, systemic illness, such as that associated with yellow fever vaccine. Adverse events following specific vaccines and toxoids are discussed in detail in each ACIP statement. In the United States, clinicians are required by law to report selected adverse events occurring after vaccination with any vaccine. In addition, CDC strongly recommends that all vaccine adverse events be reported to the Vaccine Adverse Event Reporting System (VAERS), even if a causal relation to vaccination is not certain. VAERS reporting forms and information are available electronically at www.vaers.hhs.gov, or they may be requested by telephone: 800-822-7967 (toll-free). Clinicians are encouraged to report electronically at www.vaers.hhs.gov/esub/step1.

Yellow fever vaccine

Yellow fever vaccine is a live, weakened virus. It is given as a single shot. For people who remain at risk, a booster dose is recommended every 10 years.

Yellow fever vaccine may be given at the same time as most other vaccines.

Who should get yellow fever vaccine?

- Persons 9 months through 59 years of age traveling to or living in an area where risk of yellow fever is known to exist, or traveling to a country with an entry requirement for the vaccination.

- Laboratory personnel who might be exposed to yellow fever virus or vaccine virus.

What are the risks from yellow fever vaccine?

A vaccine, like any medicine, could cause a serious reaction. But the risk of a vaccine causing serious harm, or death, is extremely low.

Mild problems

Yellow fever vaccine has been associated with fever, and with aches, soreness, redness or swelling where the shot was given.

These problems occur in up to 1 person out of 4. They usually begin soon after the shot, and can last up to a week.

Severe problems

- Severe allergic reaction to a vaccine component (about 1 person in 55,000).

- Severe nervous system reaction (about 1 person in 125,000).

- Life-threatening severe illness with organ failure (about 1 person in 250,000). More than half the people who suffer this side effect die.

These last two problems have never been reported after a booster dose.

What if there is a serious reaction?

What should I look for?

- Look for anything that concerns you, such as signs of a severe allergic reaction, very high fever, or behavior changes.

  - Signs of a severe allergic reaction can include hives, swelling of the face and throat, difficulty breathing, a fast heartbeat, dizziness, and weakness.

  - These would start a few minutes to a few hours after the vaccination.

What should I do?

- If you think it is a severe allergic reaction or other emergency that can't wait, call 9-1-1 or get the person to the nearest hospital. Otherwise, call your doctor.

- Afterward, the reaction should be reported to the Vaccine Adverse Event Reporting System (VAERS). Your doctor might file this report, or you can do it yourself through the VAERS website (www.vaers.hhs.gov), or by calling **800-822-7967**.

VAERS is only for reporting reactions. They do not give medical advice.

Part Five

Diagnosing and Treating Allergies

Chapter 37

When You Should See an Allergist

Allergy/immunology is the field of medicine that deals with the human body's immune system. The immune system is a network of cells, tissues, and organs that defends the body against potentially harmful foreign organisms and particles. A physician specializing in this field of medicine is called an allergist/immunologist.

The human body is well equipped to defend itself against disease-causing organisms such as bacteria, viruses, or fungi. It also defends itself from foreign particles such as dust or mold. When the body encounters substances that it recognizes as potentially harmful, the immune system produces antibodies to eliminate them.

Under normal circumstances, this defense mechanism does a good job of protecting the body and keeping it healthy. Sometimes, though, the immune system overreacts to harmless substances—like a certain food or pollen—by releasing chemicals and triggering changes in the body to destroy the invaders. This process is called an allergic reaction. When the reaction is severe enough to require medical care, an allergist/immunologist is usually involved in diagnosing and treating the patient's condition.

"When You Should See an Allergist," © 2015 Omnigraphics, Inc. Reviewed November 2015.

Types of Allergic Reactions

Allergic reactions tend to happen in locations where the immune system has concentrated its defenses to protect against foreign substances entering the body. They frequently affect the skin, the eyes, the respiratory system (nose, sinuses, throat, lungs), and the digestive system (stomach, intestines). Some common types of allergic reactions include contact dermatitis or skin allergies, allergic rhinitis (inflammation of the lining of the nose and sinuses), and asthma. Anaphylaxis is a sudden, severe, whole-body allergic reaction that can be life-threatening without immediate medical attention.

People can develop allergies to a variety of ordinary substances that they are exposed to daily. Common types of allergens include: foods such as milk, wheat, nuts, fish, soy, and eggs; airborne particles such as dust, pollen, mold, and animal dander; insect bites and stings; certain chemicals and medications; and substances like latex. Certain plants, like poison ivy, can also trigger severe allergic reactions.

Seeing an Allergist/Immunologist

The symptoms of allergic reactions can range from a mild runny nose or skin rash to diarrhea and vomiting or anaphylaxis. Sometimes the symptoms can be controlled with occasional doses of over-the-counter allergy medications, and sometimes they get worse over time and detract from the person's quality of life. Generally speaking, patients should consider seeing an allergist/immunologist under the following circumstances:

- an abnormal reaction to inhaling, ingesting, or coming into contact with something;

- symptoms of asthma such as wheezing, difficulty breathing, or chest pressure;

- more than three infections of the ear, nose, throat, or lungs per year;

- skin conditions like rashes or hives that appear frequently or without a known cause;

- a severe reaction to a bee sting or an insect bite;

- allergic reactions that interfere with performing activities of daily living;

- symptoms that do not improve with the use of over-the-counter medications.

An allergist/immunologist has to undergo a minimum of nine years of medical education and training, including four years of medical school, three years of residency training as an internist or pediatrician, and two years of specialized study in the field of allergy/immunology. The physician then has to pass a certification examination conducted by the American Board of Allergy and Immunology.

An allergist will conduct a medical history and physical examination and perform certain tests to identify the allergen responsible for the patient's reaction. One of the most common tests is the skin-prick test, in which the allergist uses a small needle to prick the patient's skin and insert tiny quantities of allergy-causing substances. If the patient is allergic to a specific substance, they will develop a bump on the skin similar to a mosquito bite. Another test that is often performed by allergists is a challenge test, in which the patient inhales or ingests a very small quantity of allergen under medical supervision to see if they have a reaction. Finally, an allergist may conduct blood tests to check for immunoglobulin E (IgE) antibodies, which are indicators of an allergic reaction.

To prepare for a visit to an allergist, it may be helpful to keep a diary of allergic reactions, recording details about symptoms, exposure to potential allergens, and timing. This information makes it easier for the allergist to diagnose and treat the condition. Prompt diagnosis and identification of allergens will help the patient avoid exposure to these substances or control their reactions if they are exposed to them. Patients with severe allergies may be required to carry emergency medication, like an epinephrine auto-injector or an inhaler, with them at all times.

References

1. "Allergy Testing." American College of Allergy, Asthma, and Immunology, 2015.

2. "When to See an Allergist." American College of Allergy, Asthma, and Immunology, 2014.

Chapter 38

Allergy Testing

Chapter Contents

Section 38.1

Tests to Diagnose Environmental Allergies

Text in this section is excerpted from "Diagnosis of Environmental
Allergies," National Institute of Allergy and Infectious Diseases
(NIAID), May 12, 2015.

Diagnosis of Environmental Allergies

A healthcare professional may perform skin, blood, or allergy component tests to help diagnose environmental allergies.

Skin Tests

A skin prick test can detect if a person is sensitive to a specific
allergen. Being "sensitive" means that the immune system produces
a type of antibody called IgE against that allergen. IgE attaches to
specialized cells called mast cells. This happens throughout the body,
including the lining of the nose and the airways, as well as the skin.

During a skin prick test, a healthcare professional uses a piece of plastic to prick the skin on the arm or back and place a tiny amount of allergen
extract just below the skin's surface. In sensitive people, the allergen binds
to IgE on mast cells in the skin and causes them to release histamine
and other chemicals that produce itching, redness, and minor swelling.

A positive skin test to a particular allergen does not necessarily
indicate that a person has allergic rhinitis or asthma caused by that
allergen. Up to 50 percent of the U.S. population may have at least
one positive skin test to a common allergen, but less than half of those
people have allergic rhinitis or asthma. Therefore, healthcare professionals often will try to match skin test results with the kind of
allergen exposures person may have had.

Blood Tests

Instead of performing a skin test, doctors may take a blood sample
to measure levels of allergen-specific IgE antibodies. Most people who
are sensitive to a particular allergen will have IgE antibodies detectable by both skin and blood tests.

As with skin testing, a positive blood test to an allergen does not necessarily mean that a person's symptoms are caused by that allergen.

Allergy Component Tests

One reason why a positive skin or blood test does not always indicate that a person's symptoms are caused by a particular allergen is that allergens comprise many different components, some of which are more likely to cause symptoms than others. For example, birch tree pollen contains proteins, sugars, and fats. IgE antibodies to birch pollen proteins are likely to cause allergic reactions, but IgE antibodies to the sugars in birch pollen, although common, are less likely to cause allergic reactions. Allergy component tests are blood tests that can determine exactly which component of an allergen the IgE in a person's blood recognizes. This can help a health professional determine whether the allergen is likely to cause symptoms.

Section 38.2

Allergenics

Text in this section is excerpted from "Allergenics," U.S. Food and Drug Administration (FDA), April 18, 2014.

The Center for Biologics Evaluation and Research (CBER) regulates allergenic products. There are currently three types of allergenic products licensed for use: allergen extracts, allergen patch tests, and antigen skin tests.

Allergen extracts are used for the diagnosis and/or treatment of allergic diseases such as allergic rhinitis ("hay fever"), allergic sinusitis, allergic conjunctivitis, bee venom allergy and food allergy. Currently, there are two types of licensed allergen extracts:

- **Injectable allergen extracts** are used for both diagnosis and treatment and are sterile liquids that are manufactured from

311

natural substances (such as molds, pollens, insects, insect venoms, and animal hair) known to elicit allergic reactions in susceptible individuals. Injectable allergen extracts for food allergies are used only for diagnostic purposes. Among the injectable allergen extracts, some are standardized; for these products there is an established method to determine the potency (or strength) of the product on a lot-by-lot basis. For the other injectable allergen extracts there is no measure of potency, and these are called "non-standardized."

- **Sublingual allergen extract tablets** are used for treatment only and are also derived from natural substances known to elicit allergic reactions in susceptible individuals, and are intended for the treatment of allergic rhinitis with or without allergic conjunctivitis.

Allergen patch tests are diagnostic tests applied to the surface of the skin. Patch tests are used by healthcare providers to determine the specific cause of contact dermatitis, and are manufactured from natural substances or chemicals (such as nickel, rubber, and fragrance mixes) that are known to cause contact dermatitis.

Antigen skin tests are diagnostic tests injected into the skin to aid in the diagnosis of infection with certain pathogens.

Allergen extracts

- Injectable allergen extracts
  - Injectable Allergen Extracts – Standardized
  - Injectable Allergen Extracts – Non-Standardized
- Allergen extract sublingual tablets
  - GRASTEK
  - Oralair
  - RAGWITEK

Allergen patch tests

- T.R.U.E. Test

Antigen skin tests

- Candin

- Spherusol

- Tuberculin, Purified Protein Derivative – Tubersol

- Tuberculin, Purified Protein Derivative – Aplisol

Section 38.3

Improving Safety and Potency Testing of Allergen Extracts

Text in this section is excerpted from "Vaccines, Blood & Biologics–Improving Safety and Potency Testing of Allergen Extracts," U.S. Food and Drug Administration (FDA), December 12, 2015.

General Overview

Allergen extracts are used in the United States to diagnose and treat allergic diseases. Skin tests containing these extracts determine the causes of allergies. "Allergy shots" containing them are used to reduce or eliminate allergic symptoms. As with all drugs and biologics, good quality controls are needed to ensure that allergen extracts are safe and effective. The goal of this research is to provide new tools and data that allow allergen extract manufacturers to maintain and improve the quality of these important products.

This research work has two major areas of focus. First, attempting to improve the methods by which U.S. Food and Drug Administration (FDA) and manufacturers measure the potency, or strength, of an allergen extract. Existing methods either measure a single, dominant protein in the extract, or determine the potency by measuring several undefined proteins as one group. In contrast, the research team is developing a method that will measure many specific proteins simultaneously. In this way, not only the overall potency but also the levels of individual proteins can be measured.

In the research team's second project the presence of endotoxin in certain allergen extracts are being investigated. Endotoxins are ubiquitous in our environment, and are even present in some biological

313

products; but their presence in allergen extracts has not been studied. The team is using sophisticated laboratory techniques to identify the sources of endotoxins and the factors that affect endotoxin levels in these extracts.

Scientific Overview

The existing competition enzyme-linked immunosorbent assay (ELISA test) is a sensitive and specific method of determining overall potency, but its performance characteristics for each component allergen is uncertain. When an individual allergen is removed from the extract, the polyvalent sera cannot reliably discern its absence. Until each relevant allergen in a mixture is identified, regulators must ask manufacturers to measure overall potency. Once important allergens are determined, their measurement requires a change in technology that can be time-consuming and difficult.

The purpose of this study is to construct an assay that will have the strengths of both the RIDA and the competition ELISA, and that will allow manufacturers and regulators to determine the amounts of specific allergens in a mixture, as well as its overall allergenicity. Multiplex assays have been used with success for a variety of assays, such as detecting allergen-specific IgE and the amount of allergen in the environment. Following this approach, the team has designed a multiplex allergen extract potency assay (MAEPA). In work so far, the assay has been optimized for cat hair and short ragweed pollen allergen extracts. The team is currently developing the assay for German cockroach allergens, as well as to detect allergens in Neurospora crassa, Agarigus bisporus, and Nicotiana benthamiana/excelsiana.

The team is also working to identify endotoxins in allergen extracts using bacterial genotyping by specific PCR and sequencing, and specific LPS-typing.

Section 38.4

Tests to Diagnose Asthma

Text in this section is excerpted from "Asthma: How Is Asthma
Diagnosed?" National Heart, Lung, and Blood Institute (NHLBI),
August 4, 2014.

How Is Asthma Diagnosed?

Your primary care doctor will diagnose asthma based on your medical and family histories, a physical exam, and test results

Your doctor also will figure out the severity of your asthma—that is, whether it's intermittent, mild, moderate, or severe. The level of severity will determine what treatment you'll start on.

You may need to see an asthma specialist if:

- You need special tests to help diagnose asthma

- You've had a life-threatening asthma attack

- You need more than one kind of medicine or higher doses of medicine to control your asthma, or if you have overall problems getting your asthma well controlled

- You're thinking about getting allergy treatments

Medical and Family Histories

Your doctor may ask about your family history of asthma and allergies. He or she also may ask whether you have asthma symptoms and when and how often they occur.

Let your doctor know whether your symptoms seem to happen only during certain times of the year or in certain places, or if they get worse at night.

Your doctor also may want to know what factors seem to trigger your symptoms or worsen them.

Your doctor may ask you about related health conditions that can interfere with asthma management. These conditions include a runny nose, sinus infections, reflux disease, psychological stress, and sleep apnea.

Physical Exam

Your doctor will listen to your breathing and look for signs of asthma or allergies. These signs include wheezing, a runny nose or swollen nasal passages, and allergic skin conditions (such as eczema).

Keep in mind that you can still have asthma even if you don't have these signs on the day that your doctor examines you.

Diagnostic Tests

Lung Function Test

Your doctor will use a test called spirometry to check how your lungs are working. This test measures how much air you can breathe in and out. It also measures how fast you can blow air out.

Your doctor also may give you medicine and then test you again to see whether the results have improved.

If the starting results are lower than normal and improve with the medicine, and if your medical history shows a pattern of asthma symptoms, your diagnosis will likely be asthma.

Other Tests

Your doctor may recommend other tests if he or she needs more information to make a diagnosis. Other tests may include:

- Allergy testing to find out which allergens affect you, if any.

- A test to measure how sensitive your airways are. This is called a bronchoprovocation test. Using spirometry, this test repeatedly measures your lung function during physical activity or after you receive increasing doses of cold air or a special chemical to breathe in.

- A test to show whether you have another condition with the same symptoms as asthma, such as reflux disease, vocal cord dysfunction, or sleep apnea.

- A chest X-ray or an EKG (electrocardiogram). These tests will help find out whether a foreign object or other disease may be causing your symptoms.

Diagnosing Asthma in Young Children

Most children who have asthma develop their first symptoms before 5 years of age. However, asthma in young children (aged up to 5 years) can be hard to diagnose.

Sometimes it's hard to tell whether a child has asthma or another childhood condition. This is because the symptoms of asthma also occur with other conditions.

Also, many young children who wheeze when they get colds or respiratory infections don't go on to have asthma after they're 6 years old.

A child may wheeze because he or she has small airways that become even narrower during colds or respiratory infections. The airways grow as the child grows older, so wheezing no longer occurs when the child gets colds.

A young child who has frequent wheezing with colds or respiratory infections is more likely to have asthma if:

- One or both parents have asthma

- The child has signs of allergies, including the allergic skin condition eczema

- The child has allergic reactions to pollens or other airborne allergens

- The child wheezes even when he or she doesn't have a cold or other infection

The most certain way to diagnose asthma is with a lung function test, a medical history, and a physical exam. However, it's hard to do lung function tests in children younger than 5 years. Thus, doctors must rely on children's medical histories, signs and symptoms, and physical exams to make a diagnosis.

Doctors also may use a 4–6 week trial of asthma medicines to see how well a child responds.

Section 38.5

Important Issues for Allergen-Specific IgE Testing

Text in this section is excerpted from "Medical Devices – Important Issues for Allergen-Specific IgE Testing," U.S. Food and Drug Administration (FDA), May 8, 2015.

Immunoglobulin E (IgE) is a distinct class of serum antibody which mediates Type 1 hypersensitivity reactions, also known as atopic allergy. In sensitized individuals suffering from this immediate (atopic or anaphylactic) type of allergy, IgE molecules act as points of contact between the allergen and mast cells or basophilic leukocytes that release histamine and other agents upon exposure. This initiates the events recognized as allergic reactions, the most common clinical manifestations being sinusitis, asthma, dermatitis, hives and, in rare cases, anaphylactic shock. Assessing the level of allergen-specific IgE in a patient's serum in conjunction with a clinical evaluation based on patient history and other testing can help a physician confirm a diagnosis of atopic allergy and assist in the treatment of the patient.

Limitations of the Testing

Clinicians and laboratorians should be aware of inherent problems with currently available allergen-specific IgE tests. Following pre-market review, U.S. Food and Drug Administration (FDA) allows these tests on the market but suggests that manufacturers and distributors include limitations in the labeling (package insert) that accompanies each test kit to the clinical laboratories/physicians.

- A definite clinical diagnosis should not be made solely on the basis of an in vitro allergen-specific IgE result. Diagnosis should be made by the physician only after all clinical and laboratory findings have been evaluated.

- The results of an allergen-specific IgE antibody test should not be used as a definitive guide to select an initial dose for immunotherapy. Prior to implementing such therapy, a skin test with the planned initial dilution of the immunotherapy solution should be performed to prove that the patient tolerates in vivo administration of this allergenic extract.

- Very low levels of allergen-specific IgE antibodies should be evaluated with caution when total IgE values are above 1000 kU/L.

- In food allergies, circulating IgE antibodies may remain undetectable despite a convincing clinical history because these antibodies may be directed toward allergens that are revealed or altered during industrial processing, cooking or digestion and therefore do not exist in the original food for which the patient is tested.

- False positive test results in persons who are tested for food allergies may lead to inappropriate dietary restrictions while false negative results in food sensitive persons may result in anaphylactic reactions of varying severity.

- A positive result may be due to cross-reactivity with other similar allergens and not to the specific allergen tested. The user should be aware of the possibility of clinical cross-reactivity within an allergen family.

- Latex specific IgE antibodies may show cross-reactivity with ragweed and certain food allergens such as banana, avocado, kiwi and chestnut. Since a latex assay measures allergen-specific IgE, type IV delayed reaction or irritation from latex will not be detected.

- Results below the limit of quantitation obtained for a drug-specific IgE determination indicate the absence or undetectable levels of specific IgE antibodies to the drug, as is found in nonsensitized individuals. However, negative specific IgE results can also be found in patients who are nevertheless hypersensitive to drugs, for example when:

  - The symptoms are mediated without IgE involvement.

  - The blood sample was collected a long time after the latest adverse reaction to a therapeutic treatment procedure. The concentration of IgE antibodies can decrease over time after the allergic reaction.

  - The blood sample was collected very soon after the allergic reaction. An interval between the time of the allergic reaction and the appearance of measurable specific IgE antibodies can occur and can lead to "false" negative results for drug-specific IgE determinations. Such results can be checked by collecting a new blood sample and repeating the test two weeks after the allergic reaction.

- Allergen-specific IgE antibody results below the limit of quantitation for venom-specific IgE indicate absent or undetectable levels. Such results do not preclude existence of current or future clinical hypersensitivity to insect sting.

- Identical results for different allergens may not be associated with clinically equivalent manifestations, due to differences in patient sensitivities and IgE binding capacities.

Allergens as Analyte Specific Reagents (ASRs)

What is the definition of an ASR? ASRs may be thought of as the "active ingredients" of tests that are used to identify one specific disease or condition. They are defined as "antibodies, both polyclonal and monoclonal, specific receptor proteins, ligands, nucleic acid sequences, and similar reagents which, through specific binding or chemical reactions with substances in a specimen, are intended for use in a diagnostic application for identification and quantification of an individual chemical substance or ligand in biological specimens" (21 CFR 864.4020). ASRs are components of in vitro diagnostic devices that are regulated by FDA.

ASRs may be purchased by a clinical laboratory to develop in-house tests used exclusively by that laboratory. In this case, the laboratory would perform all necessary verification and validation of the assays. Laboratories using ASRs should be regulated under the Clinical Laboratory Improvement Amendments of 1988 (CLIA) as qualified to perform high complexity testing or they should be clinical laboratories regulated under VHA Directive 1106.

FDA views an ASR as having the following characteristics:

- used to detect a single ligand or target (e.g., protein, single nucleotide change, epitope);

- not labeled with instructions for use or performance claims; and

- not promoted for use on specific designated instruments or in specific tests.

Are allergens considered ASRs? Allergens would not be considered ASRs: if more than one allergen is combined together by the manufacturer, e.g., AgA + AgB in the same vial; if more than one ASR is bundled together in a single pre-configured or optimized mixture so that they must be used together in the resulting laboratory developed test; if the product marketed includes some or all of the products needed to conduct a particular test; if they are designed or formatted to be used only on a specific instrument; if they are promoted for use with specific named reagents (e.g., buffers, diluents or controls) used with that instrument; or if they are marketed with analytical or clinical performance claims.

Chapter 39

Lung Function Tests

What Are Lung Function Tests?

Lung function tests, also called pulmonary function tests, measure how well your lungs work. These tests are used to look for the cause of breathing problems, such as shortness of breath.

Lung function tests measure:

- How much air you can take into your lungs. This amount is compared with that of other people your age, height, and sex. This allows your doctor to see whether you're in the normal range.

- How much air you can blow out of your lungs and how fast you can do it.

- How well your lungs deliver oxygen to your blood.

- The strength of your breathing muscles.

Doctors use lung function tests to help diagnose conditions such as asthma, pulmonary fibrosis (scarring of the lung tissue), and COPD (chronic obstructive pulmonary disease).

Lung function tests also are used to check the extent of damage caused by conditions such as pulmonary fibrosis and sarcoidosis. Also, these tests might be used to check how well treatments, such as asthma medicines, are working.

Text in this chapter is excerpted from "What Are Lung Function Tests?" National Heart, Lung, and Blood Institute (NHLBI), September 17, 2012.

Overview

Lung function tests include breathing tests and tests that measure the oxygen level in your blood. The breathing tests most often used are:

- Spirometry. This test measures how much air you can breathe in and out. It also measures how fast you can blow air out.

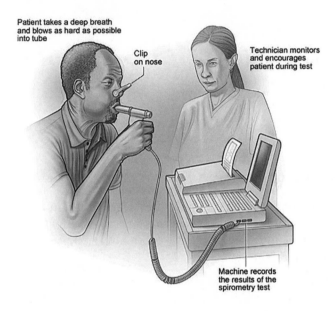

Figure 39.1. *Spirometry*

- Body plethysmography. This test measures how much air is present in your lungs when you take a deep breath. It also measures how much air remains in your lungs after you breathe out fully.

- Lung diffusion capacity. This test measures how well oxygen passes from your lungs to your bloodstream.

These tests may not show what's causing breathing problems. So, you may have other tests as well, such as an exercise stress test. This test measures how well your lungs and heart work while you exercise on a treadmill or bicycle.

Two tests that measure the oxygen level in your blood are pulse oximetry and arterial blood gas tests. These tests also are called blood oxygen tests.

Pulse oximetry measures your blood oxygen level using a special light. For an arterial blood gas test, your doctor takes a sample of your blood, usually from an artery in your wrist. The sample is sent to a laboratory, where its oxygen level is measured.

Outlook

Lung function tests usually are painless and rarely cause side effects. You may feel some discomfort during an arterial blood gas test when the blood sample is taken.

Chapter 40

Allergy Medication and Therapies

Chapter Contents

Section 40.1

Allergy Medicines for Children

Text in this section is excerpted from "Allergy Relief for Your Child,"
U.S. Food and Drug Administration (FDA), August 30, 2015.

Children are magnets for colds. But when the "cold" won't go away
for weeks, the culprit may be allergies.

Long-lasting sneezing, with a stuffy or runny nose, may signal the
presence of allergic rhinitis—the collection of symptoms that affect the
nose when you have an allergic reaction to something you breathe in
and that lands on the lining inside the nose.

Allergies may be seasonal or they can strike year-round (perennial).
In most parts of the United States, plant pollens are often the cause
of seasonal allergic rhinitis—more commonly called hay fever. Indoor
substances, such as mold, dust mites, and animal dander, may cause
the perennial kind.

Up to 40 percent of children suffer from allergic rhinitis, according
to the National Institute of Allergy and Infectious Diseases (NIAID).
And children are more likely to develop allergies if one or both parents
have allergies.

The U.S. Food and Drug Administration (FDA) regulates both over-
the-counter (OTC) and prescription medicines that offer allergy relief
as well as allergen extracts used to diagnose and treat allergies.

Immune System Reaction

An allergy is a reaction of the immune system to a specific substance, or allergen. The immune system responds to the invading
allergen by releasing histamine and other chemicals that typically
trigger symptoms in the nose, lungs, throat, sinuses, ears, eyes, skin,
or stomach lining, according to the American Academy of Allergy,
Asthma and Immunology.

In some children, allergies can also trigger symptoms of asthma—a
disease that causes wheezing or difficulty breathing.

If a child has allergies and asthma, "not controlling the allergies
can make asthma worse," says Anthony Durmowicz, M.D., a pediatric

pulmonary doctor in FDA's Division of Pulmonary, Allergy, and Rheumatology Products.

Avoiding the Culprit

If your child has seasonal allergies, you may want to pay attention to pollen counts and try to keep your child inside when the levels are high.

- In the late summer and early fall, during ragweed pollen season, pollen levels are highest in the morning.

- In the spring and summer, during the grass pollen season, pollen levels are highest in the evening.

- Some molds, another allergy trigger, may also be seasonal. For example, leaf mold is more common in the fall.

- Sunny, windy days can be especially troublesome for pollen allergy sufferers.

- It may also help to keep windows closed in your house and car and run the air conditioner when pollen counts are high.

Allergy Medicines

For most children, symptoms may be controlled by avoiding the allergen, if known, and using OTC medicines. However, if a child's symptoms are persistent and not relieved by OTC medicines, it is wise to see a health care professional to assess your child's symptoms and see if other treatments, including prescription medicines, may be appropriate. Five types of drugs are generally available to help bring your child relief.

While some allergy medicines are approved for use in children as young as six months, Dianne Murphy, M.D., director of FDA's Office of Pediatric Therapeutics, cautions, "Always read the label to make sure the product is appropriate for your child's age. Just because a product's box says that it is intended for children does not mean it is intended for children of all ages."

"Children are more sensitive than adults to many drugs," adds Murphy. "For example, some antihistamines can have adverse effects at lower doses on young patients, causing excitability or excessive drowsiness."

More Child-Friendly Medicines

Recent pediatric legislation, including a combination of incentives and requirements for drug companies, has significantly increased research and development of drugs for children and has led to more products with new pediatric information in their labeling. Since 1997, a combination of legislative activities has helped generate studies in children for 400 products.

Many of the older drugs were only tested in adults, says Durmowicz, "but we now have more information available for the newer allergy medications. With the passing of this legislation, there should be more confidence in pediatric dosing and safety with the newer drugs."

The legislation also requires drugs for children to be in a child-friendly formulation, adds Durmowicz. So if the drug was initially developed as a capsule, it has to also be made in a form that a child can take, such as a liquid with cherry flavoring, rapidly dissolving tablets, or strips for placing under the tongue.

Allergy Shots

Children who don't respond to either OTC or prescription medications, or who suffer from frequent complications of allergic rhinitis, may be candidates for allergen immunotherapy—commonly known as allergy shots. According to NIAID, about 80 percent of people with allergic rhinitis will see their symptoms and need for medicine drop significantly within a year of starting allergy shots.

After allergy testing, typically by skin testing to detect what allergens your child may react to, a health care professional injects the child with "extracts"—small amounts of the allergens that trigger a reaction. The doses are gradually increased so that the body builds up immunity to these allergens.

Allergen extracts are manufactured from natural substances, such as pollens, insect venoms, animal hair, and foods. More than 1,200 extracts are licensed by FDA.

Some doctors are buying extracts licensed for injection and instructing the parents to administer the extracts using a dropper under the child's tongue, says Jay E. Slater, M.D., director of FDA's Division of Bacterial, Parasitic and Allergenic Products. "While FDA considers this the practice of medicine (and the agency does not regulate the practice of medicine), parents and patients should be aware that there are no allergenic extracts currently licensed by FDA for oral use."

"Allergy shots are never appropriate for food allergies," adds Slater, who is also a pediatrician and allergist. But it's common to use extracts to test for food allergies so the child can avoid those foods.

Transformation in Treatment

"In the last 20 years, there has been a remarkable transformation in allergy treatments," says Slater. "Kids used to be miserable for months out of the year, and drugs made them incredibly sleepy. But today's products are outstanding in terms of safety and efficacy."

Forgoing treatment can make for an irritable, sleepless, and unhappy child, adds Slater, recalling a mother saying, after her child's successful treatment, "I didn't realize I had a nice kid!"

Table 40.1. FDA-Approved Drug Options for Treatment of Allergic Rhinitis (Hay Fever) in Children

Drug Type	How Used	Some Examples of Over-the-Counter (OTC) or Prescription (Rx) Drugs (many are available in generic form)	Common Side Effects
Nasal corticosteroids	Usually sprayed in nose once a day	Rx: • Nasonex (mometasone furoate) • Flonase (fluticasone propionate)	Stinging in nose
Oral and topical antihistamines	Orally (pills, liquid, or strip placed under the tongue), nasally (spray or drops), or eye drops	Oral OTC: • Benadryl (diphenhydramine) • Chlor-Trimeton (chlorpheniramine) • Allegra* (fexofenadine) • Claritin* (loratadine) • Zyrtec* (cetirizine) Oral Rx: • Clarinex (desloratadine) Nasal Rx: • Astelin (azelastine) * non-sedating	Some antihistamines may cause drowsiness Some nasal sprays may cause a bitter taste in mouth, headache, and stinging in nose
Decongestants	Orally and nasally (some-times taken with antihistamines, which used alone do not treat nasal congestion)	Oral Sudafed (pseudoephedrine*), Sudafed PE (phenylephrine)Oral Rx: • Allegra D, which has both an antihistamine (fexofenadine) and decongestant (pseudoephedrine*) Nasal OTC: • Neo-Synephrine (phenylephrine) • Afrin (oxymetazoline)	Using nose sprays or drops more than a few days may cause "rebound" effect, in which nasal congestion gets worse

Table 40.1. Continued

Drug Type	How Used	Some Examples of Over-the-Counter (OTC) or Prescription (Rx) Drugs (many are available in generic form)	Common Side Effects
		* Drugs that contain pseudoephedrine are non-prescription but are kept behind the pharmacy counter because of their illegal use to make methamphetamine. You'll need to ask your pharmacist and show identification to buy these drugs.	
Non-steroidal nasal sprays	Nasally used 3–4 times a day	OTC: • NasalCrom (cromolyn sodium) Rx: • Atrovent (ipratropium bromide)	Stinging in nose or sneezing; can help prevent symptoms of allergic rhinitis if used before symptoms start
Leukotriene receptor antagonist	Orally once a day (comes in granules to mix with food, and chewable tablets)	Rx: • Singulair (montelukast sodium)	Headache, ear infection, sore throat, upper respiratory infection

Section 40.2

Allergy Shots and Allergy Drops

Text in this section is excerpted from "Allergy Shots and Allergy Drops for Adults and Children," Agency for Healthcare Research and Quality (AHRQ), August 22, 2013.

This type of treatment works differently than allergy medicines. Allergy shots and drops work to lessen your body's reaction to an allergen. Your doctor may suggest allergy shots or drops to make your symptoms happen less often or to make them less severe.

- Allergy shots: shots that are given under the skin (often in the upper arm) usually at the doctor's office

- Allergy drops: a liquid you put under your tongue that you can take at home (this is called "sublingual immunotherapy")

What are allergy shots and allergy drops?

Allergy shots and allergy drops help your immune system become less sensitive to allergens. The shots and drops contain a tiny amount of the allergens that cause your allergies. For example, if you are allergic to oak tree pollen, your shots or drops will have a tiny amount of oak tree pollen in them. Allergy shots and drops both contain the allergens that cause your allergies. The difference between them is simply in how they are given.

The amount of the allergen in allergy shots or drops is so small that your immune system likely will not react strongly to it. Your doctor will talk with you about what to do if you have a strong reaction.

Your doctor will slowly put more of the allergen into your shots or drops until your immune system becomes less sensitive to the allergen. This means your immune system will not react strongly when you breathe in the allergen. Over time, your immune system will start to tolerate the allergen, and your allergy symptoms will get better.

Note

Some people may not be able to take allergy shots or drops.

You should talk with your doctor if:

- You (or your child) have severe asthma
- You (or your child) take a type of medicine called a "beta-blocker," used to treat high blood pressure
- You (or your child) have heart problems
- You are pregnant or are thinking of becoming pregnant
- You are considering allergy shots or allergy drops for a child under 5 years of age

Table 40.2. Comparing Allergy Shots and Allergy Drops

Questions	Allergy Shots	Allergy Drops
How are they taken?	The shots are given under the skin (often in the upper arm) usually at the doctor's office	The liquid drops are placed under the tongue and are usually taken at home
	One or more shots each time you go to the doctor's office	A few times a week or every day
	Once or twice a week for the first few months	
	Once or twice a month after that	
How long do you take them?	3 to 5 years (or sometimes longer)	Typically 3 to 5 years (or sometimes longer)
Are they approved by the U.S. Food and Drug Administration (FDA) to treat allergies and asthma caused by allergies?	Yes	No, allergy drops are not yet approved by the FDA.* But they are approved and commonly used in Europe and other parts of the world. Allergy drops are available in the United States, and doctors are starting to prescribe them.

* Because allergy drops are not yet approved by the FDA, they may not be covered by your health insurance.

What have researchers found about how well allergy shots and allergy drops work?

In adults:

- Both allergy shots and allergy drops improve allergy and mild asthma symptoms.

- Both allergy shots and allergy drops lessen the need to take allergy and asthma medicines.

- Both allergy shots and allergy drops improve quality of life.

In children:

- Both allergy shots and allergy drops improve allergy and mild asthma symptoms.

- Allergy drops lessen the need to take allergy and asthma medicines.

- Allergy shots also appear to lessen the need to take allergy and asthma medicines, but more research is needed to know this for sure.

Researchers also found:

- There is not enough research to know if allergy shots or allergy drops work better.

What are the possible side effects of allergy shots and allergy drops?

Allergy shots and allergy drops are safe, and side effects are usually mild.

Common side effects of allergy shots include:

- Itching, swelling, and redness at the place where the shot was given

- Headache

- Coughing

- Tiredness

- Mucus dripping down your throat

- Sneezing

Common side effects of allergy drops include:

* Throat irritation

* Itching or mild swelling in the mouth

Note

Although it is rare, allergy shots and allergy drops could cause a life threatening allergic reaction called "anaphylaxis". Symptoms of anaphylaxis can include severe swelling of the face, throat, or tongue; itching; a skin rash; trouble breathing; tightness in the chest; wheezing; dizziness; nausea; diarrhea; or loss of consciousness.

If you or your child has any of these symptoms after getting an allergy shot or taking allergy drops, call the doctor right away. Anaphylaxis must be treated immediately with a shot of epinephrine, a type of hormone that regulates your heart rate and breathing passages.

What are the costs of allergy shots and allergy drops?

The costs to you for allergy shots and allergy drops depend on your health insurance. Because allergy drops are not yet approved by the U.S. Food and Drug Administration (FDA), they may not be covered by your health insurance. The costs also depend on how many allergens are in your allergy shots or allergy drops. Because allergy shots are usually given at the doctor's office, you may have to pay for an office visit each time you go for a shot.

Making a Decision

What should I think about when deciding?

There are many things to think about when deciding if allergy shots or allergy drops are right for you or your child. You may want to talk with your doctor about:

* How severe your (or your child's) allergy or asthma symptoms are

* How well you are able to avoid or reduce allergens in your environment (for example, cleaning carpets and drapes or using an air filter, mattress cover, or special pillow case)

337

- How well allergy medicines (antihistamines or steroid nasal spray) work to improve your (or your child's) symptoms

- Possible benefits and side effects of allergy shots or allergy drops

- Which might work better to improve your (or your child's) allergy or asthma symptoms—allergy shots or allergy drops

- Which better fits your preferences and lifestyle—allergy shots or allergy drops

  - For example, would it be easier to take allergy drops every day or go to the doctor's office every few days for a shot?

- The costs of allergy shots or allergy drops

Ask your doctor

- What are the best ways for me to avoid or reduce allergens in my environment?

- Could allergy shots or drops help me (or my child)?

- Do any of my (or my child's) medical conditions affect my (or my child's) ability to take allergy shots or allergy drops?

- Which do you think would be better—allergy shots or allergy drops?

- How long will it take for the allergy shots or allergy drops to start helping?

- How long will I (or my child) need to take the allergy shots or allergy drops?

- How long will allergy shots or allergy drops improve my (or my child's) allergy or asthma symptoms?

- How much would allergy shots cost? How much would allergy drops cost?

- Are there side effects that I need to call you about right away or that would require me to go to an emergency room? If so, what are they? What should I do? When are they likely to happen?

Section 40.3

Anti-Immunoglobulin E Therapy

Text in this section is excerpted from "Omalizumab," LiverTox, National Library of Medicine (NLM), 18 June 2015.

Introduction

Omalizumab is a monoclonal antibody to human immunoglobulin E (IgE), which leads to a decrease in IgE binding to mast cells and basophils and a reduction in allergic symptoms of asthma and seasonal rhinitis. Omalizumab therapy has not been associated with serum enzyme elevations during therapy and has yet to be implicated in cases of clinically apparent drug induced liver injury with jaundice.

Background

Omalizumab is a recombinant, human monoclonal antibody to IgE which binds avidly to circulating immunoglobulin E, preventing its attachment to high affinity receptors on mast cells and basophils. This receptor inhibition prevents the release of histamine and other mediators of the allergic immune response, reducing airway inflammation and spasm and alleviating symptoms of asthma and allergic rhinitis. Therapy with omalizumab has been shown to reduce the requirement for inhaled corticosteroids and lower the frequency of exacerbations of asthma and to decrease the severity and symptoms of chronic urticaria of unknown cause. Omalizumab was approved for use in the United States in 2003 for therapy of patients with severe and persistent asthma despite corticosteroid inhalation therapy. The indications were extended in 2014 to include chronic idiopathic urticaria. Omalizumab has been evaluated in patients with seasonal rhinitis, but has yet to be approved for that use. Omalizumab is available in single use vials of 150 mg under the brand name Xolair. The recommended dose is 150 to 300 mg intravenously every 4 weeks or 225 to 375 mg every 2 weeks based upon body weight and IgE levels. Common side effects include injection site reactions, rash, diarrhea, nausea and vomiting and epistaxis. Rarely, omalizumab can cause serious acute

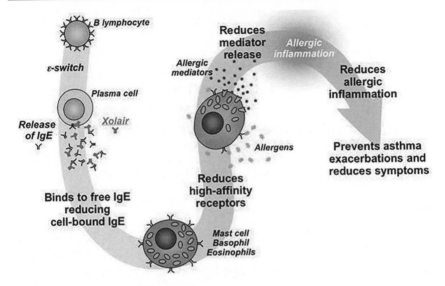

Figure 40.1. *Omalizumab Mechanism of Action*

Source: U.S. Food and Drug Administration (FDA)

anaphylaxis or anaphylactoid reactions (~ 0.1%) and should be given under close medical supervision.

Hepatotoxicity

In large clinical trials, omalizumab was not associated with changes in serum aminotransferase levels during therapy, and rates of most adverse reactions were similar in patients who received omalizumab or placebo. There have been no published reports of clinically apparent acute liver injury attributed to omalizumab therapy. Thus, liver injury from omalizumab must be very rare, if it occurs at all.

Mechanism of Injury

Omalizumab is a human monoclonal antibody and is unlikely to be inherently hepatotoxic. While most recombinant proteins are metabolized by the liver, the metabolism leads largely to small peptides and amino acids which may be reused to synthesize proteins and are unlikely to be toxic or immunogenic. Omalizumab lowers serum levels of IgE, which seems to have no adverse effects on the liver and does not result in significant immunosuppression.

Section 40.4

Therapies for Asthma

Text in this section is excerpted from "How Is Asthma Treated and Controlled?" National Heart, Lung, and Blood Institute (NHLBI), August 4, 2014.

How Is Asthma Treated and Controlled?

Asthma is a long-term disease that has no cure. The goal of asthma treatment is to control the disease. Good asthma control will:

- Prevent chronic and troublesome symptoms, such as coughing and shortness of breath

- Reduce your need for quick-relief medicines

- Help you maintain good lung function

- Let you maintain your normal activity level and sleep through the night

- Prevent asthma attacks that could result in an emergency room visit or hospital stay

To control asthma, partner with your doctor to manage your asthma or your child's asthma. Children aged 10 or older—and younger children who are able—should take an active role in their asthma care.
Taking an active role to control your asthma involves:

- Working with your doctor to treat other conditions that can interfere with asthma management.

- Avoiding things that worsen your asthma (asthma triggers). However, one trigger you should not avoid is physical activity. Physical activity is an important part of a healthy lifestyle. Talk with your doctor about medicines that can help you stay active.

- Working with your doctor and other health care providers to create and follow an asthma action plan.

An asthma action plan gives guidance on taking your medicines properly, avoiding asthma triggers (except physical activity), tracking your level of asthma control, responding to worsening symptoms, and seeking emergency care when needed.

Asthma is treated with two types of medicines: long-term control and quick-relief medicines. Long-term control medicines help reduce airway inflammation and prevent asthma symptoms. Quick-relief, or "rescue," medicines relieve asthma symptoms that may flare up.

Your initial treatment will depend on the severity of your asthma. Followup asthma treatment will depend on how well your asthma action plan is controlling your symptoms and preventing asthma attacks.

Your level of asthma control can vary over time and with changes in your home, school, or work environments. These changes can alter how often you're exposed to the factors that can worsen your asthma.

Your doctor may need to increase your medicine if your asthma doesn't stay under control. On the other hand, if your asthma is well controlled for several months, your doctor may decrease your medicine. These adjustments to your medicine will help you maintain the best control possible with the least amount of medicine necessary.

Asthma treatment for certain groups of people—such as children, pregnant women, or those for whom exercise brings on asthma symptoms—will be adjusted to meet their special needs.

Follow an Asthma Action Plan

You can work with your doctor to create a personal asthma action plan. The plan will describe your daily treatments, such as which medicines to take and when to take them. The plan also will explain when to call your doctor or go to the emergency room.

If your child has asthma, all of the people who care for him or her should know about the child's asthma action plan. This includes babysitters and workers at daycare centers, schools, and camps. These caretakers can help your child follow his or her action plan.

Avoid Things That Can Worsen Your Asthma

Many common things (called asthma triggers) can set off or worsen your asthma symptoms. Once you know what these things are, you can take steps to control many of them.

For example, exposure to pollens or air pollution might make your asthma worse. If so, try to limit time outdoors when the levels of these substances in the outdoor air are high. If animal fur triggers your asthma symptoms, keep pets with fur out of your home or bedroom.

One possible asthma trigger you shouldn't avoid is physical activity. Physical activity is an important part of a healthy lifestyle. Talk with your doctor about medicines that can help you stay active.

The National Heart, Lung, and Blood Institute (NHLBI) offers many useful tips for controlling asthma triggers.

If your asthma symptoms are clearly related to allergens, and you can't avoid exposure to those allergens, your doctor may advise you to get allergy shots.

You may need to see a specialist if you're thinking about getting allergy shots. These shots can lessen or prevent your asthma symptoms, but they can't cure your asthma.

Several health conditions can make asthma harder to manage. These conditions include runny nose, sinus infections, reflux disease, psychological stress, and sleep apnea. Your doctor will treat these conditions as well.

Medicines

Your doctor will consider many things when deciding which asthma medicines are best for you. He or she will check to see how well a medicine works for you. Then, he or she will adjust the dose or medicine as needed.

Asthma medicines can be taken in pill form, but most are taken using a device called an inhaler. An inhaler allows the medicine to go directly to your lungs.

Not all inhalers are used the same way. Ask your doctor or another health care provider to show you the right way to use your inhaler. Review the way you use your inhaler at every medical visit.

Long-Term Control Medicines

Most people who have asthma need to take long-term control medicines daily to help prevent symptoms. The most effective long-term medicines reduce airway inflammation, which helps prevent symptoms from starting. These medicines don't give you quick relief from symptoms.

Inhaled corticosteroids. Inhaled corticosteroids are the preferred medicine for long-term control of asthma. They're the most effective option for long-term relief of the inflammation and swelling that makes your airways sensitive to certain inhaled substances.

Reducing inflammation helps prevent the chain reaction that causes asthma symptoms. Most people who take these medicines daily find they greatly reduce the severity of symptoms and how often they occur.

Inhaled corticosteroids generally are safe when taken as prescribed. These medicines are different from the illegal anabolic steroids taken by some athletes. Inhaled corticosteroids aren't habit-forming, even if you take them every day for many years.

Like many other medicines, though, inhaled corticosteroids can have side effects. Most doctors agree that the benefits of taking inhaled corticosteroids and preventing asthma attacks far outweigh the risk of side effects.

One common side effect from inhaled corticosteroids is a mouth infection called thrush. You might be able to use a spacer or holding chamber on your inhaler to avoid thrush. These devices attach to your inhaler. They help prevent the medicine from landing in your mouth or on the back of your throat.

Check with your doctor to see whether a spacer or holding chamber should be used with the inhaler you have. Also, work with your health care team if you have any questions about how to use a spacer or holding chamber. Rinsing your mouth out with water after taking inhaled corticosteroids also can lower your risk for thrush.

If you have severe asthma, you may have to take corticosteroid pills or liquid for short periods to get your asthma under control.

If taken for long periods, these medicines raise your risk for cataracts and osteoporosis. A cataract is the clouding of the lens in your eye. Osteoporosis is a disorder that makes your bones weak and more likely to break.

Your doctor may have you add another long-term asthma control medicine so he or she can lower your dose of corticosteroids. Or, your doctor may suggest you take calcium and vitamin D pills to protect your bones.

Other long-term control medicines. Other long-term control medicines include:

- Cromolyn. This medicine is taken using a device called a nebulizer. As you breathe in, the nebulizer sends a fine mist of medicine to your lungs. Cromolyn helps prevent airway inflammation.

- Omalizumab (anti-IgE). This medicine is given as a shot (injection) one or two times a month. It helps prevent your body from reacting to asthma triggers, such as pollen and dust mites. Anti-IgE might be used if other asthma medicines have not worked well.

A rare, but possibly life-threatening allergic reaction called anaphylaxis might occur when the Omalizumab injection is given. If you take this medication, work with your doctor to make sure you understand the signs and symptoms of anaphylaxis and what actions you should take.

- Inhaled long-acting beta2-agonists. These medicines open the airways. They might be added to inhaled corticosteroids to improve asthma control. Inhaled long-acting beta2-agonists should never be used on their own for long-term asthma control. They must used with inhaled corticosteroids.

- Leukotriene modifiers. These medicines are taken by mouth. They help block the chain reaction that increases inflammation in your airways.

- Theophylline. This medicine is taken by mouth. Theophylline helps open the airways.

If your doctor prescribes a long-term control medicine, take it every day to control your asthma. Your asthma symptoms will likely return or get worse if you stop taking your medicine.

Long-term control medicines can have side effects. Talk with your doctor about these side effects and ways to reduce or avoid them.

With some medicines, like theophylline, your doctor will check the level of medicine in your blood. This helps ensure that you're getting enough medicine to relieve your asthma symptoms, but not so much that it causes dangerous side effects.

Quick-Relief Medicines

All people who have asthma need quick-relief medicines to help relieve asthma symptoms that may flare up. Inhaled short-acting beta2-agonists are the first choice for quick relief.

These medicines act quickly to relax tight muscles around your airways when you're having a flareup. This allows the airways to open up so air can flow through them.

You should take your quick-relief medicine when you first notice asthma symptoms. If you use this medicine more than 2 days a week, talk with your doctor about your asthma control. You may need to make changes to your asthma action plan.

Carry your quick-relief inhaler with you at all times in case you need it. If your child has asthma, make sure that anyone caring for him or her has the child's quick-relief medicines, including staff at the child's school. They should understand when and how to use these medicines and when to seek medical care for your child.

You shouldn't use quick-relief medicines in place of prescribed long-term control medicines. Quick-relief medicines don't reduce inflammation.

Track Your Asthma

To track your asthma, keep records of your symptoms, check your peak flow number using a peak flow meter, and get regular asthma checkups.

Record Your Symptoms

You can record your asthma symptoms in a diary to see how well your treatments are controlling your asthma.

Asthma is well controlled if:

You have symptoms no more than 2 days a week, and these symptoms don't wake you from sleep more than 1 or 2 nights a month.

- You can do all your normal activities.

- You take quick-relief medicines no more than 2 days a week.

- You have no more than one asthma attack a year that requires you to take corticosteroids by mouth.

- Your peak flow doesn't drop below 80 percent of your personal best number.

If your asthma isn't well controlled, contact your doctor. He or she may need to change your asthma action plan.

Use a Peak Flow Meter

This small, hand-held device shows how well air moves out of your lungs. You blow into the device and it gives you a score, or peak flow number. Your score shows how well your lungs are working at the time of the test.

Your doctor will tell you how and when to use your peak flow meter. He or she also will teach you how to take your medicines based on your score.

Your doctor and other health care providers may ask you to use your peak flow meter each morning and keep a record of your results. You may find it very useful to record peak flow scores for a couple of weeks before each medical visit and take the results with you.

When you're first diagnosed with asthma, it's important to find your "personal best" peak flow number. To do this, you record your score each day for a 2- to 3-week period when your asthma is well-controlled. The highest number you get during that time is your personal best. You can compare this number to future numbers to make sure your asthma is controlled.

Your peak flow meter can help warn you of an asthma attack, even before you notice symptoms. If your score shows that your breathing is getting worse, you should take your quick-relief medicines the way your asthma action plan directs. Then you can use the peak flow meter to check how well the medicine worked.

Get Asthma Checkups

When you first begin treatment, you'll see your doctor about every 2 to 6 weeks. Once your asthma is controlled, your doctor may want to see you from once a month to twice a year.

During these checkups, your doctor may ask whether you've had an asthma attack since the last visit or any changes in symptoms or peak flow measurements. He or she also may ask about your daily activities. This information will help your doctor assess your level of asthma control.

Your doctor also may ask whether you have any problems or concerns with taking your medicines or following your asthma action plan. Based on your answers to these questions, your doctor may change the dose of your medicine or give you a new medicine.

If your control is very good, you might be able to take less medicine. The goal is to use the least amount of medicine needed to control your asthma.

Emergency Care

Most people who have asthma, including many children, can safely manage their symptoms by following their asthma action plans. However, you might need medical attention at times.

Call your doctor for advice if:

- Your medicines don't relieve an asthma attack.

- Your peak flow is less than half of your personal best peak flow number.

Call 911 for emergency care if:

- You have trouble walking and talking because you're out of breath.
- You have blue lips or fingernails.

At the hospital, you'll be closely watched and given oxygen and more medicines, as well as medicines at higher doses than you take at home. Such treatment can save your life.

Asthma Treatment for Special Groups

The treatments described above generally apply to all people who have asthma. However, some aspects of treatment differ for people in certain age groups and those who have special needs.

Children

It's hard to diagnose asthma in children younger than 5 years. Thus, it's hard to know whether young children who wheeze or have other asthma symptoms will benefit from long-term control medicines. (Quick-relief medicines tend to relieve wheezing in young children whether they have asthma or not.)

Doctors will treat infants and young children who have asthma symptoms with long-term control medicines if, after assessing a child, they feel that the symptoms are persistent and likely to continue after 6 years of age.

Inhaled corticosteroids are the preferred treatment for young children. Montelukast and cromolyn are other options. Treatment might be given for a trial period of 1 month to 6 weeks. Treatment usually is stopped if benefits aren't seen during that time and the doctor and parents are confident the medicine was used properly.

Inhaled corticosteroids can possibly slow the growth of children of all ages. Slowed growth usually is apparent in the first several months of treatment, is generally small, and doesn't get worse over time. Poorly controlled asthma also may reduce a child's growth rate.

Many experts think the benefits of inhaled corticosteroids for children who need them to control their asthma far outweigh the risk of slowed growth.

Older Adults

Doctors may need to adjust asthma treatment for older adults who take certain other medicines, such as beta blockers, aspirin and other pain relievers, and anti-inflammatory medicines. These medicines can prevent asthma medicines from working well and may worsen asthma symptoms.

Be sure to tell your doctor about all of the medicines you take, including over-the-counter (OTC) medicines.

Older adults may develop weak bones from using inhaled corticosteroids, especially at high doses. Talk with your doctor about taking calcium and vitamin D pills, as well as other ways to help keep your bones strong.

Doctors may need to adjust asthma treatment for older adults who take certain other medicines, such as beta blockers, aspirin and other pain relievers, and anti-inflammatory medicines. These medicines can prevent asthma medicines from working well and may worsen asthma symptoms.

Be sure to tell your doctor about all of the medicines you take, including over-the-counter medicines.

Older adults may develop weak bones from using inhaled corticosteroids, especially at high doses. Talk with your doctor about taking calcium and vitamin D pills, as well as other ways to help keep your bones strong.

Pregnant Women

Pregnant women who have asthma need to control the disease to ensure a good supply of oxygen to their babies. Poor asthma control increases the risk of preeclampsia, a condition in which a pregnant woman develops high blood pressure and protein in the urine. Poor asthma control also increases the risk that a baby will be born early and have a low birth weight.

Studies show that it's safer to take asthma medicines while pregnant than to risk having an asthma attack.

Talk with your doctor if you have asthma and are pregnant or planning a pregnancy. Your level of asthma control may get better or it may get worse while you're pregnant. Your health care team will check your asthma control often and adjust your treatment as needed.

People Whose Asthma Symptoms Occur with Physical Activity

Physical activity is an important part of a healthy lifestyle. Adults need physical activity to maintain good health. Children need it for growth and development.

In some people, however, physical activity can trigger asthma symptoms. If this happens to you or your child, talk with your doctor about the best ways to control asthma so you can stay active.

The following medicines may help prevent asthma symptoms caused by physical activity:

- Short-acting beta2-agonists (quick-relief medicine) taken shortly before physical activity can last 2 to 3 hours and prevent exercise-related symptoms in most people who take them.

- Long-acting beta2-agonists can be protective for up to 12 hours. However, with daily use, they'll no longer give up to 12 hours of protection. Also, frequent use of these medicines for physical activity might be a sign that asthma is poorly controlled.

- Leukotriene modifiers. These pills are taken several hours before physical activity. They can help relieve asthma symptoms brought on by physical activity.

- Long-term control medicines. Frequent or severe symptoms due to physical activity may suggest poorly controlled asthma and the need to either start or increase long-term control medicines that reduce inflammation. This will help prevent exercise-related symptoms.

Easing into physical activity with a warmup period may be helpful. You also may want to wear a mask or scarf over your mouth when exercising in cold weather.

If you use your asthma medicines as your doctor directs, you should be able to take part in any physical activity or sport you choose.

People Having Surgery

Asthma may add to the risk of having problems during and after surgery. For instance, having a tube put into your throat may cause an asthma attack.

Tell your surgeon about your asthma when you first talk with him or her. The surgeon can take steps to lower your risk, such as giving you asthma medicines before or during surgery

Section 40.5

Therapies for Sinusitis

Text in this section is excerpted from "Sinusitis Treatment," National
Institute of Allergy and Infectious Diseases (NIAID), May 15, 2015.

Acute Sinusitis

Medications can help ease the symptoms of acute sinusitis. Healthcare providers may recommend pain relievers or decongestants—medicines that shrink the swollen membranes in the nose and make it
easier to breathe. Decongestant nose drops and sprays should be used
for only a few days, as longer term use can lead to even more congestion
and swelling of the nasal passages. A doctor may prescribe antibiotics
if the sinusitis is caused by a bacterial infection.

Chronic Rhinosinusitis

Chronic rhinosinusitis can be difficult to treat. Medicines may offer
some symptom relief. Surgery can be helpful if medication fails.

Medicine

Nasal steroid sprays are helpful for many people, but most still
do not get full relief of symptoms with these medicines. Saline (salt
water) washes or nasal sprays can be helpful in chronic rhinosinusitis
because they remove thick secretions and allow the sinuses to drain.
Doctors may prescribe oral steroids, such as prednisone, for severe
chronic rhinosinusitis. However, oral steroids are powerful medicines
that can cause side effects such as weight gain and high blood pressure if used long-term. Oral steroids typically are prescribed when
other medicines have failed. Desensitization to aspirin may be helpful for patients with aspirin-exacerbated respiratory disease. During
desensitization, which is performed under close medical supervision,
a person is given gradually increasing doses of aspirin over time to
induce tolerance to the drug.

Surgery

When medicine fails, surgery may be the only alternative for treating chronic rhinosinusitis. The goal of surgery is to improve sinus drainage and reduce blockage of the nasal passages. Sinus surgery usually is performed to

- Enlarge the natural openings of the sinuses

- Remove nasal polyps

- Correct significant structural problems inside the nose and the sinuses if they contribute to sinus obstruction

Although most people have fewer symptoms and a better quality of life after surgery, problems can recur, sometimes after a short period of time.

In children, problems can sometimes be eliminated by removing the adenoids. These gland-like tissues, located high in the throat behind and above the roof of the mouth, can obstruct the nasal passages.

Section 40.6

Treatments for Seasonal Allergic Rhinitis (SAR)

Text in this section is excerpted from "Treatments for Seasonal Allergic Rhinitis," Agency for Healthcare Research and Quality (AHRQ), July 16, 2013.

Seasonal allergic rhinitis (SAR), also known as hay fever, is an allergic reaction in the upper airways that occurs when sensitized individuals encounter airborne allergens (typically tree, grass, and weed pollens and some molds). SAR afflicts approximately 10 percent of the U.S. population, or 30 million individuals. Although pollen seasons vary across the United States, generally, tree pollens emerge in the spring, grass pollens in the summer, and weed pollens in the fall. Outdoor molds generally are prevalent in the summer and fall. SAR is distinguished from perennial allergic rhinitis (PAR), which is triggered by continuous exposure to house dust mites, animal dander, and other allergens generally found in an individual's indoor environment. Patients may have either SAR or PAR or both (i.e., PAR with seasonal exacerbations). The four defining symptoms of allergic rhinitis are nasal congestion, nasal discharge (rhinorrhea), sneezing, and/or nasal itch. Many patients also experience eye symptoms, such as itching, tearing, and redness. Additional signs of rhinitis include the "allergic salute" (rubbing the hand against the nose in response to itching and rhinorrhea), "allergic shiner" (bruised appearance of the skin under one or both eyes), and "allergic crease" (a wrinkle across the bridge of the nose caused by repeated allergic salute). SAR can adversely affect quality of life, sleep, cognition, emotional life, and work or school performance. Treatment improves symptoms and quality of life.

Treatments for SAR include allergen avoidance, pharmacotherapy, and immunotherapy. Although allergen avoidance may be the preferred treatment, for SAR, total allergen avoidance may be an unrealistic approach, as it may require limiting time spent outdoors. Thus, pharmacotherapy is preferable to allergen avoidance for SAR symptom relief. Allergen-specific immunotherapy is the subject of a separate review, also sponsored by the Agency for Healthcare Research and Quality (AHRQ) and posted on the Effective Health Care Web site (www.effectivehealthcare.ahrq.gov/reports/final/cfm).

Six classes of drugs and nasal saline are used to treat SAR.

1. *Antihistamines* used to treat allergic rhinitis bind *peripheral* H1 histamine receptors selectively or nonselectively. Nonselective binding to other receptor types can cause dry mouth, dry eyes, urinary retention, constipation, and tachycardia. Sedation results from the nonselective binding to *central* H1 receptors. In contrast, selective antihistamines may have reduced incidence of adverse effects. Both selective and nonselective antihistamines interact with drugs that inhibit cytochrome P450 isoenzymes, which may impact patient selection. Two nasal antihistamines—azelastine and olopatadine—are approved by the U.S. Food and Drug Administration (FDA) for the treatment of SAR. Adverse effects of nasal antihistamines may include a bitter aftertaste.

2. *Corticosteroids* are potent anti-inflammatory drugs. Intranasal corticosteroids are recommended as first-line treatment for moderate/severe or persistent allergic rhinitis. However, their efficacy for the symptom of nasal congestion compared with

nasal antihistamine is uncertain particularly in patients with mild allergic rhinitis. For patients with unresponsive symptoms, it is unclear whether adding oral or nasal antihistamine provides any additional benefit. Little is known about cumulative corticosteroid effects in patients who take concomitant oral or inhaled formulations for other diseases. Intranasal corticosteroids do not appear to cause adverse events associated with systemic absorption (e.g., adrenal suppression, bone fracture among the elderly, and reduced bone growth and height in children). Adverse local effects may include increased intraocular pressure and nasal stinging, burning, bleeding, and dryness. Oral and intramuscular corticosteroids are not reviewed in this report.

3. *Decongestants* stimulate the sympathetic nervous system to produce vasoconstriction, which results in decreased nasal swelling and decreased congestion. After several days of nasal decongestant use, rebound congestion (rhinitis medicamentosa) may occur. Other local adverse effects may include nosebleeds, stinging, burning, and dryness. Oral decongestants are used alone and in combination, often with antihistamines. Systemic adverse effects of decongestants may include hypertension, tachycardia, insomnia, headaches, and irritability. Decongestants are used with caution, if at all, in patients with diabetes mellitus, ischemic heart disease, unstable hypertension, prostatic hypertrophy, hyperthyroidism, and narrow-angle glaucoma. Oral decongestants are contraindicated with coadministered monoamine oxidase inhibitors and in patients with uncontrolled hypertension or severe coronary artery disease.

4. *Ipratropium* nasal spray is an anticholinergic drug approved by the FDA for treating rhinorrhea associated with SAR. Postmarketing experience suggests that there may be some systemic absorption. Cautious use is advised for patients with narrow-angle glaucoma, prostatic hypertrophy, or bladder neck obstruction, particularly if another anticholinergic is coadministered. Local adverse effects may include nosebleeds and nasal and oral dryness.

5. Nasal mast cell stabilizers are commonly administered prophylactically, before an allergic reaction is triggered, although as-needed use has been described and may be of benefit. Cromolyn is the only mast cell stabilizer approved by the FDA for the

354

treatment of SAR. For prophylaxis, it requires a loading period during which it is applied four times daily for several weeks. Systemic absorption is minimal. Local adverse effects may include nasal irritation, sneezing, and an unpleasant taste.

6. *Leukotriene* receptor antagonists are oral medications that reduce allergy symptoms by reducing inflammation. Montelukast is the only leukotriene receptor antagonist approved by the FDA for the treatment of SAR. Potential adverse effects include upper respiratory tract infection and headache.

Nasal saline has been shown to be beneficial in treating nasal SAR symptoms. Because it is associated with few adverse effects, nasal saline may be particularly well suited for treating SAR symptoms during pregnancy, in children, and in those whose treatment choices are restricted due to comorbidities, such as hypertension and urinary retention.

The optimal treatment of SAR during pregnancy is unknown. Drugs effective before pregnancy may be effective during pregnancy, but their use may be restricted because of concerns about maternal and fetal safety. Preferred treatments are Pregnancy Category B drugs (nasal cromolyn, budesonide, and ipratropium; several oral selective and nonselective antihistamines; and the oral leukotriene receptor antagonist montelukast) commencing in the second trimester, after organogenesis.

Chapter 41

Complementary and Alternative Medicine (CAM) for Allergies

Chapter Contents

Section 41.1

Complementary and Alternative Medicine (CAM) for Seasonal Allergies

Text in this section is excerpted from "Seasonal Allergies at a Glance," National Center for Complementary and Integrative Health (NCCIH), April 2013.

Seasonal Allergies at a Glance

Seasonal allergies, also called allergic rhinitis or hay fever, are common among both adults and children. They occur when the immune system, which defends the body against foreign invaders such as bacteria, responds to a false alarm. In a person who has an allergy, the immune system treats a normally harmless substance as a threat and attacks it, producing symptoms of an allergic reaction.

What the Science Says

Many complementary health approaches have been studied for allergic rhinitis. There is some evidence that a few may be helpful.

- Rinsing the sinuses with a neti pot (a device that comes from the Ayurvedic tradition) or with other devices, such as bottles, sprays, pumps, or nebulizers, may be a useful addition to conventional treatment for allergic rhinitis.

- There have been several studies in Europe of the herb butterbur for allergic rhinitis, most of which indicated that butterbur may be helpful.

- It has been thought that eating honey might help to relieve seasonal allergies because honey contains small amounts of pollen and might act as a form of immunotherapy. Another possibility is that honey could act as an antihistamine or anti-inflammatory agent. Only a few studies have examined the effects of honey in people with seasonal allergies, and there is no convincing evidence that honey can relieve allergy symptoms.

- Many other natural products have been studied for allergic rhinitis, including astragalus, capsaicin, grape seed extract, omega-3 fatty acids, probiotics, Pycnogenol (French maritime pine bark extract), quercetin, spirulina, stinging nettle, and an herb used in Ayurvedic medicine called tinospora or guduchi. In all instances, the evidence is either inconsistent or too limited to show whether these products are helpful.

- It is uncertain whether acupuncture can be helpful for allergic rhinitis. A few studies have evaluated acupuncture for this condition, but their results have been inconsistent.

Side Effects and Risks

- People can get infections if they use neti pots or other nasal rinsing devices improperly. The U.S. Food and Drug Administration (FDA) has information on how to rinse your sinuses safely.

  - Most important is the source of water that is used with nasal rinsing devices. According to the FDA, tap water that is not filtered, treated, or processed in specific ways is not safe for use as a nasal rinse. Sterile water is safe; over-the-counter nasal rinsing products that contain sterile saline (salt water) are available.

  - Some tap water contains low levels of organisms, such as bacteria and protozoa, including amoebas, that may be safe to swallow because stomach acid kills them. But these organisms can stay alive in nasal passages and cause potentially serious infections. Improper use of neti pots may have caused two deaths in 2011 in Louisiana from a rare brain infection that the state health department linked to tap water contaminated with an amoeba called *Naegleria fowleri*.

- Raw butterbur extracts contain pyrrolizidine alkaloids, which can cause liver damage and cancer. Extracts of butterbur that are almost completely free from these alkaloids are available. However, no studies have proven that the long-term use of butterbur products, including the reduced-alkaloid products, is safe.

- Acupuncture is generally considered safe when performed by an experienced practitioner using sterile needles. Improperly performed acupuncture can cause potentially serious side effects.

- Be cautious about using herbs or bee products for any purpose. Some herbs, such as chamomile and echinacea, may cause allergic reactions in people who are allergic to related plants. Also, people with pollen allergies may have allergic reactions to bee products, such as bee pollen, honey, royal jelly, and propolis (a hive sealant made by bees from plant resins). Children under 1 year of age should not eat honey.

Talk to your health care provider about the best way to manage your seasonal allergies, especially if you are considering or using a dietary supplement. Be aware that some supplements may interact with medications or other supplements or have side effects of their own. Keep in mind that most dietary supplements have not been tested in pregnant women, nursing mothers, or children.

Section 41.2

Complementary Health Approaches for Asthma

Text in this section is excerpted from "Asthma and Complementary Health Approaches," National Center for Complementary and Integrative Health (NCCIH), April 2013.

Most people are able to control their asthma with conventional therapies and by avoiding the substances that can set off asthma attacks. Even so, some people turn to complementary health approaches in their efforts to relieve symptoms. According to the 2002 National Health Interview Survey (NHIS), which included a comprehensive survey on the use of complementary health approaches by Americans, asthma ranked 13th as a condition prompting use of complementary health approaches by adults; 1.1 percent of respondents (an estimated 788,000 adults) said they had used a complementary approach for asthma in the past year. In the 2007 NHIS survey, which included adults and children, asthma ranked eighth among conditions prompting use of complementary health approaches by children, but did not appear in a similar ranking for adults.

What the Science Says about Complementary Health Approaches and Asthma

According to reviewers who have assessed the research, there is not enough evidence to support the use of any complementary health approaches for the relief of asthma.

- Several studies have looked at actual or true **acupuncture**—stimulation of specific points on the body with thin metal needles—for asthma. Although a few studies showed some reduction in medication use and improvements in symptoms and quality of life, the majority showed no difference between actual acupuncture and simulated or sham acupuncture on asthma symptoms. At this point, there is little evidence that acupuncture is an effective treatment for asthma.

- There has been renewed patient interest in **breathing exercises** or **retraining** to reduce hyperventilation, regulate breathing, and achieve a better balance of carbon dioxide and oxygen in the blood. A review of seven randomized controlled trials found a trend toward improvement in symptoms with breathing techniques but not enough evidence for firm conclusions.

- A 2011 study examined the placebo response in patients with chronic asthma and found that patients receiving a placebo (placebo inhaler and simulated acupuncture) reported significant improvement in symptoms such as chest tightness and perception of difficulty breathing. However, lung function did not improve in these patients. This is an important distinction because although the patients felt better, their risk for becoming very sick from untreated asthma was not lessened.

NCCIH-Funded Research

NCCIH is currently funding studies to determine whether:

- Mindfulness meditation practices might help manage symptoms or improve quality of life for people with asthma

- Vitamin E might reduce lung inflammation in mice and humans with allergic asthma

- Borage oil or *Ginkgo biloba* might reduce airway inflammation

- Under-the-tongue (sublingual) immunotherapy might build tolerance to substances that trigger allergic asthma.

If You Are Considering Complementary Health Approaches for Asthma

- Conventional medical treatments are very effective for managing asthma symptoms. See your health care provider to discuss a comprehensive medical treatment plan for your asthma.

- Do not use any complementary approaches to postpone seeing your health care provider about asthma-like symptoms or any health problem.

- Do not replace conventional treatments for asthma with unproven products or practices.

- Keep in mind that dietary supplements can act in the same way as drugs. They can cause health problems if not used correctly or if used in large amounts, and some may interact with medications you take. Your health care provider can advise you. If you are pregnant or nursing a child, or if you are considering giving a child a dietary supplement, it is especially important to consult your (or your child's) health care provider.

- Tell all your health care providers about any complementary health approaches you use. Give them a full picture of what you do to manage your health. This will help ensure coordinated and safe care.

Section 41.3

Nasal Decongestants

Text in this section is excerpted from "Is Rinsing Your Sinuses Safe?"
U.S. Food and Drug Administration (FDA), August 2012.

Is Rinsing Your Sinuses Safe?

Little teapots with long spouts have become a fixture in many homes for reasons that have nothing to do with tea.

Called neti pots, they are used to rinse the nasal passages with a saline (salt-based) solution, and have become popular as a treatment for congested sinuses, colds and allergies, and for moistening nasal passages exposed to dry indoor air.

However, the U.S. Food and Drug Administration (FDA) has concerns about the risk of infection tied to the improper use of neti pots and other nasal rinsing devices. The agency is informing consumers, manufacturers and health care professionals about safe practices for using all nasal rinsing devices, which include bulb syringes, squeeze bottles, and batteryoperated pulsed water devices.

These devices are generally safe and useful products, says Steven Osborne, M.D., a medical officer in FDA's Center for Devices and Radiological Health (CDRH). But they must be used and cleaned properly.

Most important is the source of water that is used with nasal rinsing devices. Tap water that is not filtered, treated, or processed in specific ways is not safe for use as a nasal rinse.

Some tap water contains low levels of organisms, such as bacteria and protozoa, including amoebas, which may be safe to swallow because stomach acid kills them. But these "bugs" can stay alive in nasal passages and cause potentially serious infections, according to the Centers for Disease Control and Prevention (CDC).

Improper use of neti pots may have caused two deaths in 2011 in Louisiana from a rare brain infection that the state health department linked to tap water contaminated with an amoeba called *Naegleria fowleri*.

Misleading, Missing Information

Information included with the device might give more specific instructions about its use and care. However, FDA staff has found that some manufacturers' instructions provide misleading or contradictory information, or lack any guidelines.

For example, some manufacturers have recommended using plain tap water; others warn against using it in printed directions, but show its use in pictures or videos.

The device might also come without instructions. If you order a custom neti pot made by an artist, for example, that person might assume you know how to use it.

The procedure for nasal rinsing may vary slightly by device, but generally involves these steps:

- Leaning over a sink, tilt your head sideways with your forehead and chin roughly level to avoid liquid flowing into your mouth.

- Breathing through your open mouth, insert the spout of the saline-filled container into your upper nostril so that the liquid drains through the lower nostril.

- Clear your nostrils, then repeat the procedure, tilting your head sideways, on the other side.

Nasal rinsing can remove dirt, dust, pollen, and other debris, as well as help to loosen thick mucus. It can also help relieve nasal symptoms of allergies, colds and flu.

"The nose is like a car filter or home air filter that traps debris. Rinsing the nose with saline solution is similar to using saline eye drops to rinse out pollen," Osborne says. The saline, he adds, enables the water to pass through delicate nasal membranes with little or no burning or irritation.

FDA staff recommends that you consult a health care provider or pharmacist if the instructions do not clearly state how to use the device or the types of water to use, if instructions are missing, or if you have any questions.

Questions and Answers

What types of water are safe to use in nasal rinsing devices?

- Distilled or sterile water, which you can buy in stores. The label will state "distilled" or "sterile."

- Boiled and cooled tap water—boiled for 3-5 minutes, then cooled until it is lukewarm. Previously boiled water can be stored in a clean, closed container for use within 24 hours.

- Water passed through a filter with an absolute pore size of 1 micron or smaller, which traps potentially infectious organisms. CDC has information on selecting these filters, which you can buy from some hardware and discount stores, or online.

How do I use and care for my device?

- Wash and dry hands.

- Check that the device is clean and completely dry.

- Use the appropriate water as recommended above to prepare the saline rinse, either with the prepared mixture supplied with the device, or one you make yourself.

- Follow the manufacturer's directions for use.

- Wash the device with distilled, sterile, or boiled and cooled tap water, and then dry the inside with a paper towel or let it air dry between uses

Are nasal rinsing devices safe for children?

"Some children are diagnosed with nasal allergies as early as age 2," Osborne says, "and could use nasal rinsing devices at that time, if a pediatrician recommends it." However, he adds that very young children might not tolerate the procedure as easily as would older children or adults.

What are some negative effects to watch out for when using nasal rinsing devices?

Talk to your health care provider to determine if nasal rinsing will be safe or effective for your condition. If symptoms are not relieved or worsen after nasal rinsing, then return to your health care provider, especially if you had any of these symptoms while using the nasal rinse:

- fever

- nosebleed

- headaches

FDA asks health care professionals and patients to report complaints about nasal rinsing devices to the FDA's MedWatch (www.fda.gov/Safety/MedWatch) Safety Information and Adverse Event Reporting Program.

Section 41.4

Probiotics as a Complementary Health Approach

Text in this section is excerpted from "Probiotics," National Center for Complementary and Integrative Health (NCCIH), July 2015.

What Are Probiotics?

Probiotics are live microorganisms that are intended to have health benefits. Products sold as probiotics include foods (such as yogurt), dietary supplements, and products that are not used orally, such as skin creams.

Although people often think of bacteria and other microorganisms as harmful "germs," many microorganisms help our bodies function properly. For example, bacteria that are normally present in our intestines help digest food, destroy disease-causing microorganisms, and produce vitamins. Large numbers of microorganisms live on and in our bodies. In fact, microorganisms in the human body outnumber human cells by 10 to 1. Many of the microorganisms in probiotic products are the same as or similar to microorganisms that naturally live in our bodies.

What's the Bottom Line

How much do we know about probiotics?

Although a great deal of research has been done on probiotics, much remains to be learned.

What do we know about the usefulness of probiotics?

Some probiotics may help to prevent diarrhea that is caused by infections or antibiotics. They may also help with symptoms of irritable bowel syndrome. However, benefits have not been conclusively demonstrated, and not all probiotics have the same effects.

What do we know about the safety of probiotics?

In healthy people, probiotics usually have only minor side effects, if any. However, in people with underlying health problems (for example, weakened immune systems), serious complications such as infections have occasionally been reported.

The History of Probiotics

The concept behind probiotics was introduced in the early 20th century, when Nobel laureate Elie Metchnikoff, known as the "father of probiotics," proposed that consuming beneficial microorganisms could improve people's health. Researchers continued to investigate this idea, and the term "probiotics"—meaning "for life"—eventually came into use.

What Kinds of Microorganisms Are in Probiotics?

Probiotics may contain a variety of microorganisms. The most common are bacteria that belong to groups called *Lactobacillus* and *Bifidobacterium*. Each of these two broad groups includes many types of bacteria. Other bacteria may also be used as probiotics, and so may yeasts such as *Saccharomyces boulardii*.

Probiotics, Prebiotics, and Synbiotics

Prebiotics are not the same as probiotics. The term "prebiotics" refers to dietary substances that favor the growth of beneficial bacteria over harmful ones. The term "synbiotics" refers to products that combine probiotics and prebiotics.

How Popular Are Probiotics?

Data from the 2012 National Health Interview Survey (NHIS) show that about 4 million (1.6 percent) U.S. adults had used probiotics or prebiotics in the past 30 days. Among adults, probiotics or prebiotics were the third most commonly used dietary supplement other than vitamins and minerals, and the use of probiotics quadrupled between 2007 and 2012. The 2012 NHIS also showed that 300,000 children age 4 to 17 (0.5 percent) had used probiotics or prebiotics in the 30 days before the survey.

What the Science Says about the Effectiveness of Probiotics

Researchers have studied probiotics to find out whether they might help prevent or treat a variety of health problems, including:

- Digestive disorders such as diarrhea caused by infections, antibiotic-associated diarrhea, irritable bowel syndrome, and inflammatory bowel disease

- Allergic disorders such as atopic dermatitis (eczema) and allergic rhinitis (hay fever)

- Tooth decay, periodontal disease, and other oral health problems

- Colic in infants

- Liver disease

- The common cold

- Prevention of necrotizing enterocolitis in very low birth weight infants

There's preliminary evidence that some probiotics are helpful in preventing diarrhea caused by infections and antibiotics and in improving symptoms of irritable bowel syndrome, but more needs to be learned. We still don't know which probiotics are helpful and which are not. We also don't know how much of the probiotic people would have to take or who would most likely benefit from taking probiotics. Even for the conditions that have been studied the most, researchers are still working toward finding the answers to these questions.

Probiotics are not all alike. For example, if a specific kind of *Lactobacillus* helps prevent an illness, that doesn't necessarily mean that another kind of Lactobacillus would have the same effect or that any of the *Bifidobacterium* probiotics would do the same thing.

Although some probiotics have shown promise in research studies, strong scientific evidence to support specific uses of probiotics for most health conditions is lacking. The U.S. Food and Drug Administration (FDA) has not approved any probiotics for preventing or treating any health problem. Some experts have cautioned that the rapid growth in marketing and use of probiotics may have outpaced scientific research for many of their proposed uses and benefits.

How Might Probiotics Work?

Government Regulation of Probiotics

Many probiotics are sold as dietary supplements, which do not require FDA approval before they are marketed. Dietary supplement labels may make claims about how the product affects the structure or function of the body without FDA approval, but they cannot make health claims (claims that the product reduces the risk of a disease) without the FDA's consent.

If a probiotic is marketed as a drug for specific treatment of a disease or disorder in the future, it will be required to meet more stringent requirements. It must be proven safe and effective for its intended use through clinical trials and be approved by the FDA before it can be sold.

What the Science Says about the Safety and Side Effects of Probiotics

Whether probiotics are likely to be safe for you depends on the state of your health.

- In people who are generally healthy, probiotics have a good safety record. Side effects, if they occur at all, usually consist only of mild digestive symptoms such as gas.

- On the other hand, there have been reports linking probiotics to severe side effects, such as dangerous infections, in people with serious underlying medical problems.

  - The people who are most at risk of severe side effects include critically ill patients, those who have had surgery, very sick infants, and people with weakened immune systems

  - The people who are most at risk of severe side effects include critically ill patients, those who have had surgery, very sick infants, and people with weakened immune systems

Even for healthy people, there are uncertainties about the safety of probiotics. Because many research studies on probiotics haven't looked closely at safety, there isn't enough information right now to answer some safety questions. Most of our knowledge about safety comes from studies of *Lactobacillus* and *Bifidobacterium*; less is known about other probiotics. Information on the long-term safety of probiotics is limited, and safety may differ from one type of probiotic to another. For example, even though a National Center for Complementary and Integrative Health (NCCIH)-funded study showed that a particular kind of *Lactobacillus* appears safe in healthy adults age 65 and older, this does not mean that all probiotics would necessarily be safe for people in this age group.

Quality Concerns about Probiotic Products

NCCIH-Funded Research

NCCIH is sponsoring a variety of research projects related to probiotics.

- Whether a specific probiotic is helpful for irritable bowel syndrome

- The mechanisms by which certain probiotics may enhance the response to vaccines

- How prebiotics influence probiotic bacteria

- Whether a yogurt beverage can be used as a way of giving probiotics to children.

NCCIH participates in the National Institutes of Health (NIH) Probiotic and Prebiotic Working Group, a joint effort by several NIH agencies to identify gaps and challenges in research on probiotics and prebiotics. NCCIH also partially funded an Agency for Healthcare Research and Quality review of the safety of probiotics.

More to Consider

- Don't replace scientifically proven treatments with unproven products and practices. Don't use a complementary health product, such as probiotics, as a reason to postpone seeing your health care provider about any health problem.

- If you're considering a probiotic dietary supplement, consult your health care provider first. This is especially important if you have health problems. Anyone with a serious underlying health condition should be monitored closely while taking probiotics.

- If you're pregnant or nursing a child, or if you're considering giving a child a dietary supplement, such as probiotics, it's especially important to consult your (or your child's) health care provider.

- Tell all your health care providers about any complementary or integrative health approaches you use. Give them a full picture of what you do to manage your health. This will help ensure coordinated and safe care.

Part Six

Avoiding Allergy Triggers, Preventing Symptoms, and Getting Support

Chapter 42

Improving Indoor Air Quality and Reducing Environmental Triggers

Improving Indoor Air Quality

There are three basic strategies to improve indoor air quality

1. Source control

2. Improved ventilation

3. Air cleaners

Source Control

Usually the most effective way to improve indoor air quality is to eliminate individual sources of pollution or to reduce their emissions.

Some sources, like those that contain asbestos, can be sealed or enclosed; others, like gas stoves, can be adjusted to decrease the amount of emissions. In many cases, source control is also a more cost-efficient approach to protecting indoor air quality than increasing ventilation because increasing ventilation can increase energy costs.

Text in this chapter is excerpted from "Indoor Air Quality (IAQ)," U.S. Environmental Protection Agency (EPA), September 28, 2015.

Ventilation Improvements

Another approach to lowering the concentrations of indoor air pollutants in your home is to increase the amount of outdoor air coming indoors.

> For most indoor air quality problems in the home, source control is the most effective solution.

Most home heating and cooling systems, including forced air heating systems, do not mechanically bring fresh air into the house. Opening windows and doors, operating window or attic fans, when the weather permits, or running a window air conditioner with the vent control open increases the outdoor ventilation rate. Local bathroom or kitchen fans that exhaust outdoors remove contaminants directly from the room where the fan is located and also increase the outdoor air ventilation rate.

It is particularly important to take as many of these steps as possible while you are involved in short-term activities that can generate high levels of pollutants—for example, painting, paint stripping, heating with kerosene heaters, cooking, or engaging in maintenance and hobby activities such as welding, soldering, or sanding. You might also choose to do some of these activities outdoors, if you can and if weather permits.

Advanced designs of new homes are starting to feature mechanical systems that bring outdoor air into the home. Some of these designs include energy-efficient heat recovery ventilators (also known as air-to-air heat exchangers).

Ventilation and shading can help control indoor temperatures. Ventilation also helps remove or dilute indoor airborne pollutants coming from indoor sources. This reduces the level of contaminants and improves indoor air quality (IAQ). Carefully evaluate using ventilation to reduce indoor air pollutants where there may be outdoor sources of pollutants, such as smoke or refuse, nearby.

The introduction of outdoor air is one important factor in promoting good air quality. Air may enter a home in several different ways, including:

- through natural ventilation, such as through windows and doors

- through mechanical means, such as through outdoor air intakes associated with the heating, ventilation and air conditioning (HVAC) system

- through infiltration, a process by which outdoor air flows into the house through openings, joints and cracks in walls, floors and ceilings, and around windows and doors.

Infiltration occurs in all homes to some extent.

Natural ventilation describes air movement through open windows and doors. If used properly natural ventilation can at times help moderate the indoor air temperature, which may become too hot in homes without air-conditioning systems or when power outages or brownouts limit or make the use of air conditioning impossible.

Natural ventilation can also improve indoor air quality by reducing pollutants that are indoors. Examples of natural ventilation are:

- opening windows and doors
- window shading such as closing the blinds

Most residential forced air-heating systems and air-conditioning systems do not bring outdoor air into the house mechanically, and infiltration and natural ventilation are relied upon to bring outdoor air into the home. Advanced designs for new homes are starting to add a mechanical feature that brings outdoor air into the home through the HVAC system. Some of these designs include energy efficient heat recovery ventilators to mitigate the cost of cooling and heating this air during the summer and winter.

Air Cleaners

There are many types and sizes of air cleaners on the market, ranging from relatively inexpensive table-top models to sophisticated and expensive whole-house systems. Some air cleaners are highly effective at particle removal, while others, including most table-top models, are much less so. Air cleaners are generally not designed to remove gaseous pollutants.

The effectiveness of an air cleaner depends on how well it collects pollutants from indoor air (expressed as a percentage efficiency rate) and how much air it draws through the cleaning or filtering element (expressed in cubic feet per minute).

A very efficient collector with a low air-circulation rate will not be effective, nor will a cleaner with a high air-circulation rate but a less efficient collector. The long-term performance of any air cleaner depends on maintaining it according to the manufacturer's directions.

Another important factor in determining the effectiveness of an air cleaner is the strength of the pollutant source. Table-top air cleaners, in particular, may not remove satisfactory amounts of pollutants from strong nearby sources. People with a sensitivity to particular sources may find that air cleaners are helpful only in conjunction with concerted efforts to remove the source.

Over the past few years, there has been some publicity suggesting that houseplants have been shown to reduce levels of some chemicals in laboratory experiments. There is currently no evidence, however, that a reasonable number of houseplants remove significant quantities of pollutants in homes and offices. Indoor houseplants should not be over-watered because overly damp soil may promote the growth of microorganisms which can affect allergic individuals.

At present, EPA does not recommend using air cleaners to reduce levels of radon and its decay products. The effectiveness of these devices is uncertain because they only partially remove the radon decay products and do not diminish the amount of radon entering the home. EPA plans to do additional research on whether air cleaners are, or could become, a reliable means of reducing the health risk from radon.

Chapter 43

Air Cleaners and Indoor Air Pollutants

Introduction

Indoor air pollutants are unwanted, sometimes harmful materials in the air. Indoor air pollution is among the top five environmental health risks. Usually the best way to address this risk is to control or eliminate the sources of pollutants, and to ventilate a home with clean outdoor air. The ventilation method may, however, be limited by weather conditions or undesirable levels of contaminants contained in outdoor air. If these measures are insufficient, an air cleaning device may be useful. Air cleaning devices are intended to remove pollutants from indoor air.

Some air cleaning devices are designed to be installed in the ductwork of a home's central heating, ventilating and air-conditioning (HVAC) system to clean the air in the whole house. Portable room air cleaners can be used to clean the air in a single room or specific areas, but they are not intended for whole-house filtration. The following pages will provide information on different types of air cleaning devices and how they work.

Text in this chapter is excerpted from "Guide to Air Cleaners in the Home," United States Environmental Protection Agency (EPA), October 14, 2015.

Indoor Air Pollutants

Pollutants that can affect air quality in a home fall into the following categories:

- Particulate matter includes dust, smoke, pollen, animal dander, tobacco smoke, particles generated from combustion appliances such as cooking stoves, and particles associated with tiny organisms such as:

    - dust mites

    - molds

    - bacteria

    - viruses

- Gaseous pollutants come from combustion processes. Sources include gas cooking stoves, vehicle exhaust and tobacco smoke. They also come from:

    - building materials

    - furnishings

    - the use of products such as

        - adhesives

        - paints

        - varnishes

        - cleaning products

        - pesticides

What Types of Pollutants Can an Air Cleaner Remove?

There are several types of air cleaning devices available, each designed to remove certain types of pollutants.

Particle Removal

Two types of air cleaning devices can remove particles from the air—mechanical air filters and electronic air cleaners. **Mechanical air filters** remove particles by capturing them on filter materials. High efficiency particulate air (HEPA) filters are in this category. **Electronic air cleaners** such as electrostatic precipitators use a process called electrostatic attraction to trap charged particles. They draw air through an ionization section where particles obtain an electrical charge. The charged particles then accumulate on a series of flat plates called a collector that is oppositely charged. Ion generators, or ionizers, disperse charged ions into the air, similar to the electronic air cleaners but without a collector. These ions attach to airborne particles, giving them a charge so that they attach to nearby surfaces such as walls or furniture, or attach to one another and settle faster.

Gaseous Pollutant Removal

Gas-phase air filters remove gases and odors by using a material called a sorbent, such as activated carbon, which adsorbs the pollutants. These filters are typically intended to remove one or more gaseous pollutants from the airstream that passes through them. Because gas-phase filters are specific to one or a limited number of gaseous pollutants, they will not reduce concentrations of pollutants for which they were not designed. Some air cleaning devices with gas-phase filters may remove a portion of the gaseous pollutants and some of the related hazards, at least on a temporary basis. However, none are expected to remove all of the gaseous pollutants present in the air of a typical home.

For example, carbon monoxide is a dangerous gaseous pollutant that is produced whenever any fuel such as gas, oil, kerosene, wood or charcoal is burned, and it is not readily captured using currently available residential gas-phase filtration products.

Pollutant Destruction

Some air cleaners use ultraviolet (UV) light technology intended to destroy pollutants in indoor air. These air cleaners are called ultraviolet germicidal irradiation (UVGI) cleaners and photocatalytic oxidation (PCO) cleaners. Ozone generators that are sold as air cleaners intentionally produce ozone gas, a lung irritant, to destroy pollutants.

> Ozone is a lung irritant that can cause adverse health effects.

UVGI cleaners use ultraviolet radiation from UV lamps that may destroy biological pollutants such as viruses, bacteria, allergens and molds that are airborne or growing on HVAC surfaces (e.g., found on cooling coils, drain pans, or ductwork). If used, they should be applied with, but not as a replacement for, filtration systems.

- PCO cleaners use a UV lamp along with a substance, called a catalyst, that reacts with the light. They are intended to destroy gaseous pollutants by converting them into harmless products, but are not designed to remove particulate pollutants.

- Ozone generators use UV light or an electrical discharge to intentionally produce ozone. Ozone is a lung irritant that can cause adverse health effects. At concentrations that do not exceed public health standards, ozone has little effect in removing most indoor air contaminants. Thus, ozone generators are not always safe and effective in controlling indoor air pollutants. Consumers should instead use methods proven to be both safe and effective to reduce pollutant concentrations, which include eliminating or controlling pollutant sources and increasing outdoor air ventilation.

Table 43.1. Air Cleaning Technologies

Air Cleaning Technologies		Pollutants Addressed	Limitations
Filtration	Air filters	Particles	Ineffective in removing larger particles because most settle from the air quickly and never reach filters.
	Gas-phase filters	Gases	Used much less frequently in homes than particle air filters. The lifetime for removing pollutants may be short.
Other Air Cleaners	UVGI	Biologicals	Bacterial and mold spores tend to be resistant to UV radiation and require more light or longer time of exposure, or both, to be killed.
	PCO	Gases	Application for homes is limited because currently available catalysts are ineffective in destroying gaseous pollutants from indoor air.
	Ozone generators	Particles, gases, biologicals	Sold as air cleaners, they are not always safe and effective in removing pollutants. By design, they produce ozone, a lung irritant.

Table 43.1 provides a brief summary of air cleaning technologies and the pollutants they are designed to control.

In addition to understanding the different types of air cleaning devices, consumers should consider their performance.

How Is the Performance of an Air Cleaner Measured?

There are different ways to measure how well air cleaning devices work, which depend on the type of device and the basic configuration. Air cleaning devices are configured either in the ductwork of HVAC systems (i.e., in-duct) or as portable air cleaners.

In-duct Particle Removal

Most **mechanical air filters** are good at capturing larger airborne particles, such as dust, pollen, dust mite and cockroach allergens, some molds and animal dander. However, because these particles settle rather quickly, air filters are not very good at removing them completely from indoor areas. Although human activities such as walking and vacuuming can stir up particles, most of the larger particles will resettle before an air filter can remove them.

Consumers can select a particle removal air filter by looking at its efficiency in removing airborne particles from the air stream that passes through it. This efficiency is measured by the minimum efficiency reporting value (MERV) for air filters installed in the ductwork of HVAC systems. The American Society of Heating, Refrigerating and Air-Conditioning Engineers, or ASHRAE developed this measurement method. MERV ratings (ranging from a low of 1 to a high of 20) also allow comparison of air filters made by different companies.

> Filters with a MERV between 7 and 13 are likely to be nearly as effective as true HEPA filters.

- **Flat or panel air filters** with a MERV of 1 to 4 are commonly used in residential furnaces and air conditioners. For the most part, such filters are used to protect the HVAC equipment from the buildup of unwanted materials on the surfaces such as fan motors and heating or cooling coils, and not for direct indoor air quality reasons. They have low efficiency on smaller airborne particles and medium efficiency on larger particles, as long as they remain airborne and pass through the filter.

Some smaller particles found within a house include:

- viruses

- bacteria

- some mold spores

- a significant fraction of cat and dog allergens

- a small portion of dust mite allergens

- **Pleated or extended surface filters**

  - Medium efficiency filters with a MERV of 5 to 13 are reasonably efficient at removing small to large airborne particles. Filters with a MERV between 7 and 13 are likely to be nearly as effective as true HEPA filters at controlling most airborne indoor particles. Medium efficiency air filters are generally less expensive than HEPA filters, and allow quieter HVAC fan operation and higher airflow rates than HEPA filters since they have less airflow resistance.

  - Higher efficiency filters with a MERV of 14 to 16, sometimes misidentified as HEPA filters, are similar in appearance to true HEPA filters, which have MERV values of 17 to 20. True HEPA filters are normally not installed in residential HVAC systems; installation of a HEPA filter in an existing HVAC system would probably require professional modification of the system. A typical residential air handling unit and the associated ductwork would not be able to accommodate such filters because of their physical dimensions and increase in airflow resistance.

Some residential HVAC systems may not have enough fan or motor capacity to accommodate higher efficiency filters. Therefore, the HVAC manufacturer's information should be checked prior to upgrading filters to determine whether it is feasible to use more efficient filters. Specially built high performance homes may occasionally be equipped with true HEPA filters installed in a properly designed HVAC system.

There is no standard measurement for the effectiveness of **electronic air cleaners**. While they may remove small particles, they may be ineffective in removing large particles. Electronic air cleaners can produce ozone—a lung irritant. The amount of ozone produced varies among models. Electronic air cleaners may also produce ultrafine particles resulting from reaction of ozone with indoor chemicals such as those coming from household cleaning products, air fresheners, certain paints, wood flooring, or carpets. Ultrafine particles may be linked with adverse health effects in some sensitive populations.

In-duct Gaseous Pollutant Removal

Although there is no standard measurement for the effectiveness of gas-phase air filters, ASHRAE is developing a standard method to be used in choosing gas-phase filters installed in home HVAC systems. Gas-phase filters are much less commonly used in homes than particle air filters. The useful lifetime of gas-phase filters can be short because the filter material can quickly become overloaded and may need to be replaced often. There is also concern that, when full, these filters may release trapped pollutants back into the air. Finally, a properly designed and built gas-phase filtration system would be unlikely to fit in a typical home HVAC system or portable air cleaner.

In-duct Pollutant Destruction

> UVGI cleaners may not reduce allergy or asthma symptoms.

There is no standard measurement for the effectiveness of UVGI cleaners. Typical UVGI cleaners used in homes have limited effectiveness in killing bacteria and molds. Effective destruction of some viruses and most mold and bacterial spores usually requires much higher UV exposure than is provided in a typical home unit. Furthermore, dead mold spores can still produce allergic reactions, so UVGI cleaners may not be effective in reducing allergy and asthma symptoms.

There is no standard measurement for the effectiveness of PCO cleaners. The use of PCO cleaners in homes is limited because currently available catalysts are ineffective in destroying gaseous pollutants from indoor air. Some PCO cleaners fail to destroy pollutants completely and instead produce new indoor pollutants that may cause irritation of the eyes, throat and nose.

Portable Air Cleaners

Portable air cleaners generally contain a fan to circulate the air and use one or more of the air cleaning devices discussed above. Portable air cleaners may be moved from room to room and used when continuous and localized air cleaning is needed. They may be an option if a home is not equipped with a central HVAC system or forced air heating system.

Portable air cleaners can be evaluated by their effectiveness in reducing airborne pollutants. This effectiveness is measured by the clean air delivery rate, or CADR, developed by the Association of Home Appliance Manufacturers, or AHAM. The CADR is a measure of a portable air cleaner's delivery of contaminant-free air, expressed in cubic feet per minute. For example, if an air cleaner has a CADR of 250 for dust particles, it may reduce dust particle levels to the same concentration as would be achieved by adding 250 cubic feet of clean air each minute. While a portable air cleaner may not achieve its rated CADR under all circumstances, the CADR value does allow comparison across different portable air cleaners.

Many of the portable air cleaners tested by AHAM have moderate to large CADR ratings for small particles. However, for typical room sizes, most portable air cleaners currently on the market do not have high enough CADR values to effectively remove large particles such as pollen, dust mite and cockroach allergens.

Some portable air cleaners using electronic air cleaners might produce ozone, which is a lung irritant. AHAM has a portable air cleaner certification program, and provides a complete listing of all certified cleaners with their CADR values on its Website.

Will Air Cleaning Reduce Adverse Health Effects?

The ability to remove particles, including microorganisms, is not, in itself, an indication of the ability of an air cleaning device to reduce adverse health effects from indoor pollutants. The use of air cleaning devices may help to reduce levels of smaller airborne allergens or particles. However, air cleaners may not reduce adverse health effects completely in sensitive population such as children, the elderly and people with asthma and allergies.

For example, the evidence is weak that air cleaning devices are effective in reducing asthma symptoms associated with small particles that remain in the air, such as those from some airborne cat dander and dust mite allergens. Larger particles, which may contain allergens, settle rapidly before they can be removed by filtration, so effective allergen control measures require washing sheets weekly, frequent vacuuming of carpets and furniture, and dusting and cleaning of hard surfaces.

There are no studies to date linking gas-phase filtration, UVGI and PCO systems in homes to reduced health symptoms in sensitive populations.

Additional Factors to Consider

When making decisions about using air cleaning devices, consumers should also consider:

- **Installation:** In-duct air cleaning devices have certain installation requirements that must be met, such as sufficient access for inspection during use, repairs, or maintenance.

- **Major Costs:** These include the initial purchase, maintenance (such as cleaning or replacing filters and parts), and operation (such as electricity).

- **Odors:** Air cleaning devices designed for particle removal are incapable of controlling gases and some odors. The odor and many of the carcinogenic gas-phase pollutants from tobacco smoke will still remain.

- **Soiling of Walls and Other Surfaces:** Ion generators generally are not designed to remove the charged particles that they generate from the air. These charged particles may deposit on room surfaces, soiling walls and other surfaces.

- **Noise:** Noise may be a problem with portable air cleaners containing a fan. Portable air cleaners without a fan are typically much less effective than units with a fan.

Conclusion

Indoor air pollution is among the top five environmental health risks. The best way to address this risk is to control or eliminate the sources of pollutants, and to ventilate a home with clean outdoor air. The ventilation method may, however, be limited by weather conditions or undesirable levels of contaminants in outdoor air. If these measures are insufficient, an air cleaning device may be useful.

While air cleaning devices may help to control the levels of airborne allergens, particles, or, in some cases, gaseous pollutants in a home, they may not decrease adverse health effects from indoor air pollutants.

Note: EPA neither certifies nor recommends particular brands of home air cleaning devices. While some home air cleaning devices may be useful in some circumstances, EPA makes no broad endorsement of their use, nor specific endorsement of any brand or model. This document describes performance characteristics associated with several types of air cleaners sold to consumers for home use. It does not discuss the effectiveness of air cleaners installed in the HVAC systems of large buildings, such as apartments, offices, schools or public buildings.

Under Federal pesticide law, manufacturers of ozone generators must list an EPA establishment number on the packaging. This number merely identifies the facility that manufactured the product. Display of this number implies neither EPA endorsement nor that EPA has found the product to be safe or effective.

Some portable air cleaners sold in the consumer market are ENERGY STAR® qualified. Please note the following disclaimer on their packaging: "This product earned the ENERGY STAR® by meeting strict energy efficiency guidelines set by EPA. EPA does not endorse any manufacturer claims of healthier indoor air from the use of this product."

Chapter 44

Cleaning up Mold in Your Home, School, and Commercial Buildings

You Can Control Mold

Mold can cause many health effects. For some people, mold can cause a stuffy nose, sore throat, coughing or wheezing, burning eyes, or skin rash. People with asthma or who are allergic to mold may have severe reactions. Immune-compromised people and people with chronic lung disease may get infections in their lungs from mold.

There is always some mold around. Molds have been on the earth for millions of years. Mold can get in your home through open doors, windows, vents, and heating and air conditioning systems. Mold in the air outside can be brought indoors on clothing, shoes, bags, and even pets.

Mold will grow where there is moisture, such as around leaks in roofs, windows, or pipes, or where there has been a flood. Mold grows on paper, cardboard, ceiling tiles, and wood. Mold can also grow in dust, paints, wallpaper, insulation, drywall, carpet, fabric, and upholstery.

This chapter includes excerpts from "You Can Control Mold," Centers for Disease Control and Prevention (CDC), February 10, 2015; and text from "Mold Remediation in Schools and Commercial Buildings Guide," U.S. Environmental Protection Agency (EPA), October 29, 2015.

If You Have Mold in Your Home

Mold can look like spots. It can be many different colors, and it can smell musty. If you see or smell mold, you should remove it. You do not need to know the type of mold.

If mold is growing in your home, you need to clean up the mold and fix the moisture problem. Mold can be removed from hard surfaces with household products, soap and water, or a bleach solution of no more than 1 cup of household laundry bleach in 1 gallon of water.

If You Use Bleach to Clean up Mold

- Never mix bleach with ammonia or other household cleaners. Mixing bleach with ammonia or other cleaning products will produce a poisonous gas. Always follow the manufacturer's instructions when you use bleach or any other cleaning product.

- Open windows and doors to provide fresh air.

- Wear waterproof gloves and eye protection.

- If you need to clean more than 10 square feet, check the *Mold Remediation in Schools and Commercial Buildings*, which gives advice on all building types. You can go to the EPA web site at www.epa.gov/mold/mold_remediation.html

To Prevent Mold Growth in Your Home

- Keep humidity levels in your home as low as you can—no higher than 50%—all day long. An air conditioner or dehumidifier will help you keep the level low. You can buy a meter to check your home's humidity at a home improvement store. Humidity levels change over the course of a day so you will need to check the humidity levels more than once a day.

- Be sure the air in your home flows freely. Use exhaust fans that vent outside your home in the kitchen and bathroom. Make sure your clothes dryer vents outside your home.

- Fix any leaks in your home's roof, walls, or plumbing so mold does not have moisture to grow.

- Clean up and dry out your home fully and quickly (within 24–48 hours) after a flood.

- Add mold inhibitors to paints before painting. You can buy mold inhibitors at paint and home improvement stores.

- Clean bathrooms with mold-killing products.

- Remove or replace carpets and upholstery that have been soaked and cannot be dried right away. Think about not using carpet in places like bathrooms or basements that may have a lot of moisture.

Mold Remediation in Schools and Commercial Buildings

Concern about indoor exposure to mold has been increasing as the public becomes aware that exposure to mold can cause a variety of health effects and symptoms, including allergic reactions. These are the guidelines for the remediation/cleanup of mold and moisture problems in schools and commercial buildings; these guidelines include measures designed to protect the health of building occupants and remediators. It has been designed primarily for:

- Building managers

- Custodians

- Others who are responsible for commercial building and school maintenance

> Molds gradually destroy the things they grow on. By controlling moisture and eliminating mold growth you can:
>
> - Prevent damage to building materials and furnishings
> - Save money
> - Avoid potential health risks

It should serve as a reference for potential mold and moisture remediators. Using this content, individuals with little or no experience with mold remediation should be able to make a reasonable judgment as to whether the situation can be handled in-house. It will help those in charge of maintenance to evaluate an in-house remediation plan or a remediation plan submitted by an outside contractor. Contractors and other professionals who respond to mold and moisture situations in commercial buildings and schools may also want to refer to these guidelines.

Molds can be found almost anywhere; they can grow on virtually any organic substance, as long as moisture and oxygen are present. There are molds that can grow on wood, paper, carpet, foods, and insulation. When excessive moisture accumulates in buildings or on building materials, mold growth will often occur, particularly if the moisture problem remains undiscovered or unaddressed. **It is impossible to eliminate all mold and mold spores in the indoor environment. However, mold growth can be controlled indoors by controlling moisture indoors.**

Molds reproduce by making spores that usually cannot be seen without magnification. Mold spores waft through the indoor and outdoor air continually. When mold spores land on a damp spot indoors, they may begin growing and digesting whatever they are growing on in order to survive. Molds gradually destroy the things they grow on.

Many types of molds exist. **All molds have the potential to cause health effects.** Molds can produce allergens that can trigger allergic reactions or even asthma attacks in people allergic to mold. Others are known to produce potent toxins and/or irritants. Potential health concerns are an important reason to prevent mold growth and to remediate/clean up any existing indoor mold growth.

Since mold requires water to grow, it is important to prevent moisture problems in buildings. Moisture problems can have many causes, including uncontrolled humidity. Some moisture problems in buildings have been linked to changes in building construction practices during the 1970s, 80s and 90s. Some of these changes have resulted in buildings that are tightly sealed, but may lack adequate ventilation, potentially leading to moisture buildup. Building materials, such as drywall, may not allow moisture to escape easily. Moisture problems may include:

- Roof leaks

- Landscaping or gutters that direct water into or under the building

- Unvented combustion appliances

- Delayed maintenance or insufficient maintenance are also associated with moisture problems in schools and large buildings

When mold growth occurs in buildings, adverse health problems may be reported by some building occupants, particularly those with allergies or respiratory problems. Remediators should avoid exposing themselves and others to mold-laden dusts as they conduct their cleanup activities. Caution should be used to prevent mold and mold spores from being dispersed throughout the air where they can be inhaled by building occupants.

Chapter 45

Avoiding Skin Allergies: Choosing Safe Cosmetics

Chapter Contents

Section 45.1

Hypoallergenic Cosmetics and Its Historical Background

Text in this section is excerpted from "Hypoallergenic Cosmetics,"
U.S. Food and Drug Administration (FDA), March 23, 2014.

Hypoallergenic Cosmetics

Hypoallergenic cosmetics are products that manufacturers claim produce fewer allergic reactions than other cosmetic products. Consumers with hypersensitive skin, and even those with "normal" skin, may be led to believe that these products will be gentler to their skin than non-hypoallergenic cosmetics.

There are no federal standards or definitions that govern the use of the term "hypoallergenic." The term means whatever a particular company wants it to mean. Manufacturers of cosmetics labeled as hypoallergenic are not required to submit substantiation of their hypoallergenicity claims to U.S. Food and Drug Administration (FDA).

The term "hypoallergenic" may have considerable market value in promoting cosmetic products to consumers on a retail basis, but dermatologists say it has very little meaning.

Historical Background

Ever since the days when "She's lovely, she's engaged, she uses Ponds" became one of the best known advertising slogans in America, cosmetics manufacturers have pursued consumers with promises of everything from new beauty to a new lifestyle. Indeed, with cosmetics—perhaps more than with any other type of product—promotion is the key to sales success. Recognizing this, manufacturers have used a wide variety of appeals to break into or increase their share in this lucrative market.

For many years, companies have been producing products which they claim are "hypoallergenic" or "safe for sensitive skin" or "allergy tested." These statements imply that the products making the claims are less likely to cause allergic reactions than competing products.

But there has been no assurance to consumers that this actually was the case.

For the past few years, the U.S. Food and Drug Administration (FDA) has been working to clear up this confusion of claims by establishing testing requirements that would determine which products really are "hypoallergenic." But recently, the U.S. Court of Appeals for the District of Columbia ruled that FDA's regulation defining "hypoallergenic" was invalid. This means there is now no regulation specifically defining or governing the use of the term "hypoallergenic" or similar claims. And because of the lengthy procedural steps required to establish a new regulation, that is likely to be the situation for some time to come.

Where does that leave consumers?

Consumers concerned about allergic reactions from cosmetics should understand one basic fact: there is no such thing as a "nonallergenic" cosmetic—that is, a cosmetic that can be guaranteed never to produce an allergic reaction.

But are some cosmetics less likely to produce adverse reactions than competing products?

By and large, the basic ingredients in so-called "hypoallergenic" cosmetics are the same as those used in other cosmetics sold for the same purposes. Years ago, some cosmetics contained harsh ingredients that had a high potential for causing adverse reactions. But these ingredients are no longer used. FDA knows of no scientific studies which show that "hypoallergenic" cosmetics or products making similar claims actually cause fewer adverse reactions than competing conventional products.

FDA's ill-fated regulation on "hypoallergenic" cosmetics was first issued as a proposal in February 1974. It said that a cosmetic would be permitted to be labeled "hypoallergenic" or make similar claims only if scientific studies on human subjects showed that it caused a significantly lower rate of adverse skin reactions than similar products not making such claims. The manufacturers of cosmetics claiming to be "hypoallergenic" were to be responsible for carrying out the required tests.

Numerous comments on the proposal were received from consumers, consumer groups and cosmetic manufacturers. Some people urged a ban on the use of the term "hypoallergenic" on grounds that most consumers don't have allergies. Others suggested that the term be banned because allergic individuals cannot use "hypoallergenic" products with any assurance of safety. A number of cosmetic manufacturers complained about the requirement for product comparison tests to validate claims of hypoallergenicity. Among other things, they said the tests would pose an undue economic burden on them.

In responding to the comments, FDA pointed out that the proposed regulation was not intended to solve all problems concerning cosmetic safety. The primary purpose of the regulation, the Agency said, was to clear up confusion about the term "hypoallergenic" and to establish a definition that could be used uniformly by manufacturers and understood by consumers.

FDA issued its final regulation on "hypoallergenic" cosmetics on June 6, 1975. Although the final regulation did require comparative tests, procedures for carrying out the tests were changed to reduce the costs to the manufacturers.

The new regulation was quickly challenged in the U.S. District Court for the District of Columbia by Almay and Clinique, makers of "hypoallergenic" cosmetics. The two firms charged that FDA had no authority to issue the regulation, but the court upheld FDA.

The firms then appealed to the U.S. Court of Appeals for the District of Columbia, which ruled that the regulation was invalid. The appeals court held that FDA's definition of the term "hypoallergenic" was unreasonable because the Agency had not demonstrated that consumers perceive the term "hypoallergenic" in the way described in the regulation.

As a result of the decision, manufacturers may continue to label and advertise their cosmetics as "hypoallergenic" or make similar claims without any supporting evidence. Consumers will have no assurance that such claims are valid.

However, cosmetics users who know they are allergic to certain ingredients can take steps to protect themselves. FDA regulations now require the ingredients used in cosmetics to be listed on the product label, so consumers can avoid substances that have caused them problems.

Section 45.2

Bad Reaction to Cosmetics? Tell FDA

Text in this section is excerpted from "Bad Reaction to
Cosmetics? Tell FDA," U.S. Food and Drug Administration (FDA),
November 5, 2015.

You break out in a head-to-toe rash after applying a sunless tanning lotion. Your son's skin is red and blotchy after he gets his face painted at the school carnival. Your daughter's scalp is burned after using a hair relaxer.

If you've had a negative reaction to a beauty, personal hygiene, or makeup product, the U.S. Food and Drug Administration (FDA) wants to hear from you.

From morning until night—styling our hair for work to showering before bed—Americans depend upon personal care products. Most are safe, but some cause problems, and that's when FDA gets involved.

Even though these products are widely used, most don't require FDA approval before they're sold in stores, salons, and at makeup counters. So, consumers are one of FDA's most important resources when it comes to identifying problems.

The federal Food, Drug, and Cosmetic Act defines "cosmetics" as products that are intended to be applied to the body "for cleansing, beautifying, promoting attractiveness, or altering the appearance." But the legal definition includes items that most Americans might not ordinarily think of as cosmetics, including:

- face and body cleansers

- deodorants

- moisturizers and other skin lotions and creams

- baby lotions and oils

- hair care products, dyes, conditioners, straighteners, perms

- makeup

- hair removal creams

- nail polishes

- shaving products

- perfumes and colognes

- face paints and temporary tattoos

- permanent tattoos and permanent makeup

What to Report to FDA

Consumers should contact FDA if they experience a rash, hair loss, infection, or other problem—even if they didn't follow product directions. FDA also wants to know if a product has a bad smell or unusual color—which could signal contamination—or if the item's label is incomplete or inaccurate.

If you have any concerns about a cosmetic, contact MedWatch, FDA's problem-reporting program, on the Web or at 1-800-332-1088; or contact the consumer complaint coordinator in your area.

When you contact FDA, include the following information in your report:

- the name and contact information for the person who had the reaction;

- the age, gender, and ethnicity of the product's user;

- the name of the product and manufacturer;

- a description of the reaction—and treatment, if any;

- the healthcare provider's name and contact information, if medical attention was provided; and

- when and where the product was purchased.

When a consumer report is received, FDA enters the information into a database of negative reactions. Experts then look for reports related to the same product or similar ones. FDA scientists will use the information to determine if the product has a history of problems and represents a public health concern that needs to be addressed.

If you file a consumer report, your identity will remain confidential.

Cosmetics are usually safe, but when they aren't, consumer reporting is essential so FDA can take action when appropriate. Those actions could—depending upon the product and the problem—range from issuing a consumer safety advisory to taking legal action.

Chapter 46

Asthma and Physical Activity in School Settings

Help Students Control Their Asthma

Good asthma management is essential for getting control of asthma. In school settings, it means helping students to:

- Follow their written asthma action plan;

- Have quick and easy access to their asthma medications;

- Recognize their asthma triggers (the factors that make asthma worse or cause an asthma attack); and

- Avoid or control asthma triggers.

You can also help by modifying physical activities to match students' current asthma status.

Good asthma management offers important benefits, including allowing students who have asthma to participate fully in physical activities and other regular school activities.

Text in this chapter is excerpted from "Asthma and Physical Activity in the School," National Heart, Lung, and Blood Institute (NHLBI), 2012.

Benefits of Asthma Control

With good asthma management, students with asthma should:

- Be free from troublesome symptoms day and night:
  - no coughing or wheezing
  - no difficulty breathing or chest tightness
  - no night time awakening due to asthma
- Have the best possible lung function
- Be able to participate fully in any activities of their choice
- Not miss work or school because of asthma symptoms
- Need fewer or no urgent care visits or hospitalizations for asthma
- Use medications to control asthma with as few side effects as possible
- Be satisfied with their asthma care

Follow the Asthma Action Plan

Everyone who has asthma should have a written asthma action plan. The student's health care provider, together with the student and his or her parent or guardian, develops the student's written asthma action plan.

It should provide instructions for daily management of asthma (including medications and control of triggers) and explain how to recognize and handle worsening asthma symptoms.

Depending on the student's needs, the school may also develop a more extensive individualized health plan (IHP) or individualized education plan (IEP). A copy of the student's asthma action plan should be on file in the school office or health services office, with additional copies provided to the student's teachers and coaches.

You can help a student to follow his or her written asthma action plan in two ways: 1) by monitoring the student's asthma symptoms and/or 2) by having the student use a peak flow meter, which is a small, handheld device that measures how **hard** and **fast** the student can blow air out of the lungs. A drop in peak flow can warn of worsening asthma even before symptoms appear.

Asthma Action Plan Contents

Daily management:

- What medication to take daily, including the specific names and dosages of the medications.
- What actions to take to control environmental factors (triggers) that worsen the student's asthma.

Recognizing and handling signs of worsening asthma:

- What signs, symptoms, and peak flow readings (if peak flow monitoring is used) indicate worsening asthma.
- What medications and dosages to take in response to these signs of worsening asthma.
- What symptoms and peak flow readings indicate the need for urgent medical attention.

Administrative issues:

- Emergency telephone numbers for the physician, emergency department, and person or service to transport the student rapidly for medical care.
- Written authorization for students to carry and self-administer asthma medication, when considered appropriate by the health care provider and the parent or guardian.
- Written authorization for schools to administer the student's asthma medication.

Asthma action plans are most commonly divided into three colored zones—green, yellow, and red—like a traffic light. The individual zones correspond with a range of symptoms and/or peak flow numbers determined by the student's health care provider and listed on the asthma action plan. As described on the next page, an increase in asthma symptoms, or a drop in peak flow compared with the student's personal best peak flow number, indicates the need for prompt action to prevent or treat an asthma attack.

- **GREEN ZONE = Go.** The green zone means that the student has no asthma symptoms and/or has a peak flow reading at 80% or more of the student's personal best peak flow number. The student should continue taking his or her daily long-term control medication, if prescribed.

- **YELLOW ZONE = Caution.** The yellow zone means that the student is experiencing worsening asthma symptoms and/or has a peak flow reading between 50% and 79% of the student's best peak flow number. Typically, this means the student needs a quick-relief (bronchodilator) medication—inhaled albuterol, for example—to temporarily open the airways. In the meantime, the student should continue the medication listed in the green zone.

  Follow any additional instructions provided in the asthma action plan.

- **RED ZONE = Medical Alert!** Begin emergency steps and get medical help now. A student in the red zone has severe asthma symptoms and/or a peak flow reading of less than 50% of the student's best peak flow number. The student needs a quick-relief (bronchodilator) medication, such as inhaled albuterol, to open the airways. Seek medical help right away. Your quick action could help save a life.

Supporting and encouraging each student's efforts to follow his or her written asthma action plan is essential for the student's active participation in physical activities.

Actions for School Staff

Classroom Teachers, Physical Education Teachers, or Coaches:

- Take steps to support the use of written asthma action plans:
  - **Know how to easily access the student's asthma action plan or ask for a copy from the school nurse or designee.** You may need to assist a student to follow pre-medication procedures before the student exercises, or to help a student who has worsening asthma. Consult with the school nurse or designee for clarification.
  - **Establish good communication among all parties involved in the student's care.** Engage parents or guardians, students, health care providers, and school health

staff in following the asthma action plan to help maximize the student's participation and minimize risks.

- **Be responsive to the needs of students who have asthma.**
- **Teach students asthma awareness and peer sensitivity.** As students learn more about asthma, they can more easily offer support instead of barriers to their classmates who have asthma.

School Health Personnel:

- Ensure that all students who have asthma have an asthma action plan on file at school, and appropriate medications available at school.

Ensure Students Have Easy Access to Their Medication

Asthma Medications

Many students who have asthma require both long-term control medications and quick-relief medications. These medications prevent as well as treat symptoms and enable the student to participate safely and fully in physical activities.

All students who have asthma must have quick-relief medication available at school to take as needed to relieve symptoms, and, if directed, to take before exposure to an asthma trigger, such as exercise.

Most asthma medications are inhaled as sprays or powders and may be taken using metered-dose inhalers, dry powder inhalers, or nebulizers. A metered dose inhaler is a pressurized canister that delivers a dose of medication and does not require deep and fast breathing. A dry powder inhaler is another kind of inhaler that does require deep and fast breathing to get the medication into the lungs. A nebulizer is a machine that turns liquid medication into a fine mist. Whichever delivery method is used, it is important for students to take their medications correctly.

Long-Term Control Medications are usually taken daily to control underlying airway infl ammation and thereby prevent asthma symptoms. They can significantly reduce a student's need for quick-relief medication.

Inhaled corticosteroids are the most effective long-term control medications for asthma. It is important to remember that inhaled corticosteroids are generally safe for long-term use when taken as prescribed. They are **not** addictive and are not the same as illegal anabolic steroids used by some athletes to build muscles.

Quick-Relief Medications (also known as short-acting bronchodilators) are taken when needed for rapid, short-term relief of asthma symptoms. They help stop asthma attacks by temporarily relaxing the muscles around the airways. However, they do nothing to treat the underlying airway infl ammation that caused the symptoms to flare up.

An additional use for quick-relief medications is the prevention of asthma symptoms in students who have exercise-induced asthma. These students may be directed by their health care provider to take their quick-relief medication inhaler 5 minutes before participating in physical activities.

Ensuring Access

Ensuring that students who have asthma have quick and easy access to their quick-relief medication is essential. These students often require medication during school to treat asthma symptoms or to take just before participating in physical activities or exposure to another asthma trigger. If accessing the medication is difficult, inconvenient, or embarrassing, the student may be discouraged and fail to use his or her quick-relief medication as needed. The student's asthma may become unnecessarily worse and his or her activities needlessly limited.

A parent or guardian should provide to the school the student's prescribed asthma medication so that it may be administered by the school nurse or other designated school personnel, according to applicable federal, state, and district laws, regulations, and policies. Federal legislation relevant to the needs and rights of students who have asthma includes the Americans with Disabilities Act (www.ada.gov), Family Educational Rights and Privacy Act of 1974, Individuals with Disabilities Education Act (http://idea.ed.gov), and Section 504 of the Rehabilitation Act of 1973. Additional information about these laws is available from the Office for Civil Rights at the U.S. Department of Education.

In addition, all 50 states and the District of Columbia have laws allowing students to carry and self-administer their prescribed quick-relief asthma medications in school settings. Required documentation usually includes having on file at the school a written asthma action plan and/or medication authorization form signed by the student's physician and parent or guardian, and in some jurisdictions, the school nurse.

The NHLBI's publication *When Should Students With Asthma or Allergies Carry and Self-Administer Emergency Medications at School?* provides useful guidance for determining when to entrust and encourage a student with diagnosed asthma to carry and self-administer prescribed emergency medications at school. In addition, the Allergy and Asthma Network/Mothers of Asthmatics has information on federal and state laws that address students' rights to carry and self-administer prescribed asthma medications. You also can look for asthma-related laws and regulations in each state and territory through the Library of Congress.

Actions for School Staff

Take Steps To Support Quick And Easy Access To Student Medications:

- **Provide students who have asthma quick and easy access to their prescribed medications** for all on- and off-site school activities before, during, and after school.

- **Make sure students have prescribed medication to take before exercise**—usually a quick-relief inhaler (bronchodilator)—if indicated by student's asthma action plan.

- **Enable students to carry and self-administer their asthma medications.** Laws in all 50 states and the District of Columbia declare students' rights to carry and use their prescribed asthma medications. Consult *When Should Students With Asthma or Allergies Carry and Self-Administer Emergency Medications at School?* (available at www.nhlbi.nih.gov/health/prof/lung/index.htm).

- **Know your school's policies and procedures for administering medications,** including emergency protocols for responding to a severe asthma attack.

Chapter 47

Preventing Allergy Symptoms during Travel

General Travel Preparation: Practical Considerations

Although traveling abroad can be relaxing and rewarding, the physical demands of travel can be stressful, particularly for travelers with underlying chronic illnesses. With adequate preparation, however, those with chronic illnesses can have safe and enjoyable trips. The following is a list of general recommendations for advising patients with chronic illnesses:

- Ensure that any chronic illnesses are well controlled. Patients with an underlying illness should see their health care providers to ensure that the management of their illness is optimized.

- Encourage patients to seek pre-travel consultation early, ≥4–6 weeks before departure, to ensure adequate time to respond to immunizations and, in some circumstances, to try medications before travel.

- Advise patients to consider a destination that is not too remote.

- Ask about previous health-related issues encountered during travel, such as complications during air travel.

Text in this chapter is excerpted from "Advising Travelers with Specific Needs," Centers for Disease Control and Prevention (CDC), July 10, 2015.

- Provide a clinician's letter. The letter should be on office letter-head stationery, outlining existing medical conditions, medications prescribed (including generic names), and any equipment required to manage the condition.

- Encourage travelers with underlying medical conditions to consider choosing a medical assistance company that allows them to store their medical history pre-departure so it can be accessed worldwide if needed.

- Advise travelers to pack medications and medical supplies (such as pouching for ostomies) in their original containers in carry-on luggage and to carry a copy of their prescriptions. Ensure the traveler has sufficient quantities of medications for the entire trip, plus extra in case of unexpected delays. Since medications should be taken based on elapsed time and not time of day, travelers may need guidance on scheduling when to take medications during and after crossing time zones.

- Advise travelers to check with the American embassy or consulate to clarify medication restrictions in the destination country. Some countries do not allow visitors to bring certain medications into the country.

- Educate travelers regarding drug interactions. Medications (such as warfarin) used to treat chronic medical illnesses may interact with medications prescribed for self-treatment of travelers' diarrhea or malaria chemoprophylaxis. Discuss all medications used, either daily or on an as-needed basis.

- Suggest supplemental insurance. Three types of insurance policies can be considered: 1) trip cancellation in the event of illness; 2) supplemental insurance so that money paid for health care abroad may be reimbursed, since most medical insurance policies do not cover health care in other countries; and 3) medical evacuation insurance. Travelers may need extra help in finding supplemental insurance, as some plans will not cover costs for preexisting conditions.

- Help travelers devise a health plan. This plan should give instructions for managing minor problems or exacerbations of underlying illnesses and should include information about medical facilities available in the destination country.

- Advise travelers to wear a medical alert bracelet or carry medical information on his or her person (various brands of jewelry or tags, even electronic, are available).

- Advise travelers to keep well-hydrated, wear loose-fitting clothing, and walk and stretch at regular intervals during long-distance travel.

- Always advise the traveler about packing a health kit.

Special considerations for travelers with Severe allergic reactions

1. Plan for managing allergic reaction while traveling and consider bringing a short course of steroids for possible allergic reactions

2. Should carry injectable epinephrine and antihistamines (H1 and H2-blockers)—always have on person

3. Many airlines already have policies in place for dealing with peanut allergies

4. Make sure to carry injectable epinephrine in case of a severe reaction while in flight

Chapter 48

Preventing Food Allergy in Infants

Healthcare experts still do not have enough conclusive evidence to tell pregnant women, nursing mothers, and mothers of infants how to prevent food allergy developing in their children. Be sure to talk with your healthcare professional before changing your diet or your baby's diet.

Here is what healthcare experts know now about

- Pregnancy
- Breastfeeding
- Introducing solid foods

Pregnancy

- When you are pregnant, you should eat a balanced diet.
- If you are allergic to a food, you should avoid it.
- If you are not allergic to foods such as egg, tree nuts, peanut, fish, or cow's milk (all highly allergenic), you should not avoid

This chapter includes excerpts from "Food Allergy: Pregnancy, Breastfeeding, and Introducing Solid Foods to Your Baby," National Institute of Allergy and Infectious Diseases (NIAID), 2012; and text from "Breastfeeding," Office on Women's Health (OWH), July 21, 2014.

them because there is no conclusive evidence that avoiding these foods will prevent food allergy developing in your infant.

Breastfeeding

- Healthcare experts recommend that mothers feed their babies only breast milk for the first four months of life because of the health benefits of breastfeeding.

- Mothers who breastfeed do not need to avoid foods that are considered to be highly allergenic because there is no conclusive evidence that avoiding these foods will prevent food allergy from developing in their infants.

Introducing Solid Foods

- Healthcare experts in the United States currently suggest that you do not introduce solid food into your baby's diet until four to six months of age.

- There is no conclusive evidence to suggest that you should delay the introduction of solid foods beyond four to six months of age.

- There is no conclusive evidence to suggest that you should delay the introduction of the most common potentially allergenic foods (milk, egg, peanut) beyond four to six months of age. Delay will not prevent your child from developing an allergy.

Can a baby be allergic to breastmilk?

Research shows that what you eat affects your milk only slightly. Babies love the flavors of foods that come through the milk. Sometimes a baby may be sensitive to something the mother eats, such as dairy products like eggs or milk and cheese.

Watch your baby for the symptoms listed below, which could indicate that your baby has an allergy or sensitivity to something you eat:

- Diarrhea, vomiting, green stools with mucus and/or blood
- Rash, eczema, dermatitis, hives, dry skin
- Fussiness during and/or after feedings
- Inconsolable crying for long periods
- Sudden waking with discomfort
- Wheezing or coughing

These signs do not mean your baby is allergic to your milk, only to something that you ate. You may need to stop eating whatever is bothering your baby or eat less of it. You may find that after a few months you can eat the food again with better results.

Chapter 49

NIAID's Role in Research

Chapter Contents

Section 49.1

Global Allergic and Infectious Diseases Research

This chapter includes excerpts from "NIAID Role in Global
Research," National Institute of Allergy and Infectious Diseases
(NIAID), June 26, 2015; and text from "Laboratory of Allergic
Diseases," National Institute of Allergy and Infectious Diseases
(NIAID), October 2, 2015.

NIAID's Role in Global Research

The National Institute of Allergy and Infectious Diseases (NIAID)
supports the conduct of global research to better understand, treat,
and ultimately prevent infectious, immunologic, and allergic diseases
and conditions. In addition to advancing these scientific goals, NIAID
global research helps to improve the health of millions of people around
the world and to promote international economic and political stability.
Together, these efforts establish NIAID as a leader in global health.

Understanding, Treating, and Preventing Diseases

Conducting research in international settings allows NIAID-supported scientists to study infectious diseases and immunology under a
variety of environmental and social conditions. It also provides opportunities to study the effectiveness of investigational drugs and vaccines in populations that vary genetically and immunologically, in the
hope of finding treatments and preventions for wide ranges of disease
strains and mutations.

Improving the Health of Millions

Often, international research is required to answer critical scientific questions, particularly regarding infectious diseases that are
less common in the United States. In today's interconnected society,
outbreaks of infectious diseases have worldwide implications, both
directly through the transmission of disease and indirectly through
the economic and political instability that these health concerns can

provoke. NIAID support of international research helps develop new knowledge to improve diagnosis, prevention, and treatment of infectious diseases that have potential global impact.

By investing in the development of biomedical research capacity around the world, NIAID also fosters the formation of long-standing research collaborations between U.S. and international scientists, many of whom are based in developing countries. NIAID supports innovative studies on infectious diseases and immunology in populations where the research may be effectively translated into medical care and public-health improvements.

Promoting International Economic and Political Stability

The impact of debilitating diseases, such as HIV/AIDS, malaria, and tuberculosis, extends from individuals to families and into the broader society. In turn, the morbidity and mortality associated with these diseases in developing countries can slow or reverse social and economic development. By helping to improve outcomes associated with infectious and immunological diseases, NIAID contributes to global development and stability.

Leading Contributions to Global Health

With infectious diseases among the primary causes of mortality and suffering worldwide, NIAID has embraced its leadership role in the global effort to defeat these diseases. By working with partners in academia, private industry, philanthropic foundations, and other research-supporting agencies, NIAID helps guide and enhance research that improves the quality of human life around the world.

Laboratory of Allergic Diseases

The Laboratory of Allergic Diseases (LAD) conducts basic, translational, and clinical research on allergic diseases including food allergy. Researchers in LAD seek to better understand the immune system components that are involved by identifying events at the clinical and molecular level that trigger and modulate allergic reactions. The expectation is that such an approach will lead to improved disease management.

Within LAD, the Food Allergy Research Unit seeks to understand the key genetic, immunologic, and biochemical pathways that lead to the development of food allergy and how they can be manipulated for therapeutic benefit. Their current research efforts are focused on the following areas:

Genetic diseases associated with the food allergy

Studying rare genetic disorders associated with food allergy and other allergic conditions provides insight into the key cellular and signaling pathways that lead to allergic inflammation. This information will help in the development of new therapies for people with allergic diseases.

Environmental and immunologic factors that influence food allergy

Multiple factors contribute to food allergy. Both genetics and the environment likely play a role and the food allergy research group is studying how these two variables interact. Emphasis is placed on the identification of immunologic markers that predict the severity and persistence of food allergy.

Section 49.2

NIAID-Funded Research Programs

This section includes excerpts from "Short-Term Additional Treatment Reduces Asthma Attacks in Inner-City Children During Fall," National Institute of Allergy and Infectious Diseases (NIAID), October 27, 2015; and text from "Gut Bacteria May Protect Against Food Allergy," ational Institute of Allergy and Infectious Diseases (NIAID), September 19, 2014; and text from "Scientists Deepen Genetic Understanding of Eosinophilic Esophagitis," National Institute of Allergy and Infectious Diseases (NIAID), July 14, 2014.

NIH-Funded Study Finds that Adding Omalizumab to Asthma Therapy Benefits Specific Population of Children

Adding the drug omalizumab to ongoing guidelines-based asthma therapy for a targeted four-month period beginning just before the start of school reduced the number of autumn asthma attacks, or exacerbations, in inner-city children, according to results from a clinical trial sponsored by the National Institutes of Health. Asthma exacerbations—worsenings of asthma symptoms—disrupt quality of life and may contribute to chronic lung disease.

The study findings, reported online on October 27, 2015 in the *Journal of Allergy and Clinical Immunology*, also show that short-term treatment with omalizumab was most effective at preventing additional exacerbations in children who had experienced an exacerbation earlier that year.

The trial was conducted by the Inner-City Asthma Consortium (ICAC), an asthma research program supported by the National Institute of Allergy and Infectious Diseases (NIAID), part of NIH. Asthma is a leading cause of childhood hospitalizations and missed school days in the United States, and disease severity is disproportionately high among children living in inner-city communities.

Asthma exacerbations typically spike in the fall, with several factors contributing to this seasonal trend, including infections with cold-causing viruses and exposure to respiratory allergens. A previous ICAC study found that adding year-round treatment with omalizumab (brand name Xolair) to guidelines-based asthma care decreased seasonal exacerbations, with the most striking effects observed during the fall. Based on these results, ICAC investigators sought to determine whether short-term treatment with omalizumab during the late summer and fall would have a similar effect. The drug currently is approved in the United States for patients ages 12 and older with moderate-to-severe persistent allergic asthma.

"Although treatment based on NIH guidelines is generally effective for asthma management, many children still experience seasonal exacerbations requiring treatment with oral steroids or even hospitalization," said NIAID Director Anthony S. Fauci, M.D. "The results of this study show that a short-term, targeted treatment initiated shortly before the greatest risk for asthma exacerbations can potentially prevent these events, improving children's health."

In the current study, researchers enrolled children 6 to 17 years of age with asthma in eight U.S. cities prior to the fall seasons of 2012 and 2013. All of the children first received four to nine months of guidelines-based care to achieve asthma control. Guidelines-based care focuses on measures to assess and monitor asthma, patient education, medications and control of environmental factors and other conditions that can worsen asthma.

Participants with the most difficult-to-control asthma were then randomly assigned to receive omalizumab or placebo. Participants with easier-to-control asthma were randomly assigned to receive omalizumab, placebo or an inhaled corticosteroid boost (in which their normal dose was doubled). These treatments began four to six weeks before the start of school and ended 90 days after school started. Participants continued to receive guidelines-based asthma care throughout the study. Complications and side effects were rare and did not differ between the study groups.

Based on analysis of data from 478 study participants, the researchers found that, overall, children treated with omalizumab were about half as likely to experience an asthma exacerbation during the first 90 days of the school year as those who did not receive the drug.

Further analysis revealed that children who had experienced an exacerbation in the four-to-nine-month period before omalizumab treatment started benefited most from the drug. Within this group, omalizumab reduced the risk of an exacerbation by more than 80 percent—36.3 percent of children who received placebo had at least one fall exacerbation, compared to only 6.4 percent of children who received omalizumab. Children who did not experience an exacerbation in the months before school were not helped by addition of the drug to their asthma regimens. In children with easier-to-control asthma, the inhaled corticosteroid boost did not help prevent exacerbations, regardless of their history of exacerbations in the previous months.

"Identifying those children who are at greatest risk for fall asthma exacerbations and who are most likely to benefit from short-term addition of omalizumab to guidelines-based care is an important step toward delivering personalized asthma treatments," said Daniel Rotrosen, M.D., director of NIAID's Division of Allergy, Immunology and Transplantation, which oversees the ICAC program.

Compared to their peers, participants who experienced an exacerbation in the months before school had evidence of higher levels of allergic inflammation. Specifically, they had high numbers of immune cells called eosinophils in the blood and increased levels of nitric oxide in the breath, two measurable markers of asthma-associated inflammation.

"This study's most exciting result demonstrates how clinicians can individualize care for young patients with certain high-risk clinical profiles. This is an important step forward in advancing asthma care, with large benefits for some of the most at-risk, underserved children," said Stephen J. Teach, M.D., M.P.H., of Children's National Health System, the lead author of the study.

The researchers also are working to understand the mechanism underlying the protective effects of omalizumab. Respiratory viruses were common in samples of nasal mucus taken from participants around the time they experienced an asthma exacerbation. By analyzing blood samples from a subset of trial participants, the scientists found that the beneficial effects of omalizumab may be partly explained by an increased release of an antiviral substance called interferon-alpha from certain immune cells. Among participants who received omalizumab, those with the greatest increase in interferon-alpha experienced fewer exacerbations. Future work may provide additional insight into the causes of fall asthma exacerbations and how best to prevent them.

Gut Bacteria May Protect Against Food Allergy

Researchers have found that certain naturally occurring gut bacteria may protect against food allergen sensitization—a key step in the development of food allergy. Using a mouse model of peanut allergy, the scientists showed that altering the bacterial communities in the gut could change the animals' immune responses to peanut allergen, suggesting potential new strategies for food allergy treatment and prevention. The study, funded in part by NIAID, appears in *Proceedings of the National Academy of Sciences.*

Background

Food allergy among children in the United States rose 18 percent from 1997 to 2007, according to the Centers for Disease Control and Prevention. Reasons for this increase remain unclear, but recent studies have suggested that environmental factors play an important role by changing the composition of the commensal bacteria that colonize the intestinal tract. These trillions of bacteria, collectively known as the intestinal microbiota, are vital for health and immune system development. The rise in antibiotic use during childhood has been linked to an increased risk of allergic diseases, suggesting that in addition to destroying infectious bacteria, these drugs also can alter the composition of the microbiota.

Results of Study

To examine how changes in the microbiota influence allergic responses to food, researchers led by Cathryn Nagler, Ph.D., of the University of Chicago exposed different groups of mice to peanut allergen. Germ-free mice—those born and raised with no microbes—and mice treated with antibiotics as newborns produced higher levels of peanut-specific antibodies than mice with normal gut bacteria.

The scientists found that introducing specific types of bacteria into the animals' guts could influence immune responses to peanut allergen exposure. Germ-free and antibiotic-treated mice given a mixture of *Clostridia*, a class of bacteria normally found in the intestinal microbiota, were protected against peanut sensitization. However, introducing *Bacteroides*, another major group of gut bacteria, did not have a similar effect, suggesting that *Clostridia* play a unique role in protecting against allergen sensitization.

Analysis of immune cell and protein levels before and after colonization with *Clostridia* revealed significant differences. *Clostridia* stimulated immune cells to produce high levels of a molecule called interleukin 22 (IL-22), which reduced the permeability of the intestinal lining, preventing the allergen from entering the bloodstream. The scientists also found that the bacteria altered the levels of cells involved in immune regulation and levels of immunoglobulin A, the major protective antibody found in mucosal tissues such as the intestine.

Significance

These findings in a mouse model of food allergy suggest that the intestinal microbiota play an important role in determining immune responses to food allergens and also provide insight into the molecular changes that result.

Next Steps

Future research will focus on gaining a more complete understanding of how *Clostridia* enables the immune system to protect against allergen sensitization and most importantly on determining whether the bacteria have a similar effect in humans. Ultimately, scientists may investigate strategies to prevent and treat food allergy by modifying the bacterial communities in the gut.

NIH-Funded Study May Help Explain Why Disease is Confined to the Esophagus

Scientists funded by the National Institutes of Health (NIH) have identified genetic markers associated with eosinophilic esophagitis (EoE), an inflammatory disease characterized by high levels of immune cells called eosinophils in the esophagus. Their findings suggest that several genes are involved in the development of EoE, which can cause difficulty eating and often is associated with food allergies. The findings also may help explain why the disease specifically affects the esophagus. The work was supported in part by the Consortium of Food Allergy Research, which is funded by NIH's National Institute of Allergy and Infectious Diseases and National Institute of Diabetes and Digestive and Kidney Diseases.

A team led by researchers at Cincinnati Children's Hospital Medical Center searched the entire human genome for variations between 9,246 healthy people and 736 people with EoE. They confirmed previous results from a smaller study that linked variations in the region on chromosome 5 containing Thymic stromal lymphopoietin *(TSLP)*, a gene associated with allergic diseases, to a higher risk of developing EoE. They also identified variations in a region on chromosome 2 containing a gene called Calcium-activated neutral proteinase 14 *(CAPN14)*, which produces an enzyme called calpain 14, that are associated with higher EoE risk. The researchers showed that *CAPN14* is expressed, or "turned on," primarily in the esophagus. *CAPN14* expression and calpain activity rose when scientists treated cultured esophageal cells with a molecule that induces allergic inflammation, suggesting that the enzyme is part of an anti-inflammatory response. People with EoE who carry the variant form of the gene may be unable to mount this response as effectively.

Further research is needed to determine if these findings might lead to identification of biomarkers to detect a person's risk of developing EoE. Understanding the factors underlying EoE may help guide development of new diagnostic and treatment strategies for the disease.

Part Seven

Additional Help and Information

Chapter 50

Glossary of Terms Related to Allergies

adrenal gland: a gland located on each kidney that secretes hormones regulating metabolism, sexual function, water balance, and stress.

air spaces: all alveolar ducts, alveolar sacs, and alveoli. To be contrasted with airways.

airways: all passageways of the respiratory tract from mouth or nose down to and including respiratory bronchioles. to be contrasted with air spaces.

allergen: a substance that causes an allergic reaction.

allergenic: describes a substance that produces an allergic reaction.

alveolus: hexagonal or spherical air cells of the lungs. An alveolus is an ultimate respiratory unit where the gas exchange takes place.

amino acids: any of the 26 building blocks of proteins.

anaphylaxis: a severe reaction to an allergen that can cause itching, fainting, and in some cases, death.

antibody: a molecule tailor-made by the immune system to lock onto and destroy specific foreign substances such as allergens.

antigen: a substance or molecule that is recognized by the immune system.

antiserum: a serum rich in antibodies against a particular microbe.

appendix: lymphoid organ in the intestine.

artery: a blood vessel that carries blood from the heart to other parts of the body.

assay: a laboratory method of measuring a substance such as immunoglobulin.

asthma: a respiratory disease of the lungs characterized by episodes of inflammation and narrowing of the lower airways in response to asthma triggers, such as infectious agents, stress, pollutants such as cigarette smoke, and common allergens such as cat dander, dust mites, and pollen.

autoimmune disease: a disease that results when the immune system mistakenly attacks the body's own tissues.

atropine: a poisonous white crystalline alkaloid, c17h23no3, from belladonna and related plants, used to relieve spasms of smooth muscles. it is an anticholinergic agent.

B cell: a small white blood cell crucial to the immune defenses. B cells come from bone marrow and develop into blood cells called plasma cells, which are the source of antibodies.

bacteria: microscopic organisms composed of a single cell. Some cause disease.

basophil: a white blood cell that contributes to inflammatory reactions. Along with mast cells, basophils are responsible for the symptoms of allergy.

beta-adrenergic agonist medication: a bronchodilator medicine that opens the airways by relaxing the muscles around the airways that may tighten during an asthma attack or in COPD (chronic obstructive pulmonary disease).

bloodborne pathogens: means pathogenic microorganisms that are present in human blood and can cause disease in humans.

blood vessel: an artery, vein, or capillary that carries blood to and from the heart and body tissues.

breathing pattern: a general term designating the characteristics of the ventilatory activity, e.g., tidal volume, frequency of breathing, and shape of the volume time curve.

bronchiole: one of the finer subdivisions of the airways, less than 1 mm in diameter, and having no cartilage in its wall.

bronchiolitis: inflammation of the bronchioles that may be acute or chronic. if the etiology is known, it should be stated. If permanent occlusion of the lumens is present, the term bronchiolitis obliterans may be used.

bronchitis: a non-neoplastic disorder of structure or function of the bronchi resulting from infectious or noninfectious irritation.

bronchoalveolar lavage: a clinical technique which removes cell samples from the lower lungs to allow assessment of inflammation and other respiratory conditions.

bronchoconstrictor: an agent that causes a reduction in the caliber (diameter) of airways.

bronchodilator: an agent that causes an increase in the caliber (diameter) of airways.

bronchus: one of the subdivisions of the trachea serving to convey air to and from the lungs.

celiac disease: a disease of the digestive system that damages the small intestine and interferes with absorption of nutritional contents of food.

cells: the smallest units of life; the basic living things that make up tissues.

chemokine: a small protein molecule that activates immune cells, stimulates their migration, and helps direct immune cell traffic throughout the body.

chronic obstructive pulmonary disease: this term refers to chronic lung disorders that result in blocked air flow in the lungs.

clonal anergy: the process of switching off the ability of potentially harmful T or B cells to participate in immune responses. Clonal anergy is essential for generating the tolerance of T and B cells to the body's "self" tissue antigens.

clonal deletion: the genetically controlled process of eliminating immune cells that could destroy the body's own cells and tissues.

clone: a group of genetically identical cells or organisms descended from a single common ancestor; or, to reproduce identical copies.

complement cascade: a precise sequence of events, usually triggered by antigen-antibody complexes, in which each component of the complement system is activated in turn.

conjunctivitis: inflammation of the lining of the eyelid, causing red-rimmed, swollen eyes, and crusting of the eyelids.

cytokines: powerful chemical substances secreted by cells that enable the body's cells to communicate with one another.

cytotoxic T lymphocyte: a subtype of T cells that carries the CD8 marker and can destroy body cells infected by viruses or transformed by cancer.

dendritic cell: an immune cell with highly branched extensions that occurs in lymphoid tissues, engulfs microbes, and stimulates T cells by displaying the foreign antigens of the microbes on their surfaces.

deoxyribonucleic acid: a long molecule found in the cell nucleus. Molecules of DNA carry the cell's genetic information.

eczema: the term for a group of allergic conditions that causes the skin to become inflamed and is characterized by redness, itching, and oozing lesions that become crusty.

elimination diet: certain foods are removed from a person's diet and a substitute food of the same type, such as another source of protein in place of eggs, is introduced.

enzyme: A protein produced by living cells that promotes the chemical processes of life without itself being altered.

eosinophil: a white blood cell containing granules filled with chemicals damaging to parasites and enzymes that affect inflammatory reactions.

epidemiology: a branch of medical science that deals with the incidence, distribution, and control of disease in a population.

epithelial cells: cells that make up the epithelium, the covering for internal and external body surfaces.

epithelium: a membranous cellular tissue that covers a free surface or lines a tube or cavity of an animal body and serves especially to enclose and protect the other parts of the body, to produce secretions and excretions, and to function in assimilation.

epinephrine: a drug form of adrenaline (a natural hormone in the body) that stimulates nerves.

esophagus: the passageway through which food moves from the throat to the stomach.

extract: A concentrated liquid preparation containing minute parts of specific foods.

fungus: A member of a class of relatively primitive vegetable organisms. Fungi include mushrooms, yeasts, rusts, molds, and smuts.

gastrointestinal (GI) tract: An area of the body that includes the stomach and intestines.

gene: A unit of genetic material (DNA) inherited from a parent that controls specific characteristics. Genes carry coded directions a cell uses to make specific proteins that perform specific functions.

genome: a full set of genes in a person or any other living thing.

graft rejection: an immune response against transplanted tissue.

graft-versus-host disease: a life-threatening reaction in which transplanted cells attack the tissues of the recipient.

granule: a grain-like part of a cell.

granulocyte: a phagocytic white blood cell filled with granules. Neutrophils, eosinophils, basophils, and mast cells are examples of granulocytes.

helper T cells (Th cells): a subset of T cells that carry the CD4 surface marker and are essential for turning on antibody production, activating cytotoxic T cells, and initiating many other immune functions.

histamine: a chemical released by mast cells and basophils.

histamine toxicity: An allergic-like reaction to eating foods containing high levels of histamine.

histocompatibility testing: a test conducted before transplant operations to find a donor whose MHC molecules are similar to the recipient's; helps reduce the strength of transplant rejection.

hives: a raised, itchy area of skin that is usually a sign of an allergic reaction.

house dust mite: either of two widely distributed mites of the genus Dermatophagoides (d. farinae and d. pteronyssinus) that commonly occur in house dust and often induce allergic responses, especially in children.

human immunodeficiency virus: the virus that causes AIDS.

human leukocyte antigen: a protein on the surfaces of human cells that identifies the cells as "self" and, like MHC antigens, performs essential roles in immune responses. HLAs are used in laboratory tests to determine whether one person's tissues are compatible with another person's, and could be used in a transplant.

immune response: a reaction of the immune system to foreign substances. Although normal immune responses are designed to protect the body from pathogens, immune dysregulation can damage normal cells and tissues, as in the case of autoimmune diseases.

immune system: A complex network of specialized cells, tissues, and organs that defends the body against attacks by disease-causing organisms.

immunoglobulin: one of a large family of proteins, also known as antibody.

immunosuppressive: capable of reducing immune responses.

induction of asthma: the process of lung sensitization and respiratory inflammation resulting in increased difficulty with breathing; it can be caused by a variety of external stimuli.

inflammation: An immune system reaction to "foreign" invader such as microbes or allergens. Signs include redness, swelling, pain, or heat.

inflammatory response: redness, warmth, and swelling produced in response to infection; the result of increased blood flow and an influx of immune cells and their secretions.

innate: an immune system function that is inborn and provides an all-purpose defense against invasion by microbes.

interferon: a protein produced by cells that stimulates antivirus immune responses or alters the physical properties of immune cells.

interleukins: a major group of lymphokines and monokines.

lactase: the enzyme responsible for breaking down lactose in the gut. Lactase is produced by cells lining the small intestine.

lactose intolerance: the inability to digest lactose, a kind of sugar found in milk and other food products. Lactose intolerance is caused by a shortage of the enzyme lactase, which is produced by the cells that line the small intestine.

latex allergy: workers exposed to latex gloves and other products containing natural rubber latex may develop allergic reactions such as skin rashes; hives; nasal, eye, or sinus symptoms; asthma; and (rarely) shock.

lymphocytes: small white blood cells that are important parts of the immune system.

lymphokines: powerful chemical substances secreted by lymphocytes. These molecules help direct and regulate the immune responses.

macrophage: a large and versatile immune cell that devours invading pathogens and other intruders. Macrophages stimulate other immune cells by presenting them with small pieces of the invaders.

major histocompatibility complex: a group of genes that controls several aspects of the immune response. MHC genes code for "self" markers on all body cells.

mast cell: a granulocyte found in tissue. The contents of mast cells, along with those of basophils, are responsible for the symptoms of allergy.

memory cells: a subset of T cells and B cells that have been exposed to antigens and can then respond more readily when the immune system encounters those same antigens again.

microbes: Tiny life forms, such as bacteria, viruses, and fungi, which may cause disease.

molecules: The building blocks of a cell. Some examples are proteins, fats, and carbohydrates.

monoclonal antibody: an antibody produced by a single B cell or its identical progeny that is specific for a given antigen.

monocyte: a large phagocytic white blood cell which, when entering tissue, develops into a macrophage.

monokines: powerful chemical substances secreted by monocytes and macrophages. These molecules help direct and regulate the immune responses.

natural killer (NK) cell: a large granule-containing lymphocyte that recognizes and kills cells lacking self antigens. These cells' target recognition molecules are different from T cells.

neutrophil: a white blood cell that is an abundant and important phagocyte.

NK T cell: a T cell that has some characteristics of NK cells. It produces large amounts of cytokines when stimulated, and is activated by fatty substances (lipids) bound to non-MHC molecules called CD1D.

organism: An individual living thing.

parasite: a plant or animal that lives, grows, and feeds on or within another living organism.

particle pollution: particle pollution (also known as "particulate matter") consists of a mixture of solids and liquid droplets. some particles are emitted directly; others form when pollutants emitted by various sources react in the atmosphere.

passive immunity: immunity resulting from the transfer of antibodies or antiserum produced by another person.

pathogen: any virus, microorganism, or etiologic agent causing disease.

perennial: describes something that occurs throughout.

phagocyte: a large white blood cell that contributes to immune defenses by ingesting microbes or other cells and foreign particles.

phagocytosis: process by which one cell engulfs another cell or large particle.

plasma cell: a large antibody-producing cell that develops from B cells.

rhinitis: inflammation of the nasal passages, which can cause a runny nose.

sinuses: hollow air spaces located within the bones of the skull surrounding the nose.

sinusitis: when sinuses are infected or inflamed.

stem cell: an immature cell from which other cells derive. Bone marrow is rich in the kind of stem cells that become specialized blood cells.

T cell or T lymphocyte: a small white blood cell that recognizes antigen fragments bound to cell surfaces by specialized antibody-like receptors. "T" stands for the thymus gland, where T cells develop and acquire their receptors.

tissues: Groups of similar cells joined to perform the same function.

tolerance: a state of immune nonresponsiveness to a particular antigen or group of antigens.

toll-like receptor: a family of proteins important for first-line immune defenses against microbes.

toxin: An agent produced in plants and bacteria, normally very damaging to cells.

ultraviolet (UV) radiation: a portion of the electromagnetic spectrum with wavelengths shorter than visible light.

upper respiratory tract: area of the body that includes the nasal passages, mouth, and throat.

vaccine: a preparation that stimulates an immune response that can prevent an infection or create resistance to an infection. Vaccines do not cause disease.

volatile organic compound: any organic compound that participates in atmospheric photochemical reactions except those designated by EPA as having negligible photochemical reactivity.

Chapter 51

Agencies That Provide Information about Allergies

Government Agencies

Celiac Disease Awareness Campaign
c/o National Digestive Diseases Information Clearinghouse
2, Information Way
Bethesda, MD 20892-3570
Phone: 800-891-5389
Fax: 301–634–0716
TTY: 866–569–1162
Website: www.celiac.nih.gov
E-mail: celiac@info.niddk.nih.gov

Center for Food Safety and Applied Nutrition (CFSAN)
FDA CFSAN Outreach and Information Center
5100 Paint Branch Pkwy., HFS-009
College Park, MD 20740-3835
Toll-Free: 888-723-3366 (SAFEFOOD)
Website: www.fda.gov/Food

Consumer Affairs Branch (CBER)
Office of Communication, Outreach and Development
Food and Drug Administration
10903, New Hampshire Ave.
Bldg. 71, Rm. 3103
Silver Spring, MD 20993-0002
Toll-Free: 800-835-4709
Phone: 240-402-8010
Website: www.fda.gov
E-mail: ocod@fda.hhs.gov

Division of Health Interview Statistics
National Center for Health Statistics
3311 Toledo Rd., Rm. 2217
Hyattsville, MD 20782-2064
Phone: 301-458-4901
Website: www.cdc.gov
E-mail: nhis@cdc.gov

Resources in this chapter were compiled from several sources deemed reliable, November 2015.

Eunice Kennedy Shriver National Institute of Child Health and Human Development (NICHD)
31 Center Dr.
Bldg. 31, Rm. 2A32
Bethesda, MD 20892-2425
Phone: 800-370-2943
Fax: 866-760-5947
TTY: 888-320-6942
Website: www.nichd.nih.gov
E-mail:
NICHDInformationResource
Center@mail.nih.gov

Food and Nutrition Service (FNS)
3101 Park Center Dr.
Alexandria, VA 22302
Phone: 703-305-2062
Website: www.fns.usda.gov

FoodSafety.gov
Website: www.foodsafety.gov

Genetic and Rare Diseases Information Center
P.O. Box 8126
Gaithersburg, MD 20898-8126
Toll-free: 888-205-2311
Phone: 301-251-4925
Fax: 301-251-4911
TTY: 888-205-3223
Website: rarediseases.info.nih.gov

LiverTox
Website: livertox.nih.gov
E-mail: LiverTox@nih.gov

National Cancer Institute (NCI)
BG 9609 MSC 9760
9609 Medical Center Dr.
Bethesda, MD 20892-9760
Toll-Free: 800-422-6237
(4-CANCER)
Website: www.cancer.gov

National Eye Institute (NEI)
Information Office
31 Center Dr., MSC 2510
Bethesda, MD 20892-2510
Phone:301-496-5248
Website: nei.nih.gov
E-mail: 2020@nei.nih.gov

National Institute of Arthritis and Musculoskeletal and Skin Diseases (NIAMS)
1 AMS Cir.
Bethesda, MD 20892-3675
Toll free: 877-226-4267
(22-NIAMS)
Phone: 301-495-4484
Fax: 301-718-6366
TTY: 301-565-2966
Website: www.niams.nih.gov
E-mail: NIAMSinfo@mail.nih.gov

National Institute of Diabetes and Digestive and Kidney Diseases (NIDDK)
2 Information Way
Bethesda, MD 20892–3570
Phone: 800–891–5389
Fax: 703–738–4929
TTY: 866–569–1162
Website: www.digestive.niddk.nih.gov
E-mail: nddic@info.niddk.nih.gov

NIH Office of Communications and Public Liaison

Bldg. 31, Rm. 5B64
Bethesda, MD 20892-2094
Phone: 301-402-7337
Website: newsinhealth.nih.gov
E-mail: nihnewsinhealth@
od.nih.gov

NTP Center for Phototoxicology

P.O. Box 12233, MD K2-05
Research Triangle Park, NC
USA 27709
Phone: 919-541-3419
Website: ntp.niehs.nih.gov

Occupational Safety & Health Administration (OSHA)

200 Constitution Ave., N.W.
Washington, DC 20210
Toll-Free: 800-321-6742 (OSHA)
TTY: 877-889-5627
Website: www.osha.gov

Office on Women's Health

U.S. Department of Health and
Human Services
200 Independence Ave., S.W.,
Rm. 712E
Washington, DC 20201
Toll-Free: 800-994-9662
Website: www.girlshealth.gov

WIC Works Resource System

USDA National Agricultural
Library
10301 Baltimore Ave.
Beltsville, MD 20705
Phone: 301-504-6096
Website: wicworks.fns.usda.gov
E-mail: wicworks@fns.usda.gov

Private Agencies That Provide Information about Allergies

Academy of Nutrition and Dietetics

120 S. Riverside Plaza, Ste. 2000
Chicago, IL 60606-6995
Toll-Free: 800-877-1600
Phone: 312-899-0040
Website: www.eatright.org

AllergenOnline.org

Website: www.allergenonline.
com

AllergicChild.com

6660 Delmonico Dr.
Ste. D249
Colorado Springs, CO 80919
Website: www.allergicchild.com

American Academy of Ophthalmology

655 Beach St.
San Francisco, CA 94109
Phone: 415-561-8500
Fax: 415-561-8533
Website: www.aao.org

American Gastroenterological Association
4930 Del Ray Ave.
Bethesda, MD 20814
Phone: 301-654-2055
Fax: 301-654-5920
Website: www.gastro.org
E-mail: member@gastro.org

Consortium of Food Allergy Research (CoFAR)
Website: www.cofargroup.org

COPD Foundation
Development, Communications
& Public Policy Dept
20 F St., N.W.
Ste. 200-A
Washington, DC 20001
Toll-Free: 866-316-2673
Website: www.copdfoundation.org
E-mail: info@copdfoundation.org

Food Allergy Research & Education
7925 Jones Branch Dr.
Ste. 1100
McLean, VA 22102
Toll-Free: 1-800-929-4040
Phone: 703-691-3179
Fax: 703-691-2713
Website: www.foodallergy.org

Gluten Intolerance Group
31214 124th Ave., S.E.
Auburn, WA 98092
Phone: 253-833-6655
Fax: 253-833-6675
Website: www.gluten.org
E-mail: customerservice@gluten.org

Immune Tolerance Network (ITN)
Benaroya Research Institute
1201 Ninth Ave.
Seattle, WA 98101-2795
Phone: 206-342-6901
Fax: 206-342-6588
Website: www.immunetolerance.org

Infectious Diseases Society of America
1300 Wilson Blvd.
Ste. 300
Arlington, VA 22209
Phone: 703-299-0200
Fax: 703-299-0204
Website: www.idsociety.org

Institute for Food Safety and Health
Illinois Institute of Technology,
Moffett Campus
6502 S. Archer Rd.
Bedford Park, IL 60501-1957
Phone: 708-563-1576
Website: www.iit.edu/ifsh

International Food Information Council Foundation
1100 Connecticut Ave., N.W.
Ste. 430
Washington, DC 20036
Phone: 202-296-6540
Website: www.foodinsight.org
E-mail: info@foodinsight.org

Kids With Food Allergies
5049 Swamp Rd., Ste. 303
P.O. Box 554
Fountainville, PA 18923
Phone: 215-230-5394
Fax: 215-230-7674
Website: www.
kidswithfoodallergies.org

La Leche League
International
35 E. Wacker Dr., Ste. 850
Chicago, IL 60601
Toll-Free: 800-525-3243
(LALECHE)
Phone: 312-646-6260
Fax: 312-644-8557
Website: www.llli.org
E-mail: info@llli.org

SelectWisely
P.O. Box 289
Sparta, NJ 07871
Phone: 888-396-9260
Fax: 888-392-5937
Website: www.selectwisely.com
E-mail: info@selectwisely.com

Chapter 52

Directory of Websites and Cookbooks for People with Food Allergies

Recipe Books for People with Food Allergies

Allergy Proof Recipes for Kids: More Than 150 Recipes That are All Wheat-Free, Gluten-Free, Nut-Free, Egg-Free and Low in Sugar. By Leslie Hammond. Fair Winds Press 2010. ISBN: 1592333834

Allergy-Free and Easy Cooking: 30-Minute Meals without Gluten, Wheat, Dairy, Eggs, Soy, Peanuts, Tree Nuts, Fish, Shellfish, and Sesame. By Cybele Pascal. Ten Speed Press: 2012. ISBN: 1607742918

Allergy-Friendly Food for Families: 120 Gluten-Free, Dairy-Free, Nut-Free, Egg-Free, and Soy-Free Recipes Everyone Will Enjoy. By Editors of Kiwi Magazine. Andrews McMeel Publishing: 2012. ISBN: 1449409768

Complete Allergy-Free Comfort Foods Cookbook: Every Recipe Is Free Of Gluten, Dairy, Soy, Nuts, And Eggs. By Elizabeth Gordon. Lyons Press: 2013. ISBN: 0762788135

Resources in this chapter were compiled from several sources deemed reliable, November 2015.

Cooking Free: 200 Flavorful Recipes for People with Food Allergies and Multiple Food Sensitivities. By Carol Fenster. Avery: 2005. ISBN: 1583332154

Danielle Walker's Against All Grain: Meals Made Simple: Gluten-Free, Dairy-Free, and Paleo Recipes to Make Anytime. By Danielle Walker. Victory Belt Publishing: 2014. ISBN: 162860042X

Flying Apron's Gluten-free & Vegan Baking Book. By Jennifer Katzinger. Sasquatch Books: 2009. ISBN: 1570616299

Go Dairy Free: The Guide and Cookbook for Milk Allergies, Lactose Intolerance, and Casein-Free Living. By Alisa Marie Fleming. Fleming Ink: 2008. ISBN: 0979128625

Great Foods without Worry. By Cindy Mosely. Aventine Press: 2003. ISBN: 1593301162

The Allergy-Free Pantry: Make Your Own Staples, Snacks, and More Without Wheat, Gluten, Dairy, Eggs, Soy or Nuts. By Colette Martin. The Experiment: 2014. ISBN: 1615192085

The Dairy-Free & Gluten-Free Kitchen. By Denise Jardine. Ten Speed Press: 2012. ISBN: 1607742241

The Food Allergen-Free Baker's Handbook. By Cybele Pascal. Celestial Arts: 2009. ISBN: 1587613484

The Food Allergy Mama's Easy, Fast Family Meals: Dairy, Egg, and Nut Free Recipes for Every Day. By Kelly Rudnicki. Avery: 2013. ISBN: 1583335005

The Healthy Gluten-Free Life: 200 Delicious Gluten-Free, Dairy-Free, Soy-Free and Egg-Free Recipes! By: Tammy Credicott. Victory Belt Publishing: 2012. ISBN: 1936608715

The Whole Life Nutrition Cookbook: Over 300 Delicious Whole Foods Recipes, Including Gluten-Free, Dairy-Free, Soy-Free, and Egg-Free Dishes. By Tom Malterre. Grand Central Life & Style: 2014. ISBN: 1455581895

Online Allergy Tools and Applications for Mobile Devices

Allergy Alert by Pollen.com
Website: www.pollen.com/android.asp
Website: www.pollen.com/iphone.asp

Allergy Ally
Website: www.tikkunolamventures.com/

Allergy FT: Allergy Food Translator
Website: allergyft.com/

AllergyEats
Website: www.allergyeats.com/

AsthmaMD
Website: www.asthmamd.org/

Allergy Journal
itunes.apple.com/us/app/allergy-journal/id455223808?mt=8

ContentChecked USA
Website: www.contentchecked.com/

Cook IT Allergy Free
Website: cookitallergyfree.com/iphone_ipad_app/

Find Me Gluten Free
Website: www.findmeglutenfree.com/

Food intolerances
Website: www.baliza.de/en/apps/histamine.html

Gluten-Free Allergy-Free Marketplace
Website: celiac.org/live-gluten-free/gluten-free-marketplace/

Healthy Diet & Gluten Free, Allergy, GMO Scanner by NxtNutrio
Website: www.nxtnutrio.com/

iCanEatOnTheGo Gluten & Allergen Free
Website: www.allergyfreepassport.com

iEatOut Gluten Free
Website: glutenfreepassport.com/allergy-gluten-free-apps/
ieatout-allergy-gluten-free-meals

Pollen.com's 2 Day Allergy Alert™ Email
Website: www.pollen.com/alert.asp

WebArtisan Food Additives
Website: webartisan.com.au/apps/index.php/iphone-apps/
food-additives

WebMD Allergy
Website: www.webmd.com/allergy-app

YoDish
Website: www.yodish.com/#!/home

Zyrtec® Allergy Cast™
Website: www.zyrtec.com/allergy-forecast-tools-apps

Index

Index

A

abdominal cramping
  egg allergy 170
  food poisoning 151
  mast cells 118
"About Air Toxics" (EPA) 265n
Academy of Nutrition and Dietetics,
  contact 441
acupuncture, allergic rhinitis 359
acute sinusitis
  described 54
  medications 351
ADA *see* Americans with Disabilities
  Act
adaptive immunity, immunization 9
adenoids
  nasal passages 352
  sinusitis 57
adrenal gland, defined 429
adrenalin
  antihistamines 185
  food allergies 140
"Advising Travelers with Specific
  Needs" (CDC) 409n
AERD *see* aspirin-exacerbated
  respiratory disease
Afrin *see also* oxymetazoline

Agency for Healthcare Research and
  Quality (AHRQ)
  publications
    allergy shots 334n
    seasonal allergic rhinitis 352n
Agency for Toxic Substances and
  Disease Registry (ATSDR)
  publication
    environmental odors 275n
AHRQ *see* Agency for Healthcare
  Research and Quality
airborne allergens
  atopic dermatitis 95
  hay fever 22
  seasonal allergic rhinitis 352
air cleaners, overview 377–86
air pollution
  air cleaners 377
  asthma triggers 342
  see also indoor air quality
"Air Quality" (EPA) 265n
air quality index (AQI), air pollution 79
air spaces, defined 429
airways, defined 429
albuterol
  allergic inflammation 247
  quick-relief medication 404

451

457

T

U